Human Rights and Standard of Living in Sub-Saharan Africa

This book offers a comprehensive and nuanced examination of the right to an adequate standard of living in Sub-Saharan Africa (SSA), shedding light on the multifaceted challenges, opportunities, and imperatives for action. The right to an adequate standard of living is a fundamental human right, essential for the dignity and well-being of all individuals. Yet, in SSA, the realisation of this right remains a complex and elusive goal, with millions of people facing poverty, inequality, and limited access to basic services.

Through a series of in-depth chapters, the book explores the various dimensions of the right to an adequate standard of living, from the pervasive impacts of poverty and inequality to the critical importance of access to healthcare, education, housing, and justice. Drawing on a rich array of case studies, data, and expert analysis, the work provides a compelling and evidence-based assessment of the current state of affairs in SSA, highlighting the urgent need for comprehensive and context-specific approaches to advancing this fundamental right.

Providing a roadmap for promoting sustainable and inclusive development, reducing poverty and inequality, and ensuring access to basic services for all, the volume offers a set of actionable recommendations for policymakers, practitioners, and researchers working in the areas of Human Rights Law, Development Law and, in particular, those focused on the United Nations Sustainable Development Goals. At the same time, it identifies key areas for further research and investigation, underscoring the importance of ongoing knowledge generation and exchange in support of evidence-based policy and practice.

Augustine Edobor Arimoro is a Senior Lecturer in Law at the School of Law, University of West London, United Kingdom and is a Research Partner of the Centre for Comparative Law in Africa, University of Cape Town, South Africa.

Routledge Studies in Law, Rights and Justice

Routledge Studies in Law, Rights and Justice seeks to publish leading monographs and edited collections that explore the interplay between rights and justice across different areas of law and legal practice. The series serves as a home for scholars working in areas such as human rights, social justice, constitutional justice, business and human rights, equality rights and civil justice. It encourages authors to address the theoretical and practical aspects of the application of rights, the achievability of justice in these uncertain times, and the methods available to individuals, organisations, and states to achieve justice. *Routledge Studies in Law, Rights and Justice* embraces both scholarship from a national and international viewpoint and encourages authors to explore rights and justice from a global perspective. It strives to break down existing disciplinary silos and encourage collaboration, which offers the opportunity to publish thought provoking, original and cutting-edge work. The aim is to foster debates, build bridges between different areas of scholarship, and encourage a wider perspective on the underlying issues that might limit the applicability of rights, or render justice difficult to achieve.

Routledge Studies in Law, Rights and Justice primarily consider rights and justice from a legal perspective, but does however, welcome submissions that take a broader view and engage with the wider socio-economic, political, and social context. The series editor is very keen to consider works by established and early-career academics, and submissions are encouraged from scholars based all around the world.

Series Editor:

Chris Monaghan is the Head of Law and a Principal Lecturer in Law at the University of Worcester, and holds a PhD from the Dickson Poon School of Law at King's College London. He has published widely on aspects of public law.

Titles in this series:

Human Rights and Standard of Living in Sub-Saharan Africa
Challenges and Prospects
Augustine Edobor Arimoro

Human Rights and Standard of Living in Sub-Saharan Africa

Challenges and Prospects

Augustine Edobor Arimoro

Routledge
Taylor & Francis Group
LONDON AND NEW YORK

First published 2025
by Routledge
4 Park Square, Milton Park, Abingdon, Oxon OX14 4RN

and by Routledge
605 Third Avenue, New York, NY 10158

Routledge is an imprint of the Taylor & Francis Group, an informa business

British Library Cataloguing-in-Publication Data
A catalogue record for this book is available from the British Library

Library of Congress Cataloging-in-Publication Data
Names: Arimoro, Augustine Edobor, author.
Title: Human rights and standard of living in Sub-Saharan Africa : challenges and prospects / Augustine Edobor Arimoro.
Other titles: Routledge studies in law, rights and justice.
Description: Abingdon, Oxon [UK] ; New York, NY : Routledge, 2025. | Series: Routledge studies in law, rights and justice | Includes bibliographical references and index. |
Identifiers: LCCN 2024042110 (print) | LCCN 2024042111 (ebook) | ISBN 9781032612140 (hardback) | ISBN 9781032628967 (paperback) | ISBN 9781032628974 (ebook)
Subjects: LCSH: Human rights–Africa, Sub-Saharan. | Cost and standard of living–Africa, Sub-Saharan. | Africa, Sub-Saharan–Social conditions–21st century. | Africa, Sub-Saharan–Economic conditions–21st century.
Classification: LCC KQC572 .A99 2025 (print) | LCC KQC572 (ebook) | DDC 341.480967–dc23/eng/20240911
LC record available at https://lccn.loc.gov/2024042110
LC ebook record available at https://lccn.loc.gov/2024042111

ISBN: 978-1-032-61214-0 (hbk)
ISBN: 978-1-032-62896-7 (pbk)
ISBN: 978-1-032-62897-4 (ebk)

DOI: 10.4324/9781032628974

Typeset in Galliard
by Deanta Global Publishing Services, Chennai, India

This book is dedicated to the loving memory of my mother, Mrs Rose Arimoro.

Contents

Acknowledgements

This book is the result of extensive research and collaboration, and I am deeply grateful to the numerous individuals and institutions that have supported this project.

First and foremost, I would like to express my sincere gratitude to the Southlands Methodist Trust for their generous funding, which made this research possible. Their support has been instrumental in bringing this project to fruition.

I am indebted to the University of Roehampton London for supporting my research trips to Nigeria and South Africa. These field visits were crucial in gathering first-hand information and insights that have enriched this work.

My heartfelt thanks go to Professor Abubakar O. Sulaiman, Director General of the Institute for Legislative and Democratic Studies (NILDS), Abuja, for hosting a roundtable on 'Combating Extreme Poverty in Sub-Saharan Africa' on 27th March 2024. The discussions during this event significantly contributed to the outcomes of this project. I am also grateful to the researchers at NILDS who participated in the roundtable, sharing their valuable expertise and perspectives. Special thanks to Dr. Osaretin Okungbowa of NILDS for his efforts in facilitating the roundtable and fostering collaboration with the institute.

I owe a debt of gratitude to my family for their unwavering support throughout this journey. To my wife, Mrs. Joke Arimoro, and my son, Jathniel Idahosa Augustine-Arimoro, thank you for your patience, understanding, and moral support. Your encouragement has been a constant source of strength.

I am profoundly grateful to my siblings—Dr. Theodora Odagwe, Professor Francis Arimoro, Rev. Samuel Arimoro, Mrs. Mercy Obasoha, and Mrs. Susan Arimoro-Moore—for their invaluable support during my research trip to Nigeria. Your assistance and hospitality made the fieldwork not only possible but also enjoyable.

I would like to express my appreciation to my former colleagues at the Roehampton Law School, University of Roehampton London. Your academic insights, constructive feedback, and collegial support have been instrumental in shaping this work.

Lastly, I extend my thanks to all those who have contributed to this project in various ways—interviewees, conference participants, and countless others who have shared their knowledge and experiences. Your contributions have been invaluable in enhancing the depth and breadth of this research.

While it is impossible to name everyone who has played a part in this journey, please know that your support, however small, has been deeply appreciated and has contributed to the realisation of this book.

Foreword

The right to an adequate standard of living stands as a cornerstone of human dignity and well-being, enshrined in international human rights laws and recognised as fundamental to the realisation of a just and equitable society. Yet, for millions of individuals across Sub-Saharan Africa (SSA), this right remains elusive, constrained by a complex web of socio-economic, political, and environmental challenges. It is against this backdrop that this timely and comprehensive monograph emerges, offering a nuanced examination of the multifaceted issues surrounding the right to an adequate standard of living in SSA.

The importance of this study cannot be overstated. As the global community strives to achieve the Sustainable Development Goals (SDGs) by 2030, with a particular focus on ending extreme poverty and reducing inequalities, the challenges faced by SSA in ensuring an adequate standard of living for its citizens have come into sharp focus. The region, home to a significant portion of the world's poor, continues to grapple with persistent poverty, widening inequalities, limited access to basic services, and the ever-increasing threats posed by climate change and environmental degradation. These challenges not only impede the realisation of fundamental human rights but also threaten to undermine the region's progress towards sustainable development and social justice.

This monograph, through its rigorous analysis and evidence-based approach, makes a significant contribution to our understanding of the complex interplay between human rights, development, and the lived experiences of individuals and communities across SSA. By adopting a multidisciplinary perspective, the authors provide a comprehensive exploration of the various dimensions of the right to an adequate standard of living, from legal and policy frameworks to on-the-ground realities and innovative approaches to addressing persistent challenges.

One of the key strengths of this work lies in its nuanced treatment of the legal framework surrounding the right to an adequate standard of living. The authors provide a thorough examination of international human rights instruments, regional mechanisms, and national constitutional provisions, offering valuable insights into the strengths and weaknesses of existing legal protections. This analysis is particularly crucial in the context of SSA, where the gap between legal commitments and practical implementation often remains wide. As noted by the UN Committee on Economic, Social, and Cultural Rights, the full realisation of socio-economic rights requires not only legal recognition but also concrete measures to ensure effective implementation.

The monograph's exploration of poverty and inequality in SSA is both timely and essential. By delving into the structural, economic, and social factors that perpetuate these issues, the author sheds light on the complex web of challenges that must be addressed to ensure the realisation of the right to an adequate standard of living. This analysis is particularly pertinent in the context of the SDGs, which call for concerted efforts to end poverty in all its forms and reduce inequality within and among countries. The author's examination of various policy interventions and initiatives aimed at addressing poverty and inequality provides valuable lessons for policymakers and practitioners working towards these goals.

The study also thoroughly addresses access to healthcare and education, which are fundamental components of the right to an adequate standard of living. The author's critical examination of the barriers to accessing these essential services in SSA, including inadequate infrastructure, limited resources, and socio-cultural factors, provides a comprehensive picture of the challenges faced by individuals and communities across the region. This analysis is especially relevant in light of the ongoing global health crisis, which has exposed and exacerbated existing inequalities in access to healthcare and education. The author's exploration of innovative approaches and best practices for expanding access to these services offers valuable insights for policymakers and practitioners working to strengthen health and education systems in resource-constrained settings.

The monograph's treatment of housing and infrastructure issues in SSA is both timely and crucial. As the region experiences rapid urbanisation, the challenges of providing adequate housing and infrastructure have become increasingly pressing. The author's examination of the multifaceted obstacles to housing and infrastructure development, including limited access to affordable housing, inadequate urban planning, and insufficient basic services, provides a comprehensive overview of the complex issues at play. This analysis is particularly relevant in the context of SDG 11, which calls for making cities and human settlements inclusive, safe, resilient, and sustainable. The author's exploration of policy interventions and urban planning strategies offers valuable insights for addressing these challenges and promoting sustainable urban development in the SSA.

Environmental degradation and climate change, as existential threats to the realisation of the right to an adequate standard of living, receive thorough treatment in this work. The author's examination of the far-reaching effects of these issues on various dimensions of socio-economic development in SSA, including agriculture, water resources, and human health, underscores the urgent need for comprehensive and integrated approaches to environmental sustainability and climate action. This analysis is particularly crucial in light of the disproportionate impact of climate change on vulnerable populations in SSA, as highlighted by the Intergovernmental Panel on Climate Change (IPCC). The author's exploration of adaptation strategies, mitigation measures, and international collaborations provides valuable insights for policymakers and practitioners working to address these pressing challenges.

Access to justice, as a critical component of realising the right to an adequate standard of living, is given due attention in this monograph. The author's examination of the multifaceted barriers to access to justice in SSA, including limited legal infrastructure, inadequate legal aid services, and corruption within the justice system, provides a comprehensive picture of the challenges faced by individuals seeking to assert and enforce their rights. This analysis is particularly relevant in light of SDG 16, which calls for promoting peaceful and inclusive societies, providing access to justice for all, and building effective, accountable, and inclusive institutions at all levels. The author's exploration of innovative approaches and legal reforms offers valuable insights for enhancing access to justice and strengthening the rule of law in SSA.

Throughout the monograph, the author draws on a rich array of case studies and empirical evidence to illustrate his arguments and highlight successful initiatives and best practices. This approach not only enhances the relevance and applicability of the work but also provides valuable lessons for policymakers, practitioners, and researchers working to advance the right to an adequate standard of living in SSA and beyond.

The concluding chapter of the monograph offers a comprehensive synthesis of key findings and recommendations, providing a roadmap for action and further research. By identifying gaps in knowledge and areas that necessitate further inquiry, the author contributes to setting a research agenda that can inform evidence-based policy interventions and scholarly discourse on the right to an adequate standard of living in SSA.

As we confront the complex challenges of the 21st century, including the ongoing global health crisis, climate change, and persistent inequalities, the importance of realising the right to an adequate standard of living for all has never been more apparent. This monograph makes a significant contribution to our understanding of these issues in the context of SSA, offering valuable insights and recommendations for advancing this fundamental right.

The author's rigorous analysis, multidisciplinary approach, and emphasis on practical solutions make this work an invaluable resource for policymakers, practitioners, researchers, and students engaged in the fields of human rights, development, and social justice. By shedding light on the complex interplay between legal frameworks, socio-economic realities, and environmental challenges, this monograph not only enhances our understanding of the right to an adequate standard of living in SSA, but also contributes to broader discussions on sustainable development, human rights, and social justice in the Global South.

As we move forward in our collective efforts to realise the right to an adequate standard of living for all, the insights and recommendations provided in this monograph will undoubtedly serve as a valuable guide. It is my hope that this work will inspire further research, inform policy interventions, and contribute to meaningful progress towards the full realisation of this fundamental right in SSA and beyond.

In conclusion, I commend the author for his comprehensive and nuanced treatment of this critical issue. This work stands as a testament to the power of rigorous scholarship in advancing our understanding of complex social challenges and informing efforts to create a more just and equitable world. As we continue to grapple with the challenges of ensuring an adequate standard of living for all, this monograph will undoubtedly serve as an essential reference point for scholars, policymakers, and practitioners alike.

Professor Abubakar O. Sulaiman
Director General,
National Institute for Legislative and Democratic Studies,
Abuja-Nigeria

1 Introduction

Introduction

Human Rights and Standard of Living in Sub-Saharan Africa: Challenges and Prospects is a thought-provoking book that delves into the pressing issue of extreme poverty in Sub-Saharan Africa (SSA) and explores how a human rights and social welfare approach can enhance the standards of the region's impoverished populations. Drawing inspiration from the United Nations Sustainable Development Goals, particularly Goal Number 1 of ending poverty in all its forms, this book seeks to provide insights and solutions for addressing the poverty challenge in SSA.

With SSA being home to the largest share of people living in extreme poverty,[1] the need for a bespoke and region-specific strategy to combat poverty becomes evident.[2] The book places SSA under the microscope, highlighting the unique challenges faced by the sub-region and the necessity of adopting approaches that suit its specific context. It recognises that solutions derived solely from Global North perspectives may not always be effective in the Global South.[3]

The central question guiding this study is: What are the main challenges to attaining an adequate standard of living in SSA, and how can the States in the sub-region address these challenges? By critically analysing the socio-economic conditions and peculiarities of the SSA countries, the book aims to offer a comprehensive understanding of the obstacles faced by the region's impoverished communities and propose viable solutions.

Taking a multidisciplinary approach, the monograph draws insights form human rights theory, social welfare perspectives, and regional studies to inform its analysis. It highlights the interconnectedness of human rights and standard

1 Augustine Edobor Arimoro, 'Beyond Economics! The (Evolving) Role of Law in the Eradication of Extreme Poverty' (2023) *Journal of Human Rights and Social Work* 1–13 https://doi.org/10.1007/s41134-023-00247-2.

2 Ibid.

3 Ada Ordor, 'Tracking the Law and Development Continuum through Multiple Intersections' (2015) 8(2) *The Law and Development Review* 333–360.

DOI: 10.4324/9781032628974-1

of living, emphasising the importance of ensuring that individuals have access to fundamental rights and resources necessary for a dignified life.

Throughout this book, in-depth case studies, empirical data, and comparative analysis will shed light on the complexities of poverty in SSA. By examining the unique dynamics of the sub-region and considering the experiences and aspirations of its diverse populations, the book seeks to develop an informed framework for addressing poverty and promoting sustainable development.

Ultimately, *Human Rights and Standard of Living in Sub-Saharan Africa: Challenges and Prospects* endeavours to contribute to academic scholarship, policy discussions, and practical interventions aimed at improving the living conditions of the poor in SSA. By highlighting the significance of human rights principles and social welfare strategies within the context of SSA, this book offers a fresh perspective on the path towards achieving an adequate standard of living and fulfilling the vision of ending extreme poverty in the sub-region.

For context, poverty is a pervasive challenge in SSA, which geographically encompasses the southern part of the African continent, excluding Northern Africa. It includes the whole of West Africa, East Africa, Central Africa, and Southern Africa.[4] SSA has simply been described as 49 of the 54 African States minus the North African States.[5] Although it has been suggested that the term 'Sub-Saharan Africa' is 'colonial in origin and used to belittled African nations south of the Sahara to separate the other countries from North Africa,'[6] other terms suggested such as 'Black Africa' or 'Tropic Africa' are not better than the term 'Sub-Saharan Africa'. For example, using the term 'Black' is even more discriminatory, and not all areas in the region are tropical. Whilst the aim of this book is not to delve into the debate of whether SSA represents a suitable term for the region, for the sake of clarity the use of the term by this author is to denote that part of the African continent that does not include North Africa.

Importance of the Right to Adequate Standard of Living

The right to an adequate standard of living is a right that has its foundation in international law. It is a part of the Universal Declaration of Human Rights (UDHR) that was accepted by the United Nations General Assembly (UNGA)

4 Katharina Lange, 'The Sub-Saharan Africa Region' (2019) available at <https://ifair.eu/2019/06/22/the-sub-saharan-africa-region/> accessed 2 January 2023.

5 Ibid.

6 Emi Eleode, 'It's Time to Drop "Sub-Saharan Africa" from our Vocabulary' (2021) available at <https://readcultured.com/its-time-to-drop-sub-saharan-africa-from-our-vocabulary-3cc0561a57cb> accessed 2 January 2023.

on 10 December 1948.[7] The right to an adequate standard of living is in the category of rights under economic, social and cultural rights.[8] Furthermore, this right is also encapsulated in Article 11 of the International Covenant on Economic, Social and Cultural Rights (ICESCR). This later international instrument was opened for signature in 1966 and came into force in January 1976. It is noted that the right to an adequate standard of living is the most central right in the ICESCR.[9] The right to an adequate standard of living encompasses the necessities of life, including food, water, housing healthcare, education, and social security. This right plays a crucial role in ensuring human dignity, equality, and social justice.[10]

The right to an adequate standard of living is tied to the concept of human dignity.[11] Every individual, irrespective of their background or circumstances, deserves to live a life of dignity.[12] As such, this book emphasises that by guaranteeing the right to an adequate standard of living, people will live with respect and be encouraged to fulfil their physical, social, and psychological needs as well as enjoy their other rights. The right to an adequate standard of living promotes equality and the opportunity for everyone to lead a decent life, free from poverty and deprivation. The right acknowledges the inherent worth and equal value of each person, irrespective of their socio-economic status. By addressing disparities and providing the basic needs of all, this right fosters a more equitable society, reducing the gaps between the affluent and the marginalised.

The right to an adequate standard of living is a critical tool in the fight against poverty.[13] Poverty is not merely the absence of material resources; it is a violation of human rights.[14] It has been noted and rightly so that:

> Poverty erodes economic and societal rights such as the right to health, adequate housing, food and safe water, and the right to education. The

7 N Jayawickrama, 'The Right to an Adequate Standard of Living' *The Judicial Application of Human Rights Law: National, Regional and International Jurisprudence* (2nd edn Cambridge University Press) 1025. See also United Nations, 'Universal Declaration of Human Rights' (2023) available at <https://www.un.org/en/about-us/universal-declaration-of-human-rights> accessed 5 June 2023.

8 Scott Leckie and Anne Gallanger, *Economic, Social and Cultural Rights: A Legal Resource Guide* (University of Pennsylvania Press) xvi.

9 Peter Bailey, 'The Right to an Adequate Standard of Living: New Issues for Australian Law' (2017) 4(1) *Australian Journal of Human Rights* 25–50.

10 Paul H Stuart, '"Economic Stabilisation of the Family: The Standard of Living": Harry Lurie's Call for an Adequate Family Income in the 1920s' (2015) 23(2) *Journal of Community Practice* 290–299.

11 Ibid.

12 R Andorno, 'Human Dignity and Human Rights' in HAMJ ten Have and B Gordijin (eds), *Handbook of Global Bioethics* (Springer 2014) https://doi.org/10.1007/978-94-007-2512-6_66.

13 Arimoro, op cit. (note 1).

14 Rod Hick, 'Material Poverty and Multiple Deprivation in Britain: The Distinctiveness of Multidimensional Assessment' (2016) 36 *Journal of Public Policy* 277.

same is true of civil and political rights, such as the right to a fair trial, political participation and security of the person.[15]

As such, this unique right provides the foundation for individuals to thrive, pursue opportunities, and contribute to their communities. Furthermore, the right to an adequate standard of living is linked to sustainable development. Sustainable development requires addressing the needs of the present generation without compromising the ability of the future generations to meet their own needs.[16] By recognising the interconnectedness between economic, social, and environmental aspects, this right encourages a holistic approach to development.[17] It emphasises the importance of sustainable resource management, equitable distribution of wealth, and the protection of the environment, thereby fostering a more sustainable and resilient society.[18]

The right to an adequate standard of living empowers individuals to actively participate in society. When basic needs are met, individuals are better positioned to exercise their civil, political, economic, and social rights. Access to education and healthcare, for example, enables individuals to develop their skills, pursue employment opportunities, and actively engage in decision-making processes that affect their lives. By promoting inclusivity and empowering individuals, this right contributes to the overall well-being and social cohesion of communities.[19]

In sum, the right to an adequate standard of living is not merely an aspirational ideal; it is a fundamental right that underpins the well-being and dignity of the individual. By guaranteeing access to basic necessities, it ensures equality, fights against poverty, and promotes sustainable development. Upholding this right requires a collective commitment from governments, civil society, and international actors to enact policies and implement measures that address inequalities and provide the basic needs of all individuals. Only through such efforts can we create a world that everyone can enjoy.

15 United Nations, 'OHCHR and the Human Rights Dimension of Poverty' (2020) available at <https://www.ohchr.org/en/poverty#:~:text=Poverty%20erodes%20economic%20and%20social,and%20security%20of%20the%20person> accessed 5 June 2023.

16 Graciela Chichilinisky, 'What is Sustainable Development?' (1997) 73(4) *Land Economics* 467–491.

17 Ben Purvis, Yao Mao and Darren Robinson, 'Three Pillars of Sustainability: In Search of Conceptual Origins' (2019) 14 *Concepts, Methodology, and Knowledge of Sustainability Science* 581–695.

18 Ibid.

19 Icelandic Human Rights Centre, 'The Right to an Adequate Standard of Living' (2023) available at <https://www.humanrights.is/en/human-rights-education-project/human-rights-concepts-ideas-and-fora/substantive-human-rights/the-right-to-an-adequate-standard-of-living> accessed 5 June 2023.

The Right to Adequate Standard of Living and the Sustainable Development Goals

The Sustainable Development Goals (SDGs) adopted by the United Nations (UN) in 2015 represent a comprehensive framework for global development.[20] Among the SDGs, the right to adequate standard of living (Goal 1) has a pivotal position in achieving sustainable and inclusive development across the globe. This book explores the interconnectedness between the right to an adequate standard of living and the SDGs, highlighting the importance of this right in realising the broader vision of a prosperous and equitable world.

- Holistic development and poverty eradication: Goal 1 of the SDGs aims to end poverty in all its forms and dimensions. The right to an adequate standard of living plays a crucial role in achieving this goal. By ensuring access to food, clean water, adequate housing, healthcare, education, and social protection, this right addresses the root causes of poverty and empowers individuals to break free from the cycle of deprivation. It promotes inclusive economic growth, reducing inequalities and fostering sustainable livelihoods.
- Health and well-being: The right to an adequate standard of living encompasses access to quality healthcare services and sanitation, which are integral to achieving Goal 3 of the SDGs: Ensure healthy lives and promote well-being for all at all ages. Without proper healthcare, individuals cannot lead productive lives or contribute fully to society. By guaranteeing access to essential healthcare services, this right enhances overall well-being, reduces preventable deaths, and promotes healthy living conditions.
- Education and human capital development: Goal 4 of the SDGs focuses on ensuring inclusive and equitable quality education for all. The right to an adequate standard of living recognises education as a fundamental component of human development. It encompasses access to quality education, vocational training, and lifelong learning opportunities. By enabling individuals to acquire knowledge and skills, this right empowers them to participate fully in society, access better employment opportunities, and contribute to sustainable development.
- Gender equality and inclusion: The right to an adequate standard of living is closely linked to Goal 5 of the SDGs: Achieve gender equality and empower all women and girls. It recognises the need to address gender disparities and promote social inclusion. Women and girls, in particular, face unique challenges in accessing an adequate standard of living due to discrimination and societal norms. By ensuring equal access to resources,

20 Ushotanefe Useh, 'Sustainable Development Goals as a Framework for Postgraduate Future Research Following COVID-19 Pandemic: A New Norm for Developing Countries' (2020) 8(1) *Higher Education for the Future* 123–132.

opportunities, and social protection, this right contributes to empowering women and promoting their active participation in all spheres of life.
- Sustainable consumption and production: Goal 12 of the SDGs emphasises responsible consumption and production patterns. The right to an adequate standard of living aligns with this goal by promoting sustainable resource management, reducing waste, and ensuring equitable access to resources. It recognises that meeting basic needs should not come at the expense of future generations. By fostering sustainable consumption and production practices, this right supports the transition towards a more environmentally sustainable and resilient world.

Based on the foregoing, it is fair to say that the right to an adequate standard of living serves as a cornerstone for achieving the SDGs. It underpins poverty eradication, promotes health and well-being, facilitates education and human capital development, fosters gender equality and social inclusion, and encourages sustainable consumption and production patterns. Upholding this right requires concerted efforts from governments, civil society, and international actors to implement policies and programmes that address inequalities, promote inclusivity, and ensure access to essential resources for all. By embracing the right to an adequate standard of living, we can pave the way towards a sustainable, prosperous, and equitable future for all individuals and generations to come.

Aims and Objectives of this Book

This book aims to examine the intersection between human rights and the right to an adequate standard of living in the context of Sub-Saharan Africa (SSA). It seeks to shed light on the unique challenges faced by the region in ensuring the realisation of this fundamental right and explore potential prospects for progress. The following objectives guides the research and analysis:

- First, the book provides a comprehensive analysis of the social, economic, and political factors that impact the realisation of the right to an adequate standard of living in SSA. It explores the region's specific challenges such as extreme poverty, inequality, limited access to basic services, inadequate housing, food insecurity, and insufficient healthcare, and examine their underlying causes.
- Secondly, the book explores the existing human rights frameworks and legal instruments relevant to the right to an adequate standard of living in SSA. It analyses the international, regional, and national mechanisms and obligations that support the protection and promotion of this right, including the African Charter on Human and Peoples' Rights and other relevant instruments.
- Thirdly, an empirical element is employed in the book as well as the use of case studies to access the gaps between existing policies, laws and their

effective implementation in relation to the right to an adequate standard of living. The book explores the role of governments, civil society and international actors in addressing these gaps and promoting accountability.

- Fourthly, the book builds on the analysis to offer policy recommendations targeted at governments, regional bodies, non-State actors as well as international stakeholders. These recommendations will focus on enhancing policy coherence, strengthening legal frameworks, allocating resources effectively, and promoting participatory approaches to address the challenges and advance the realisation of the right to an adequate standard of living in SSA.
- Finally, this book is a modest contribution to academic discourse on advocacy efforts by raising awareness about the importance of the right to an adequate standard of living in SSA. As such, the book seeks to generate evidence-based insights and promote dialogue among scholars, policymakers, activists, and practitioners, with the goal of fostering positive change and improving the lives of individuals and communities in SSA.

Use of Case Studies in the Book

The book employs a series of cases studies highlighting successful approaches in addressing the challenges that impede the realisation of the right to an adequate standard of living in SSA States. The purpose of incorporating these case studies is to provide valuable examples that SSA States can adopt and adapt within their own socio-cultural contexts. This approach aligns with the socio-economic conditions theory of law and development as articulated by YS Lee in his seminal work titled 'General Theory of Law and Development.'[21]

According to Lee's theory, developing countries should seek inspiration from models that are compatible with their specific socio-cultural settings, rather than solely relying on Western neo-liberal ideas that have been traditionally associated with the law and development paradigm. By embracing contextualised templates, SSA States can draw insights and lessons from successful initiatives implemented in similar socio-economic conditions, enabling them to tailor their approaches to better suit their unique circumstances.[22]

The utilisation of case studies serves as a practical and tangible framework for SSA States to identify promising strategies, policies, and interventions that have proven effective in addressing challenges related to the right to an adequate standard of living. These cases studies offer real-world examples and experiences that can inform decision-making and policy formulation, encouraging innovation and the sharing of best practices among countries within the region.

21 YS Lee, 'General Theory of Law and Development' (2017) 50 *Cornell International Law Journal* 415–471.

22 Ibid. See also, Ordor op cit (note 3) above.

By incorporating this approach, the book aims to foster a nuanced understanding of how socio-cultural compatibility and the adoption of successful models can contribute to the realisation of the right to an adequate standard of living in SSA States. It underscores the importance of context-specific solutions and the need to move beyond a one-size-fits-all approach to development, ultimately facilitating sustainable progress towards ensuring human rights and well-being in the region.

Structure of the Book

The book is structured into a series of nine chapters, each serving a specific purpose. The initial chapter serves as an introduction, emphasising the significance of the right to an adequate standard of living. It explores the concept of this right in depth, examining its relationship with the SDGs. Specifically, the chapter highlights the crucial connection between ensuring this fundamental right and the pursuit of achieving the UN 2030 Target Goals, with focus on SSA. By establishing this groundwork, the chapter lays the foundation for subsequent discussions that delve into the right to an adequate standard of living as a fundamental right. It concludes by outlining the aims and objectives of the book, thereby setting the stage for further exploration and analysis of this vital topic.

The second chapter of the book provides a comprehensive conceptual framework for understanding the right to an adequate standard of living. It commences by offering a precise definition of this fundamental right, elucidating its core components and underlying principles. Moreover, the chapter delves into an in-depth analysis into the intricate interplay between the right to an adequate standard of living and other essential human rights. It explores how this right intersects with rights such as the right to food, housing, health, education, and social security. Through this examination, the chapter illuminates the interconnectedness and mutually reinforcing nature of these rights, emphasising the indivisibility and interdependence of human rights. By establishing this conceptual foundation, the chapter equips readers with a solid understanding of the right to an adequate standard of living within the broader human rights framework. This clarity serves as a springboard for subsequent chapters, which will further explore the practical implications and challenges associated with realising this crucial right in various contexts.

In Chapter 3 of the book, a meticulous analysis of the legal framework surrounding the right to an adequate standard of living is conducted within the specific context of SSA. This examination encompasses a comprehensive review of the relevant international legal instruments, regional instruments, and national laws from selected SSA States pertaining to the right to an adequate standard of living. The chapter critically assesses the applicability and effectiveness of international legal instruments in safeguarding and promoting the right to an adequate standard of living within the region. It explores the extent to which regional instruments, such as those formulated by the

African Union (AU) and its affiliated bodies, contribute to the protection and realisation of this fundamental right. Furthermore, the chapter investigates the legal provisions and mechanisms embedded within the national laws of SSA countries that are designed to ensure the realisation of the right to an adequate standard of living for their citizens. This analysis entails a comprehensive examination of legislative frameworks, policy measures, and judicial decisions that impact the implementation and enforcement of this right at the national level. By undertaking this comprehensive exploration of the legal landscape, the chapter provides readers with a nuanced understanding of the legal framework surrounding the right to an adequate standard of living in SSA. This knowledge serves as a vital basis for subsequent chapters, which delve into the challenges and opportunities associated with translating these legal provisions into practical outcomes for individuals and communities within the region.

Chapter 4 of the book delves into the multifaceted theme of poverty and inequality, concentrating specifically on their manifestations in SSA. This chapter undertakes a comprehensive examination of the causes and effects of poverty and inequality within the region. In dissecting the causes, the chapter scrutinises the structural, economic, and social factors that contribute to the persistence of poverty and inequality in SSA. It delves into the intricate web of issues, including but not restricted to limited access to education, healthcare, employment opportunities, land rights, and gender disparities, that perpetuate these socio-economic disparities. The chapter also explores the wide-ranging effects of poverty and inequality on the realisation of the right to an adequate standard of living. It investigates how these disparities impact various dimensions of human well-being, including access to food, water, housing, healthcare and education, and social security. Moreover, the chapter critically analyses the efforts made thus far by several SSA States to address poverty and inequality. It examines policy initiatives, development programmes, and interventions aimed at poverty reduction and tackling inequality within the region. Drawing on cases studies, the chapter highlights successful initiatives that have effectively reduced poverty and inequality, offering valuable lessons and insights for policy formulation and implementation. By delving into these complex issues, the chapter contributes to a comprehensive understanding of poverty and inequality within the context of the right to an adequate standard of living in SSA. It sets the stage for subsequent chapters, which will explore strategies, best practices, and challenges in advancing socio-economic rights and fostering inclusive development within the region.

Chapter 5 of the book delves into the themes of access to healthcare and education within the context of SSA. This chapter critically examines the multifaceted challenges that hinder adequate access to healthcare and education in the region. The chapter analyses the socio-economic, political, and structural barriers that impede access to healthcare and education in SSA. It scrutinises factors such as inadequate infrastructure, limited resources, insufficient funding, geographical remoteness, cultural and gender biases, and disparities in the distribution of services. Through this analysis, the chapter highlights the complex interplay of these challenges and their impact on the realisation of the right to an adequate standard of living in SSA. Moreover, the chapter explores implications of inadequate access to healthcare and education on various dimensions of human well-being, including health outcomes, educational attainment, and socio-economic development. It emphasises the far-reaching consequences of these challenges, such as increased mortality rates, limited opportunities for social mobility, and perpetuation of poverty and inequality. Furthermore, the chapter delves into the efforts undertaken to improve access to healthcare and education in SSA. It critically evaluates policy interventions, institutional reforms, and initiatives aimed at expanding access to these essential services. Drawing on case studies and empirical evidence, the chapter illuminates successful initiatives that have effectively enhanced access to healthcare and education, shedding light on best practices and potential strategies for replication. By shedding light on these vital issues, the chapter contributes to a comprehensive understanding of the complexities surrounding access to healthcare and education within the context of the right to an adequate standard of living in SSA.

Chapter 6 of the book focuses on the theme of housing and infrastructure within the context of SSA. This chapter critically examines the multifaceted challenges that impede adequate housing and infrastructure development in the region. The chapter thoroughly analyses the various obstacles and constraints that hinder housing and infrastructure development in SSA. It investigates factors such as rapid urbanisation, inadequate urban planning, limited access to affordable housing, poor quality housing, insufficient basic services, inadequate transportation networks, and inadequate access to clean water and sanitation facilities. Through this analysis, the chapter sheds light on the complex dynamics that contribute to the persistent challenges in housing and infrastructure development within SSA. Furthermore, the chapter explores the implications of inadequate housing and infrastructure on the realisation of the right to an adequate standard of living. It investigates how inadequate housing conditions and deficient infrastructure systems affect individuals' well-being, social inclusion, and overall quality of life. The chapter emphasises the far-reaching consequences of these challenges, including increased vulnerability to health risks, limited economic opportunities, and reduced access to essential services. Moreover, the chapter examines the efforts undertaken to improve housing and infrastructure in SSA. It critically evaluates policy interventions, urban planning strategies, and infrastructure development initiatives aimed at addressing these challenges. The chapter draws on case studies and empirical evidence to highlight successful initiatives that have effectively improved housing conditions and infrastructure systems, offering valuable insights and lessons for replication. By addressing these critical issues, the chapter contributes to a comprehensive understanding of the complexities surrounding housing and infrastructure development within the context of the right to an adequate standard of living in SSA. It sets the stage for subsequent chapters, which will explore strategies, best practices, and challenges in advancing housing and infrastructure development to ensure the realisation of this fundamental right within the region.

Chapter 7 of the book delves into the complex and pressing issues of environmental degradation and climate change within the context of Sub-Saharan Africa (SSA). This chapter critically examines the far-reaching effects of environmental degradation and climate change in the region, highlighting their profound impact on various dimensions of socio-economic development and the right to an adequate standard of living. The chapter thoroughly explores the adverse consequences of environmental degradation and climate change in SSA, including but not limited to deforestation, desertification, loss of biodiversity, land degradation, water scarcity, and increased frequency and intensity of extreme weather events. It sheds light on how these environmental challenges directly affect vital sectors such as agriculture, water resources, energy, and human health, exacerbating poverty, inequality, and food insecurity in the region. Furthermore, the chapter emphasises the significance of addressing environmental degradation and climate change in the context of realising the right to an adequate standard of living in SSA. It analyses how these challenges disproportionately impact vulnerable populations, exacerbate existing inequalities, and undermine the enjoyment of fundamental human rights. The chapter underscores the need for comprehensive and integrated approaches that consider the interconnections between environmental sustainability, socio-economic development, and human rights. Moreover, the chapter examines the efforts made by SSA States to address environmental degradation and climate change. It evaluates policy initiatives, adaptation strategies, mitigation measures, and international collaborations aimed at mitigating the adverse impacts and building resilience to these environmental challenges. The chapter draws attention to successful initiatives and innovative approaches that have been implemented, highlighting valuable lessons and best practices for effective environmental stewardship and climate action. By addressing these critical issues, the chapter contributes to a comprehensive understanding of the intricate relationship between environmental degradation, climate change, and the realisation of the right to an adequate standard of living in SSA. It underscores the urgency for robust environmental policies, sustainable development practices, and international cooperation to address the challenges posed by environmental degradation and climate change in the region.

Chapter 8 of the book explores the complex and intricate topic of access to justice in relation to the right to an adequate standard of living. This chapter critically examines the challenges surrounding access to justice and emphasises the imperative of addressing this issue within the context of Sub-Saharan Africa (SSA). The chapter delves into the multifaceted challenges that impede access to justice in SSA, considering factors such as limited legal infrastructure, inadequate legal aid services, financial barriers, cultural and social barriers, and corruption within the justice system. It highlights the profound impact of these challenges on individuals' ability to assert and enforce their rights related to an adequate standard of living, such as housing, healthcare, education, and social security. Furthermore, the chapter emphasises the significance of addressing access to justice as an integral component of realising the right to an adequate standard of living in SSA. It examines the intersections between access to justice and the protection and enforcement of socio-economic rights, emphasising the importance of a holistic approach to justice that encompasses both civil and economic rights. Moreover, the chapter explores case studies of successful initiatives implemented in SSA to enhance access to justice. It examines innovative approaches, policy interventions, and legal reforms that have proven effective in increasing access to justice for marginalised and vulnerable populations within the region. By analysing these case studies, the chapter sheds light on best practices and lessons learned, providing valuable insights for policy formulation and implementation. By addressing these critical issues, the chapter contributes to a comprehensive understanding of the challenges and opportunities surrounding access to justice in the context of the right to an adequate standard of living in SSA. It underscores the urgent need for comprehensive and inclusive justice systems that can effectively safeguard and enforce socio-economic rights, thereby promoting social justice and equality within the region.

The concluding chapter of the monograph serves as a synthesis of the key findings presented throughout the book, providing a comprehensive overview of the insights gained regarding the realisation of the right to an adequate standard of living in Sub-Saharan Africa (SSA). Additionally, this chapter puts forth recommendations aimed at enhancing the realisation of this fundamental right within the region. It also highlights areas that require further research for a more nuanced understanding and effective policy formulation. To begin with, the chapter provides a concise summary of the major findings and arguments discussed in preceding chapters. It highlights the challenges and complexities surrounding the right to an adequate standard of living in SSA, including issues related to poverty, inequality, access to healthcare and education, housing and infrastructure, environmental degradation, climate change, and access to justice. This summary serves to reinforce the significance of addressing these challenges in order to advance the realisation of socio-economic rights in the region. Building upon the findings, the chapter proceeds to offer a series of recommendations aimed at improving the realisation of the right to an adequate standard of living in SSA. These recommendations draw upon the best practices and successful initiatives identified throughout the book, as well as insights gained from the analysis of challenges and opportunities. The recommendations may cover diverse areas such as policy formulation, institutional reforms, capacity building, international collaborations, and community engagement. They aim to guide policymakers, practitioners, and stakeholders in developing effective strategies that address the specific needs and contexts of SSA. Furthermore, the chapter identifies gaps in knowledge and areas that necessitate further research. It highlights specific research questions or areas of inquiry that would contribute to a more comprehensive understanding of the right to an adequate standard of living in SSA. These research directions may encompass exploring innovative approaches, assessing the impact of specific policies or interventions, investigating the experiences of marginalised populations, or analysing the influence of regional and international frameworks on the realisation of socio-economic rights. By providing a summary of key findings, recommendations, and avenues for further research, the final chapter of the monograph presents a conclusive and forward-looking perspective. It underscores the importance of continuous efforts, evidence-based policy interventions, and scholarly inquiry to foster progress in the realisation of the right to an adequate standard of living in Sub-Saharan Africa.

References

Andorno R, 'Human Dignity and Human Rights' in HAMJ ten Have and B Gordijin (eds), *Handbook of Global Bioethics* (Springer 2014) https://doi.org/10.1007/978-94-007-2512-6_66.

Arimoro AE, 'Beyond Economics! The (Evolving) Role of Law in the Eradication of Extreme Poverty' (2023) 8 *Journal of Human Rights and Social Work* 1–13 https://doi.org/10.1007/s41134-023-00247-2

Bailey P, 'The Right to an Adequate Standard of Living: New Issues for Australian Law' (2017) 4(1) *Australian Journal of Human Rights* 25–50.

Chichilinisky G, 'What Is Sustainable Development?' (1997) 73(4) *Land Economics* 467–491.

Eleode E, 'It's Time to Drop 'Sub-Saharan Africa' from our Vocabulary' (2021) available at <https://readcultured.com/its-time-to-drop-sub-saharan-africa-from-our-vocabulary-3cc0561a57cb> accessed 2 January 2023.

Hick R, 'Material Poverty and Multiple Deprivation in Britain: The Distinctiveness of Multidimensional Assessment' (2016) 36 *Journal of Public Policy* 277.

Icelandic Human Rights Centre, 'The Right to an Adequate Standard of Living' (2023) available at <https://www.humanrights.is/en/human-rights-education-project/human-rights-concepts-ideas-and-fora/substantive-human-rights/the-right-to-an-adequate-standard-of-living> accessed 5 June 2023.

Jayawickrama N, *The Judicial Application of Human Rights Law: National, Regional and International Jurisprudence* (2002) (2nd edn, Cambridge University Press) 1025.

Lange K, 'The Sub-Saharan Africa Region' (2019) available at <https://ifair.eu/2019/06/22/the-sub-saharan-africa-region/> accessed 2 January 2023.

Leckie S and Gallanger A, *Economic, Social and Cultural Rights: A Legal Resource Guide* (University of Pennsylvania Press 2006) xvi.

Lee YS, 'General Theory of Law and Development' (2017) 50 *Cornell International Law Journal* 415–471.

Ordor A, 'Tracking the Law and Development Continuum Through Multiple Intersections' (2015) 8(2) *The Law and Development Review* 333–360.

Purvis B, Mao Y and Robinson D, 'Three Pillars of Sustainability: In Search of Conceptual Origins' (2019) 14 *Concepts, Methodology, and Knowledge of Sustainability Science* 581–695.

Stuart PH, '"Economic Stabilisation of the Family: The Standard of Living": Harry Lurie's Call for an Adequate Family Income in the 1920s' (2015) 23(2) *Journal of Community Practice* 290–299.

United Nations, 'OHCHR and the Human Rights Dimension of Poverty' (2020) available at <https://www.ohchr.org/en/poverty#:~:text=Poverty%20erodes%20economic%20and%20social,and%20security%20of%20the%20person> accessed 5 June 2023.

United Nations, 'Universal Declaration of Human Rights' (2023) available at <https://www.un.org/en/about-us/universal-declaration-of-human-rights> accessed 5 June 2023.

Useh U, 'Sustainable Development Goals as a Framework for Postgraduate Future Research Following COVID-19 Pandemic: A New Norm for Developing Countries' (2020) 8(1) *Higher Education for the Future* 123–132.

2 Conceptual Framework

Introduction

This chapter serves as a foundational cornerstone that establishes the overarching thematic framework for the subsequent chapters of this book. The objective is to provide a comprehensive introduction to the right to an adequate standard of living, elucidating its fundamental components and conceptual underpinnings. Subsequent chapters within this book will delve into the legal framework and instrumental mechanisms that safeguard and ensure the realisation of these rights, namely the right to food, water, housing, and healthcare, thereby situating them within the broader conceptual of the right to an adequate standard of living. Particularly, this discourse is contextualised within the specific socio-political and economic milieu of Sub-Saharan Africa (SSA), further enriching our understanding of these essential rights in this regional context.

The field of human rights is considered a 'dynamic arena of struggle in law, politics, and practice.'[1] Hepner and Smith-Cannoy argue that in both the Global North and South, scholars are rethinking the future of human rights and its application.[2] There is the ever increasing need to address the human rights question and to ensure that State and non-State actors support the realisation of these rights.[3] This book argues for the guarantee of rights that promote the well-being of the ordinary citizen which is core and integral to the realisation of the United Nations Target 2030 Goals. Furthermore, the recent COVID-19 pandemic has brought to the fore the vexed problem of inequality in the society. The reality of the pandemic showed that the poor

1 Tricia Redeker Hepner and Heather Smith-Cannoy, 'Introduction to Human Rights on the Edge: The Future of International Human Rights Law and Practice' (2022) 21(2) *Journal of Human Rights* 118-122 at 118.

2 Ibid.

3 Sarita Cargas, 'Fortifying the Future of Human Rights with Human Rights Education' (2019) 18(3) *Journal of Human Rights* 293-307

DOI: 10.4324/9781032628974-2

tend to be more disadvantaged.[4] As such, the focus is on ensuring the right to an adequate standard of living for all.

At the core of human rights lies the fundamental principle of according every individual the necessary respect and dignity they deserve as human beings.[5] Human rights are inherent and do not depend on any earned status or qualification.[6] They are universally applicable, ensuring that every person is entitled to have their rights upheld.[7] This chapter aims to introduce and contextualise this right within the SSA perspective, recognising its diverse components such as the right to food, housing, water, and social security, among others. It needs to be stated, for clarity, that the realisation of the right to an adequate standard of living is a fundamental aspect of human rights.

The right to an adequate standard of living encompasses elements that are essential for individuals to live a dignified life. International law recognises the multidimensional nature of this right, acknowledging that it extends beyond mere survival.[8] It encompasses components such as access to sufficient nutritious food, secure and affordable housing, clean water and sanitation, as well as social security. These components collectively aim to ensure that individuals, regardless of their social status, have access to the basic necessities required for a decent life.

It is important to acknowledge at this point that some aspects of the right to an adequate standard of living are still evolving, especially in the light of emerging challenges such as the COVID-19 pandemic.[9] This global crisis has further underscored the importance of guaranteeing the right to an adequate standard of living, particularly in SSA, where a significant portion of the population lives in extreme poverty. Some of the challenges posed by the pandemic are enumerated below.

First, the pandemic has exposed the vulnerabilities and inequalities within the region, necessitating a deeper understanding of the right to an adequate standard of living and its implications. The COVID-19 pandemic strained healthcare systems in SSA, which were already grappling with limited resources and infrastructure.[10] Secondly, the lockdowns, restrictions, and disruptions to global supply chains caused by the pandemic led to severe economic

4 Octavio Luiz Motta Ferraz, 'Covd-19 and Inequality: The Importance of Social Rights' (2021) 32(1) *Kings Law Journal* 109-121.

5 Howard Davies, *Human Rights Law* (5th ed.) (Oxford: Oxford University Press, 2021) 4.

6 Ibid.

7 Rhona KM Smith, *International Human Rights Law* (10th ed.) (Oxford: Oxford University Press, 2021) 307.

8 Ibid.

9 Ibid.

10 Augustine Arimoro, 'The Corona Virus (COVID-19) Pandemic and the Challenge of Healthcare Infrastructure in Nigeria: What Role for Public-Private Partnerships?' (2020) 3(5) *Theoretical and Applied Law* 18-33 available at < https://papers.ssrn.com/sol3/papers.cfm?abstract_id=3813226> accessed 11 June 2023. See also, Ikechukwu Andrew Mobosi, 'Health Burdens amid COVID-19 Pandemic: A Stark Barrier to Labour Productivity in

repercussions in SSA. Many individuals, particularly those in the informal sector, lost their livelihoods, exacerbating poverty levels.[11] The economic fallout highlighted the need for social safety nets, including unemployment benefits support income, to protect vulnerable populations during crises.[12] Thirdly, COVID-19 disrupted food systems and supply chains, affecting agricultural production and access to food in SSA. Lockdowns and movement restrictions limited people's ability to earn income and purchase food, leading to increased food insecurity and malnutrition.[13] This highlighted the importance of ensuring food security and bolstering agricultural resilience to safeguard the right to adequate nutrition. Fourthly, school closures and the shift to remote learning during the pandemic highlighted stark education disparities in SSA. Many students lacked access to remote learning technologies and faced challenges in continuing their education.[14] A fifth problem was the manner in which the pandemic disproportionately affected marginalised communities in SSA, aggravating social inequalities.[15] Vulnerable groups, such as women, children, persons with disabilities, and those living within informal settlements, faced heightened risks and limited access to essential services.[16] This emphasised the importance of addressing systemic inequalities and ensuring the protection of rights of all individuals.[17]

Overall, the COVID-19 pandemic served as a wake-up call, exposing the vulnerabilities and inadequacies within SSA's socio-economic systems. It highlighted the urgent need to prioritise and invest in an adequate standard of living, encompassing access to healthcare, social protection, food security, education, and the reduction of social inequalities. By addressing these challenges, SSA can build more resilient societies and work towards realising the right to an adequate standard of living for its inhabitants.

Africa' (2022) *Health Care for Women International* available at < https://doi.org/10.1080/07399332.2022.2089146> accessed 11 June 2023.

11 Ibid.

12 Ebrahim Endris Mekonnen and Andulem Kassegn Amede, 'Food Insecurity and Unemployment Crises under COVID-19: Evidence from sub-Saharan Africa' (2022) 8(1) *Cogent Social Sciences* DOI: 10.1080/23311886.2022.2045721.

13 Priviledge Cheteni and Adrino Mazenda, 'Economic Impact of Government Intervention in Response to Covid-19 in Selected sub-Saharan African Countries' (2023) 40(2) *Development Southern Africa* 406-420.

14 Sanjo Rose, Jessleena Suri, Michael Brooks and Peter G Ryan, 'COVID-19 and Citizen Science: Lessons Learned from Southern Africa' (2020) 91(2) *Journal of African Ornithology* 188-191.

15 Reshma Sucheran, 'The COVID-19 Pandemic and Guesthouses in South Africa: Economic Impacts and Recovery Measures' (2021) 39(1) *Development Southern Africa* 35-50.

16 Rebecca Namatovu and Marcus M Larsen, 'Responding to COVID-19: Insights from African Firms' (2021) 7(1) *African Journal of Management* 104-120.

17 Chibuikem Charles Nnaeme, '"The Community comes to life': How Social Grants Enable Participation in the Local Economy and Possible Effect on Post-COVID-19 recovery in Soweto South Africa' (2022) 49(3) *Forum for Development Studies* 493-510.

Against this backdrop, this chapter aims to provide an introductory exploration of the right to an adequate standard of living, especially within the SSA context. By examining its components, emerging challenges, and the socio-economic landscape of the region, we can gain a comprehensive understanding of the complexities and prospects associated with ensuring this fundamental right in SSA.

Defining the Right to Adequate Standard of Living

The right to an adequate standard of living finds its foundation in various international human rights instruments. Notably, the Universal Declaration of Human Rights (UDHR) declares that:

> Everyone has the right to a standard of living that ensures their health, well-being, and that of their family, including access to food, clothing, housing, and medical care and social services, and the right to security in the event of unemployment, sickness, disability, widowhood, old age or other lack of livelihood in the circumstances beyond his control.[18]

Furthermore, the International Covenant on Economic, Social and Cultural Rights (ICESCR) recognises the right of every individual to an adequate standard of living, encompassing essential elements such as food, clothing, housing, and the continuous improvement of living conditions.[19]

As stated above, this chapter provides an exploration of the right to an adequate standard of living. Attention is increasingly being directed towards the different dimensions of this right, particularly in relation to inequalities and the need to make progress towards achieving the United Nations' Sustainable Development Goals (SDGs). The goals provide a roadmap towards achieving a range of interconnected objectives by the year 2030.[20]

Moreover, the right to an adequate standard of living finds expression in various treaties that address specific sectors.[21] For example, Article 5(e)(iii) and 7 of the Convention on the Elimination of All Forms of Racial Discrimination

18 UDHR, 1948, Art 25 (1).

19 ICESCR, 1966, Art 11(1).

20 Augustine Arimoro, 'Book Review: Implementing the Sustainable Development Goals in Nigeria (Routledge, 2022)' (2022) 13(1) *Journal of Sustainable Development Law and Policy* 200-206. See also, Augustine Edobor Arimoro, 'Private Sector Investment in Infrastructure in Sub-Saharan Africa Post COVID-19: The Role of Law' (2022) 27(2) *Public Works Management & Policy* 108-126. See also, Augustine Edobor Arimoro and Abba Amsami Elgujja, 'Public-Private Partnership and the Achievement of Sustainable Development Goals: The Roel of Subnational Governments' in AB Kagu and NE Attah (eds) *Perspectives on Governance and Accountability* (Damaturu: Centre for Research and Capacity Development on Humanitarian Studies, Yobe State University, 2019) 15 available at < https://works.bepress.com/augustine_arimoro/30/> accessed 11 June 2023.

21 These are discussed extensively in chapter three of this book.

(CERD), Article 14(2)(h) of the Convention on the Elimination of All Forms of Discrimination Against Women (CEDAW), Articles 24(2)(c) and 27 of the Convention on the Rights of Persons with Disabilities (CRPD) all uphold and protect this right.

The right itself encompasses a range of interconnected rights and corresponding obligations.[22] The right is not a singular, standalone human right, but rather a multifaceted framework comprising independent rights. Among these rights, some necessitate substantial resource allocations from governments while others may carry less burdensome obligations yet remain equally significant. Different aspects of this right hold distinct importance for individuals in diverse circumstances. However, safeguarding all its components is essential to ensure the provision of an adequate standard of living for all individuals.[23]

The Duty Incumbent on Governments in Sub-Saharan Africa

States bear the responsibility to uphold and fulfil international human rights standards,[24] including the right to an adequate standard of living. In the realm of socio-economic rights, comprehending these obligations is crucial, especially for States in SSA. Protecting this right involves a set of legally enforceable rights backed by remedies, while fulfilling it may require both the provision of and facilitation of the right. SSA States can fulfil these obligations through various policies, laws, and strategies. The allocation of resources becomes necessary to ensure individuals have access to the essential components of a dignified life when they are unable to secure them independently. The primary articulation of this right can be found in the ICESCR which obligates States to progressively realise that the right to the maximum of their available resources.[25] The realisation of this right varies significantly from one country to another, considering environmental, cultural, and geographical factors.

Contracting States must guarantee the minimum core standards of the various components of the right and continually strive to enhance protection and improve the standard of living of all individuals.[26] Achieving this may involve working through strategic development plans at the State level and effectively localising SDGs.

Davies notes that the Committee on Economic, Social and Cultural Rights, along with the relevant UN Special Procedures mandate holders, has developed a framework to assess realisation of the right by States.[27] For instance, the '4 As' framework (availability, accessibility, acceptability, and adaptability) can

22 Smith, op cit (n7) 308.
23 Ibid.
24 Ibid.
25 ICESCR, Art 2.
26 Smith, op cit (n7) 308.
27 Ibid.

serve as a helpful guide. Each element of the right should be available, accessible, acceptable, and adaptable, recognising that different individuals may have varying requirements. All components of the right are interconnected with other rights guaranteed by States and fundamental principles that guide the international human rights, with respect to dignity being central. Adequate housing, for instance, encompasses more than just a physical structure but includes security, peace and dignity.[28] In the same vein, food cannot be considered available if its cost is prohibitive and unaffordable to the individuals within a State.[29]

When reviewing State period performance, the Committed on Economic and Cultural Rights may examine indicators such as the Gross National Product (GNP) of the poorest sector of the population and the State's placement on the Physical Quality of Life Index. This information allows the Committee to assess the relative standard of living compared to previous reports and monitor improvements or deterioration. Some countries have established the informal minimum 'living wage' standards, which indicate the amount necessary to cover basic living expenses in specific locations. In SSA, this is often referred to as the minimum wage system.[30] Social welfare provisions present an opportunity to ensure an adequate standard of living. The COVID-19 pandemic, which began in late 2019, has highlighted the level of inequalities across jurisdictions, with intersecting inequalities often manifesting in varying rates of infection, hospitalisation, and death. This has drawn attention to the consequences of inadequate living conditions.

Components of the Right to an Adequate Standard of Living

The right to an adequate standard of living is a fundamental right that encompasses various essential components crucial for individuals to lead a dignified and fulfilling life. This right is made up of distinct component rights.[31] These include the right to food, right to water, and right to housing.[32] The right to an adequate standard of living is rooted in the principle that all individuals, irrespective of their social or economic status, should have access to basic necessities required for a standard of living.[33] Smith argues that when

28 See CESCR General Comment 4, para 7, The right to adequate housing.

29 Smith, op cit, (n7) 308.

30 Haroon Bhorat, Ravi Kanbur and Benjamin Stanwix, 'Minimum Wages in Sub-Saharan Africa: A Primer' (2017) 32(1) *Research Observer* 21-74.

31 Kasey McCall-Smith, 'Incorporation of International Human Rights Briefing Series: The Right to an Adequate Standard of Living' (2021) available at < https://hrcscotland.org/wp-content/uploads/2021/11/Final-Right-to-Adequate-Standard-of-Living-Briefing-Nov-2021.pdf> accessed 11 June 2023.

32 Ibid.

33 Asbjorn Eide and Wenche Barth Eide, *International Human Rights Law* (4th ed.) (Oxford: Oxford University Press, 2022) 187.

considering the various component rights of an adequate standard of living, it is important to take into cognisance that the requirements for adequate living differ from one jurisdiction to the other.[34] For instance, the requirements for decent housing differ from country to country and as such, there are relevant factors that determine what is adequate.

In this section, these rights that make up the right to an adequate standard of living are discussed with emphasis on how the component rights contribute to the realisation of the right to an adequate standard of living as well as their significance in promoting human well-being.

The Right to Food

The right to food entails the entitlement to consistent, enduring, and unhindered availability – either through direct means or financial transactions – of nutritionally appropriate and adequate food. Combating hunger and malnutrition is more than a moral duty or a policy choice even for SSA States. It is now, rightly so, considered as a legally binding human rights obligation under international law.[35] It is crucial to mention that the right to food is not the right to be fed after an emergency. It is the right of all citizens to have a legal framework and strategies in place to ensure that the right to food is realised both under international law and domestic law.

The right to food encompasses a comprehensive entitlement, extending beyond the mere provision of minimum calorie, protein, and nutrient requirements. It entails the entitlement to access all necessary nutritional components essential for sustaining a healthy and physically dynamic existence. Furthermore, it includes the provision of the means by which individuals can effectively obtain such nutritional elements.[36]

The right to food has been described in the following words:

> The right to adequate food is realised when every man, woman and child, alone or in community with others, has physical and economic access at all times to adequate food or means for its procurement.[37]
>
> The right to have regular, permanent, and free access, either directly or by means of financial purchases, to quantitative and qualitatively adequate and sufficient food corresponding to the cultural traditions of the

34 Smith, op cit. (n7) 309.

35 United Nations, 'The Right to Adequate Food' – Fact Sheet No. 34 (2010) available at < https://www.ohchr.org/sites/default/files/Documents/Publications/FactSheet34en.pdf> accessed 13 June 2023.

36 Ibid.

37 See OCHR Fact Sheet No. 16 (Rev. 1): The Committee on Economic, Social and Cultural Rights.

> people to which the consumer belongs, and which ensures a physical and mental, individual and collective, fulfilling and dignified life free of fear.[38]

Following the above, the Office of the High Commissioner for Human Rights (UN) has clarified the key elements of the right to food.[39] It is important that food is made available, accessible, and adequate – this means that, first, food should be available from natural resources such as land cultivation or animal husbandry or by other ways such as hunting or gathering. It also means that food should be available for purchase in markets and shops. Secondly, the accessibility requirement means that food must be available to everyone and at the same time affordable to all. This can be ensured by guaranteeing a minimum wage that allows ordinary people to provide for their food needs. It also suggests the availability of social security in the absence of employment to enable citizens have access to food. Thirdly, the requirement of adequacy is to the effect that food must satisfy dietary needs. For example, if the food given to children in any jurisdiction does not satisfy the requirement necessary for their physical and mental development, the food given is therefore, not considered adequate. It needs to be added that adequate food must be culturally acceptable. For example, food aid containing pork which is inconsistent with the eating and cultural habits of the Muslim population of SSA States will not be cultural acceptable in those communities.

In the context of SSA, it is evident that individuals living in poverty often face significant barriers in fully realising their right to food.[40] This predicament arises from their inability to afford an adequate quantity and quality of food that meets their nutritional requirements. Also, it is the case that the poor do not have the means to grow the food that they need by themselves. People suffering from poverty are those who suffer from a human condition of sustained chronic depravation of the resources, capabilities, choices, security and power necessary for the enjoyment of an adequate standard of living and other civil, cultural, economic, and political and social rights.[41] Notably the overwhelming majority of individuals experiencing extreme poverty are concentrated in SSA, making it highly plausible that a substantial proportion of those deprived of their right to an adequate standard of living are residents of this region.[42]

In order to address the issue of hunger, SSA may find it beneficial to adopt strategies employed by other regions of the Global South, specifically through the utilisation of the right to food approach. It is imperative that the right to

38 OCHR Fact Sheet No. 27.

39 United Nations, op cit (35).

40 Ibid.

41 See Poverty and the International Covenant on Economic, Social and Cultural Rights (E/C. 12/2001/10).

42 Augustine Edobor Arimoro, 'Beyond Economics! The (Evolving) Role of Law in the Eradication of Extreme Poverty' (2023) *Journal of Human Rights and Social Work* doi: 10.1007/s41134-023-00247-2.

food is not only acknowledged as a fundamental right according to international law but also established as a justiciable right within the framework of national legislation.[43] Interestingly, many countries have included the right to food as a right guaranteed under their constitutions. For example, in South America, Brazil, with a vote of a constitutional amendment by the House of Representatives on 4 February 2010 recognised the right to food. This is a major step towards ensuring greater accountability for the right to food in the country.[44] Similarly, Bolivia inserted the right to food in its Constitution under Article 16 in 2009. Also, Ecuador has recognised the right to food in its Constitution.[45] Within the SSA region, South Africa stands as an exemplary model for other countries, having directly incorporated the right to food under Article 27.1 of its Constitution.[46]

Building upon the preceding discussion, scholars have posited that the incorporation of the right to food within the domestic context can take two forms: explicit recognition, whereby the right is directly acknowledged as a fundamental human right, and implicit recognition, whereby the right is recognised as an aspirational goal within a country's constitution.[47] The latter approach is commonly referred to as a 'directive principle of State policy'. Thus, for example, the right to food is a fundamental right recognised in South Africa but a direct State principle or an aspirational goal in India.[48]

The Right to Water

Water is regarded as the source of life.[49] The right to an adequate standard of necessitates the availability of sustainable and accessible source of clean water for both personal and domestic purposes.[50] Access to water plays a vital role in promoting health and ensuring survival. However, in developing countries, rural communities frequently experience severe shortages in the provision of fresh and potable water.[51] Recognising the urgency to address the issue, the

43 Oliver de Schutter, 'Countries Tackling Hunger with a Right to Food Approach' *Briefing Note 1* May 2010 available at < https://www2.ohchr.org/english/issues/food/docs/Briefing_Note_01_May_2010_EN.pdf> accessed 25 June 2023.

44 Ibid.

45 Ibid.

46 Ibid.

47 Mathilde Cohen, 'The Right to Food' in *Max Planck Encyclopaedia of Comparative Constitutional Law* (Oxford: Oxford University Press, 2017).

48 Ibid.

49 Sila Pelon Oguz, 'Right to Water: Politics and Struggles Concerning Water' (2017) 2(1) *Research and Policy on Turkey* 25-37 doi: 10.1080/23760818.2016.1272265

50 Asbjorn Eide and Wenche BartthEide, *International Human Rights Law* (Oxford: Oxford University Press, 2022) 192.

51 Augustine Arimoro and Habiba Musa, 'Towards Sustainable Water Resource Management in Rural Nigeria: The Role of Communities' (2020) 11(1) *The Journal of Sustainable Development Law and Policy* 1-17 doi: 10.4314/jsdlp.v11i1.2.

inclusion of universal access to water as one of the SDGs for 20230 has gained significant traction. Extensive evidence demonstrates that insufficient or poor access to freshwater can lead to the proliferation of waterborne diseases and have detrimental effects on economically significant activities.[52] Water is essential for human health and survival, and access to water, is regarded as a fundamental human right. Significantly, the proportion of the world's population with access to potable water has increased from 62 percent in 2000 to 74 percent in 2020.[53] Notwithstanding, SSA continues to lag the rest of the world as far as access to potable water is concerned.

The right to water requires everyone to have access to accessible, affordable, acceptable, safe, and sufficient water for their own and domestic use.[54] This includes drinking, cooking, washing, and cleaning. It is essential that all citizens enjoy access to the minimum essential amount of water that is sufficient and safe for personal and domestic uses to prevent the outbreak or spread of diseases.

Aligned with the SDGs, particularly Goal 6, the overarching objective on a global scale is to attain comprehensive and just access to potable water that is safe and economically feasible for all individuals.[55] To realise this aspiration, it is imperative to ensure the existence of an adequate supply that fulfils domestic requirements, thereby guaranteeing its availability to households.[56] Additionally, it is essential to establish accessible water provisions in diverse settings and contexts, encompassing residential dwellings, educational institutions, medical facilities, and workplaces.[57]

As of 2020, only 64 percent of the people living in SSA had access to potable water. This is in contrast with 90 percent of the people living in the other six regions of the world.[58] However, it is not until 2010 that the General Assembly of the United Nations (UNGA) accepted the right to water as a fundamental human right.[59] The worldwide water crisis is a cause for concern. This is not unconnected with issues relating to climate change, a growing

52 Ibid.

53 The World Bank, 'World Water Day' (2023) available at < https://blogs.worldbank.org/opendata/world-water-day-two-billion-people-still-lack-access-safely-managed-water> accessed 26 June 2023.

54 Rhona KM Smith, *International Human Rights Law* (10th ed) (Oxford: Oxford University Press, 2021) 317.

55 We Are Water Foundation, 'What Do We Mean When We Talk About Access to Water' (2021) available at < https://www.wearewater.org/en/what-do-we-mean-when-we-talk-about-access-to-water_346091#:~:text=%E2%80%9CAccess%E2%80%9D%20refers%20to%20the%20existence,%2C%20health%20centers%2C%20and%20workplaces> accessed 26 June 2023.

56 Ibid.

57 Ibid.

58 The World Bank, op cit (note 53).

59 Oguz, op cit (note 49).

world population and of course an increasing demand for water.[60] In the context of SSA, it is vital to note that the right to water is not merely a luxury but should be guaranteed as a human right. This is more so as millions of people continue to face challenges in obtaining reliable and sustainable access to this essential resource. This section examines the right to water in SSA in SSA.

It is anticipated that countries in SSA will fulfil their obligations to uphold, safeguard, and realise the human right to water. The right to water should be accorded the same level of protection as the right to life, given the close interrelation between these two rights.[61] Moreover, water lies at the heart of human well-being, environmental sustainability, and economic development.[62]

The predominant challenges to water access in SSA encompasses several aspects. First, water scarcity and inequitable distribution pose significant obstacles. Despite the existence of hydro resources in abundance, there is a dearth of fresh, potable water in the region.[63] Notably the issue of inadequate supply of water is not solely a matter that if its overall availability. Rather, it brings to the forefront the question of water access disparities in SSA, where the poor face inequitable access compared to their affluent counterparts.[64] Secondly, inadequate infrastructure, encompassing storage, treatment, and distribution systems exacerbates the challenges of water access in the region. Insufficient investment in water infrastructure hampers the delivery of of clean and safe water to communities, particularly in rural areas.[65] Consequently, individuals, primarily women and children, are compelled to undertake arduous journeys to distant water sources, contributing to their disproportionate burden. Thirdly, water quality is a pressing concern in SSA. Contamination, coupled with insufficient sanitation infrastructure and poor hygiene practices results in waterborne diseases and preventable fatalities.[66] Ensuring the right to water extends beyond availability; it necessitates attention to water quality and sanitation facilities to safeguard human health and well-being.

Furthermore, in urban areas, even when water is provided to the poor, they often face financial burdens due to the reliance on water vendors, as they lack access to municipal water infrastructure. This underscores the issue of economic disparities and the need to address access inequalities within SSA. When discussing the right to water, it is crucial to approach the discourse not only from a policy perspective but also through the lens of environmental justice. Scholars such as Harris et al., contend that the pursuit of redress should foster

60 Nehaluddin Ahmad, 'Human Right to Water Under International Law Regime: An Overview' (2020) 46(3) *Commonwealth Law Bulletin* 415-439 doi: 10.1080/03050718.2020.1770618.

61 Ibid.

62 Ibid.

63 Konuralp Pamukcu, 'The Right to Water: An Assessment'(2005) 11(2-3) *Contemporary Politics* 157-167 doi: 10.1080/13569770500275155.

64 Ibid.

65 Arimoro and Musa, op cit. (note 51).

66 Ibid.

new legal foundations that strive for socially equitable and environmentally sustainable water futures for all individuals.[67]

In conclusion, it is imperative for countries in SSA to prioritise the fulfilment of the human right to water. By addressing challenges related to water scarcity, unequal distribution, inadequate infrastructure, and water quality, the region can work towards achieving socially just and environmentally sustainable water access for all.

The Right to Housing

Housing and shelter are central to human existence.[68] Smith notes that this right as a component to the right to an adequate standard of living of living involves the consideration of homelessness, forced evictions, and what constitutes adequate housing.[69] The human rights approach to housing is gaining traction around the Globe.[70] Yung and Lee note that the right to housing incorporates the following components:[71]

- The right to adequate housing.
- The right to affordable housing.
- The right to enjoy one's housing without any arbitrary interference.
- Freedom from the threat of arbitrary eviction.
- The right of choice in relation to the decision to rent or home-ownership and the neighbourhood one is to live in accordance with needs, preferences and lifestyle.

Housing is a very important subject in all regions of the world. This is especially so because it consumes a larger proportion of the household budget especially for lower income households.[72] The Office of the High Commissioner United Nations Human Rights notes that the right to adequate housing includes the following elements: security of tenure; housing land and property restitution;

67 Leila M Harris, Lucy Rodina and Cynthia Morinville, 'Revisiting the Human Right to Water from an Environmental Justice Lens' (2015) 3(4) *Politics, Groups, and Identities* 660-665 doi: 10.1080/21565503.2015.1080619

68 Smith, op cit. (note 7).

69 Ibid.

70 Sophie L Stadler and Damian Collins, 'Assessing Housing First Programs from a Right to Housing Perspective' (2021) *Housing Studies* https://doi.org/10.1080/02673037.2021.1982873.

71 Betty Yung and Fung-Ping Lee, '"Right to Housing" in Hong Kong: Perspectives from the Hong Kong Community' (2012) 29(4) *Housing, Theory and Society* 401-419 doi: 10.1080/14036096.2012.655382.

72 Chester Hartman, 'The Case for a Right to Housing' (1998) 9(2) *Housing Policy Debate* 223-246 doi: 10.1080/10511482.1998.9521292.

equal and non-discriminatory access to adequate housing; and participation in housing-related decision-making at the national and community levels.[73]

Firstly, housing cannot be considered adequate if its occupants do not have a degree of tenure security which guarantees legal protection against forced evictions.[74] Secondly, housing is not adequate if its occupants do not have safe drinking water, adequate sanitation, energy for cooking, heating, lighting, food storage or refuse disposal.[75] Thirdly, housing is not adequate if its costs threatens or compromises the occupants' enjoyment of other rights.[76] Fourthly, housing is not adequate if it does not guarantee physical safety or provide adequate space, as well as protection against the cold, damp, heat, rain, wind, other threats to health and structural hazards.[77] Fifthly, housing is not adequate if the specific needs of disadvantaged and marginalised groups are not taken into account.[78] Sixthly, housing is inadequate if it is cut off from employment opportunities, healthcare services, schools, childcare centres and other social facilities, or if located in polluted or dangerous areas.[79] Finally, housing is not adequate if it does not respect and take into account the expression of cultural identity.[80]

Forced evictions violate the right to adequate housing for two major reasons: It undermines the living standards of the people affected and it robs them off the freedom to choose where to live.[81] Furthermore, the need for better and adequate housing is acute in Africa. The population of African and SSA is rapidly growing with corresponding increase in available housing for the population.[82] In the same vein, the rapidly increasing demand for housing in SSA has also remarkably seen transformation of existing stock being transformed to meet the needs of the population.[83] There is a need to address the housing deficit in SSA particularly as about 23 percent of those living in slums in the world are in the SSA region.[84] It has been noted that poor hous-

73 Office of the High Commissioner, United Nations Human Rights, 'The Right to Adequate Housing in Human Rights Law' *Fact Sheet* 21 available at < https://www.ohchr.org/sites/default/files/Documents/Publications/FS21_rev_1_Housing_en.pdf> accessed 27 June 2023.

74 Ibid.

75 Ibid.

76 Ibid.

77 Ibid.

78 Ibid.

79 Ibid.

80 Ibid.

81 Naofumi Suzuki, Tetsuo Ogawa and Nanao Inaba, 'The Right to Adequate Housing: Evictions of the Homeless and the Elderly Caused by the 2020 Summer Olympics in Tokyo' (2018) 37(1) *Leisure Studies* 89-96 doi: 10.1080/02614367.2017.1355408.

82 Lucy S Tusting et al, 'Mapping Changes in Housing in Sub-Saharan Africa from 2000 to 2015' (2019) 568 *Nature* 391-394 doi: 10.1038/s41586-019-1050-5.

83 Ibid.

84 United Nations Statistics Division, 'Make Cities and Human Settlements Inclusive, Safe, Resilient and Sustainable' (2019) available at < https://unstats.un.org/sdgs/report/2019/goal-11/> accessed 27 June 2023.

ing accounts for health challenges in SSA. For example, Tusting et al note that poor housing is responsible for several childhood diseases and increase in child mortality rate in SSA.[85] It follows that adequate housing is directly related to healthy living and for the region, there is the need for a deliberate a clear strategy towards ensuring the realisation of this right.

The Right to Health

Health is recognised as a fundamental human right.[86] As humans, our health and those of those we care for is a matter of daily concern.[87] According to the World Health Organization, 'The enjoyment of the highest attainable standard of health is one of the fundamental rights of every human being without distinction of race, religion, political belief, economic or social condition'.[88] This right obligates States to ensure that they provide appropriate conditions for the enjoyment of health for all citizens without any form of discrimination.[89] The recent COVID-19 pandemic raised questions regarding the realisation of the right to health especially as it relates to the provision of adequate health infrastructure for the population.[90]

The right to the highest attainable standard of health means that every individual should have access to health services that are available, of high quality and acceptable to the population.[91] Following from this, every citizen irrespective of their social status should enjoy living conditions that enable them to realise optimal health through fulfilment of essential needs that include but are not limited to, access to nutritional food, adequate housing , work, education, human dignity, life, non-discrimination, equality, privacy and access to information on healthcare.[92]

85 Lucy S Tusting et al, 'Housing and Child Health in Sub-Saharan Africa: A Cross Sectional Analysis' (2020) *PLOS Medicine* available at < https://journals.plos.org/plosmedicine/article?id=10.1371/journal.pmed.1003055> accessed 27 June 2023.

86 World Health Organization, 'Health is a Fundamental Human Right' (2017) available at < https://www.who.int/news-room/commentaries/detail/health-is-a-fundamental-human-right> accessed 27 June 2023.

87 United Nations, 'The Right to Health' *Fact Sheet 31* available at < https://www.ohchr.org/sites/default/files/Documents/Publications/Factsheet31.pdf> accessed 27 June 2023.

88 Ibid. See the WHO Constitution 1946.

89 World Health Organization, 'Human Rights' (2022) available at < https://www.who.int/news-room/fact-sheets/detail/human-rights-and-health> accessed 27 June 2023.

90 Augustine Arimoro, 'The Corona Virus (COVID-19) Pandemic and the Challenge of Healthcare Infrastructure in Nigeria: What Role for Public-Private Partnerships?' (2020) 3(5) *Theoretical and Applied Law* 18-33.

91 World Health Organization, 'Right to Health 2018' (2018) available at < https://www.emro.who.int/images/stories/palestine/documents/who_right_to_health_2018_web-final.pdf?ua=1> accessed 27 June 2023.

92 Ibid.

According to the WHO disadvantaged groups are often deprived of the right to enjoy adequate healthcare.[93] For example, three of the world's most fatal communicable diseases – malaria, HIV and tuberculosis – disproportionately affect the world's poor populations and compound the problem of social inequality.[94] The right to health means functioning public healthcare facilities. States must drive policies and have the political will to provide the resources required to ensure this right.[95]

According to the United Nations, the key aspects of the right to health are that the right is inclusive, the right contains freedoms as well as entitlements.[96] Core to the right to health are aspects such as safe drinking water, safe food, adequate nutrition and housing, healthy working conditions, health-related education and gender equality.[97] Furthermore, the freedoms that flow from the right to health include the right to be free from non-consensual medical treatment, such as medical experiments, and research or forced sterilisation, and to be free from torture and other cruel, inhuman or degrading punishment.[98]

The indicators to the right to health has been subject of debate. For example, Mpinga and Chastony have argued that patient satisfaction can be considered an indicator of the right to health.[99] While this might be considered as taken a step too far, protecting the right to health should take into cognisance the need to ensure that citizens receive adequate care and have a choice about how they should receive medical treatment or assistance. This must also be under culturally acceptable circumstances. For example, in Muslim communities, where a doctor of the same gender is available to treat a patient, it is impermissible to refer that patient to a doctor of the opposite gender.[100]

Figure 2.1 is a chart representing the current health expenditure (percent of GDP) of SSA States.[101] From data reviewed, only Lesotho's figure is 10 percent. Liberia and Central African Republic have a little over 9 percent for health, while South Africa, Sierra Leone, and Guinea Bissau have about 8 percent for health. The Gambia, Angola, and Benin have a paltry 2 percent of their GDP for health. For a region with a huge infrastructure deficit, it is

93 World Health Organization, op cit (note 89).
94 Ibid.
95 Katie Jukes, 'There is a Human Right to Health, and this is How it Works' (2016) available at < https://eachother.org.uk/is-there-a-right-to-health/> accessed 27 June 2023.
96 United Nations, op cit. (note 87).
97 Ibid.
98 Ibid.
99 Emmanuel Kabengele Mpinga and Philippe Chastonay, 'Satisfaction of Patients: A Right to Health Indicator?' (2011) 100 (1-2) *Health Policy* 144-150 doi: 10.1016/j.healthpol.2010.11.001.
100 Sayyid Ali Khamene'I, 'Rules Regarding Looking, Touching and Examining' (2023) available at < https://www.al-islam.org/islamic-rulings-medical-issues-sayyid-ali-khamenei/rules-regarding-looking-touching-and-examining> accessed 27 June 2023.
101 The World Bank, 'Current health Expenditure of SSA States' (2023) available at < https://data.worldbank.org/indicator/SH.XPD.CHEX.GD.ZS> accessed 27 June 2023.

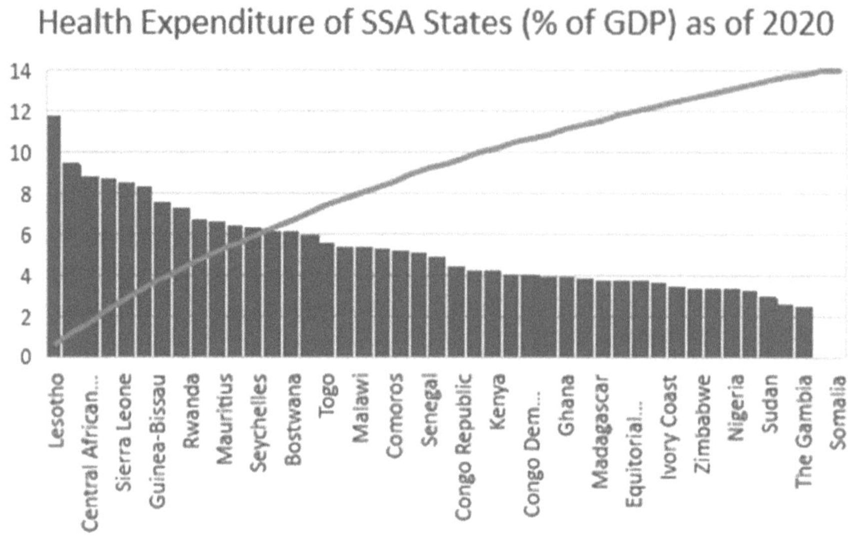

Figure 2.1 Health Expenditure of SSA States (percent of GDP) as of 2020.
Source: Author with data from the World Bank.

worrisome that policy direction is not geared towards bridging the huge deficit in the health sector.

Furthermore, World Bank data shows a continuing drop in the average spending for healthcare in SSA generally.[102] For example, while SSA States on average spent US $82 per citizen for healthcare in 2015, as of 2019 the average amount allocated per person for healthcare was down to US $79.[103]

Applying a human rights approach to healthcare requires putting in place policies and a framework to ensure that SSA States focus on healthcare as a priority.

The Right to an Adequate Standard of Living as a Socio-economic Right

The right to an adequate standard of living, along with its constituent rights mentioned earlier, pertains to a category of rights for which States acknowledge their obligations under international law.[104] However, it is evident that these rights are not accorded the same level of importance as the civil and

102 Macrotrends, 'Sub-Saharan Africa Healthcare Spending 2000-2023' (2023) available at < https://www.macrotrends.net/countries/SSF/sub-saharan-africa-/healthcare-spending> accessed 27 June 2023.
103 Ibid.
104 Tony Evans, 'A Human Right to Health?' (2002) 23(2) *Third World Quarterly* 97-215.

political rights associated with liberal freedoms.[105] Despite being legally binding at international level, these rights can be integrated into domestic law to ensure enforceability.[106]

What Are Economic, Social, and Cultural Rights?

One significant consequence following the conclusion of World War II was the establishment of the Universal Declaration of Human Rights (UDHR) in 1948, as well as the subsequent creation of two additional covenants namely the International Covenant on Economic, Social and Cultural Rights (ICESCR). Collectively referred to as the International Bill of Rights, these international rights, including civil, political, economic, social and cultural rights, which have been established through the aforementioned treaties under international law.[107] While civil and political rights encompass entitlements such as the right to life and the right to a fair trial, economic and socio-cultural rights encompass rights such as the right to education, adequate housing, food, and healthcare, among others.

However, a major challenge in many SSA States lies in their domestic legal systems, which predominantly focus on political rights, with socio-economic rights often considered as mere ideals that the State should strive for. Consequently, enforcing these socio-economic rights becomes exceedingly difficult. Therefore, in the context of SSA, it is crucial to not only recognise socio-economic rights, such as the right to and adequate standard of living and its constituent components, under international law, but also incorporate them into domestic legislation to ensure effective enforcement.[108] This implies that citizens of SSA States will be entitled to rights that guarantee improved access to a quality life, encompassing rights such as adequate housing, healthcare, education, and sufficient pensions upon retirement, among other socio-economic rights that contribute to an adequate standard of living in SSA.

The main argument put forth is that merely recognising these rights as guiding principles for the State without ensuring their enforceability creates an accountability gap, where the State is not held responsible for fulfilling its obligations in relation to these rights.

Addressing the Accountability Gap for Socio-Economic and Cultural Rights

If SSA is to address the accountability for socio-economic and cultural rights, there is the need for the domestication of international norms. There are

105 Ibid.

106 Katie Boyle, 'Models of Incorporation and Justiciability for Economic, Social and Cultural Rights' (2018) available at <https://www.scottishhumanrights.com/media/1809/models_of_incorporation_escr_vfinal_nov18.pdf> accessed 3 July 2023.

107 Ibid.

108 Ibid.

several strategies that might be employed to achieve the objective of bridging the accountability gap for socio-economic and cultural rights in SSA. For example, firstly, States in the region might chose to amend their constitutions to include these rights under the fundamental human rights chapter of their respective constitutions. Secondly, SSA States could, by way of domestic legislation, recognise these rights and make them directly enforceable by the State.

It should be noted that the incorporation of international law into domestic legislation would amount to embedding legal standards set out in international law and making them enforceable domestically. Furthermore, still in the SSA context, it is not enough to incorporate these rights domestically via legislation. There must be the political will to ensure that implementation of the rights via incorporation of international into domestic framework meets the sufficient threshold set under international norms. Also, the State must ensure that standards set under international law are not watered down. The argument here is that where international human rights norm has been domesticated in a State, the domestication of the norms must be shown to have been derived under international law and at the same time there must be a clear system under domestic law to ensure that there are remedies for rights that are violated whether by State or non-State actors.[109]

Making the Right to an Adequate Standard of Living Justifiable

Interestingly, socio-economic rights have historically been misunderstood as far as their legal status is concerned. This is not unconnected to the fact that there was no clarity regarding how the rights should be implemented. It has always been assumed that while civil and political rights are enforceable in domestic courts, socio-economic and cultural rights are not.[110] In modern times, however, both the literature and international best practice tend to show that socio-economic rights are binding international obligations that are amenable to enforcement in domestic courts.[111]

Of note, the Committee on Economic, Social and Cultural Rights,[112] as far back as 1998, has been pushing for the judicial remedies to be made available where there are violations of socio-economic rights.[113] In the view of the Committee, a refusal by a State to recognise and implement the justiciable nature of socio-economic rights is considered arbitrary.[114] Furthermore, the

109 Ibid.

110 Matthew Crave, *The International Covenant on Economic, Social, and Cultural Rights, A Perspective on its Development* (Clarendon Press OUP 1995).

111 Boyle, op cit (note 106).

112 The body responsible for overseeing the implementation of the ICESCR.

113 UN Committee on Economic, Social and Cultural Rights (CESCR), General Comment No. 9: The Domestic Application of the Covenant, 3 December 1998, E/C.12/1998/24, para.10.

114 Ibid.

Committee contends that socio-economic rights must be guaranteed and protected in the same manner as civil and political rights are preserved by States. As such, States must ensure that they implement socio-economic rights within their domestic frameworks.

It follows that SSA States have an obligation to recognise the right to an adequate standard of living and its component's part within their domestic legal framework. While it is noted that South Africa currently leads the way in terms of implementation and protection of socio-economic rights,[115] the other States in the region should seek ways to adapt or improve on the South African model. For example, the South African model adopts a hybrid of substantive rights recognition alongside safeguards and limitation clauses contained in the country's Constitution. Boyle notes that in South Africa, 'rights are also afforded protection to different degrees along the respect, protect, promote, fulfil axis.'[116] Furthermore, some rights, such as the right not to be evicted without fair procedure, enjoy immediate protection.[117] Very importantly, the South African Constitutional Court has entertained matters relating to socio-economic rights and have on many occasions ensured the enforcement of those rights by employing a 'reasonableness' review in assessing State compliance.

Comparative Overview of Non-Justiciable Constitutional Provisions in SSA States

Simply put, a non-justiciable constitutional right is a right that cannot be legally enforceable in a domestic court.[118] In this section, selected provisions across the States in SSA regarding socio-economic rights are examined. The fact that socio-economic rights are non-justiciable in several SSA States makes it challenging to hold political leaders responsible.[119] For example, who should be held responsible for the old pensioner who retires without a pension or for the out-of-school child who is ready and willing to learn but cannot secure a place in school? The answer to this question and a strategy to ensure that all citizens enjoy an adequate standard of living is central to the discussion in this chapter and subsequent chapters of this book.

115 Boyle, op cit (note 106).

116 Ibid.

117 See for example, *Occupiers of 51 Olivia Road, Berea Township and 197 Main Street, Johannesburg v City of Johannesburg and Others* CCT 24/07 Medium Neutral Citation [2008] ZACC1 – meaningful engagement and participation is required by the Constitution before an eviction order of the Court can be served. In other words, there cannot be any forced eviction without notice.

118 Chaman Law Firm, 'What Are Non-Justiciable Constitutional Provisions?' (2022) available at < https://www.chamanlawfirm.com/what-are-non-justiciable-constitutional-provisions> accessed 3 July 2023.

119 University Edih and Basil Ganagana, 'Justiciable or Non-Justiciable Rights: A Debate on Socio-Economic and Political Rights in Nigeria' (2020) 8(4) *Global Journal of Politics and Law Research* 78-85.

The selection of the countries in this section reflects what is prevalent in the region. In no order, the provisions of socio-economic rights in selected SSA States are examined below.

Nigeria

For Nigeria, socio-economic rights can be found in the second chapter of the 1999 Constitution of the Federal Republic of Nigeria (as amended). The chapter is referred to as the fundamental objectives and directive principles of State policy.[120] The chapter is made up of 12 sections.[121] The Nigerian Constitution requires all organs of government in the country to observe, and to apply the provisions of the second chapter of the Constitution.[122]

The relevant provisions of chapter II of the 1999 Constitution are sections 13,17,18, and 20.[123] The Constitution provides as follows:

1) The State social order is founded on the ideals of Freedom, Equality, and Justice.
2) In furtherance of the social order:

a) every citizen shall have equality of rights, obligations and opportunities before the law;
b) the sanctity of the human person shall be recognised, and human dignity shall be maintained and enhanced;
c) governmental actions shall be humane;
d) exploitation of human or natural resources in any form whatsoever for reason, other than the good of the community, shall be prevented; and
e) the independence, impartiality, and integrity of courts of law, and easy accessibility thereto shall be secured and maintained.[124]

The above provisions demonstrate the ideals of the Nigerian State towards equity and justice. Particularly, there is a provision that 'governmental actions shall be humane.'[125] This connotes that the Nigerian government is required under the Constitution to ensure that all actions taken by government are to the benefit of the Nigerian people. For example, government budgets should be planned to ensure that the welfare of citizens is paramount. Again, decisions

120 Constitution of the Federal Republic of Nigeria, chapter II.
121 See Ibid. sections 13 to 24.
122 Ibid. s.13.
123 Amos O Enabulele and Anthony Osaro Ewere, 'Can the Economic Community of West African States Community Court of Justice Enforce the African Charter Replicas of the Non-Justiciable Chapter II Human Rights Provisions of the Nigerian Constitution against Nigeria?' (2012) 1 *International Human Rights Law Review* 312-337.
124 Constitution of the Federal Republic of Nigeria (as amended) 1999, s. 17(1)-(2) (a-e).
125 Ibid. s.17(2)(c).

on matters that affect purchasing power like taxation should be done in a manner that does not further impoverish the poor.

Furthermore, section 17(3) of the Constitution provides unequivocally that the State shall direct its policies towards ensuring that all citizens enjoy the following:

- the opportunity for securing adequate means of livelihood as well as adequate opportunity to secure suitable employment;
- conditions of work are just and humane, and that there are adequate facilities for leisure and for social, religious and cultural life;
- the health, safety and welfare of all persons in employment are safeguarded and not endangered or abused;
- there are adequate medical and health facilities for all persons;
- there is equal pay for equal work without discrimination;
- young persons protected against any exploitation and against moral and material neglect;
- provision for public assistance in deserving cases; and
- the promotion of family life.

These goals are tandem with international norms. However, as they are provided for under chapter II of the Constitution, no citizen can require domestic courts to enforce these provisions. Interestingly, section 18 of the 1999 Constitution (as amended) states as follows:

That government shall:

- direct its policies towards ensuring that there are equal and adequate educational opportunities at all levels;
- promote science and technology; and
- strive to eradicate illiteracy by providing free, compulsory and universal primary education; free secondary education; free university education; and free adult literacy programme.

While these ideals represent the aspiration of the Nigerian State, the reality is that the same Constitution puts an encumbrance to the realisation of the ideals by way of court enforcement. According to Enabulele and Ewere, by the provision of section 6 of the Constitution, the provisions of chapter II remain non-justiciable.[126] For example, in the case of *Attorney General of Borno State & Others v Rev Joshua J Adamu & Others*,[127] the Court of Appeal of Nigeria upheld the decision of the High Court in Borno State with regards to the unenforceability of socio-economic rights under the Constitution of Nigeria. In the case, the respondents, as plaintiffs, approached the High Court of

126 Enabulele and Ewere, op cit (note 123) 316.
127 [1996] 1 NWLR (Pt 427) 681 (CA).

Borno State seeking redress. The respondents contended that it was a breach of the Constitution for their Christian children and wards to pay for religious instruction while their Muslim counterparts are not made to pay for the same instruction. This is because the Gwoza Local Government Council paid Islamic teachers but did not extend the same treatment to Christian teachers. The respondents contended that the unequal treatment is unlawful, unconstitutional, and discriminatory.

The Borno State High Court held that the case was not justiciable and therefore, dismissed it. Aggrieved, the respondents approached the Court of Appeal to upturn the decision of the lower court.[128] The Borno State Attorney General filed an application seeking the Appeal Court to refer the following questions to the Supreme Court of Nigeria to determine them in juxtaposition of the provision of section 259 of the Constitution, viz:

- Whether by the provisions of Chapter II i.e., section of 18 of the 1979 Constitution [same chapter as Chapter II of the 1999 Constitution], the duty of the government to direct its policy towards ensuring that there are equal and adequate educational opportunities at all levels is an obligation or mere directive;
- If it is an obligation on the government, it is justiciable and enforceable having regards to the unequivocal provisions of section 6(6) of the Constitution.

The Nigerian Court of Appeal rejected the referral application. Instead, it held that section 6(6) of the Constitution excludes the jurisdiction of the court in the determination of whether any authority or person is in breach of the provisions of chapter II of the Constitution.

Ghana

Ghana's 1992 Constitution contains extensive provisions on fundamental human rights, including non-justiciable socio-economic rights. One such right is the Directive Principle on the right to an 'adequate means of livelihood and suitable employment' under Article 36(2)(a).[129] This right correlates with the internationally recognised right to an adequate standard of living found in the Universal Declaration of Human Rights (UDHR) and the International Covenant on Economic, Social and Cultural Rights (ICESCR).[130]

While the right to an adequate standard of living is non-justiciable and not directly enforceable in Ghanaian courts, the State still has a duty to take steps

128 Enabulele and Ewere op cit (note 123) 317.
129 Constitution of the Republic of Ghana (1992), art 36(2)(a).
130 This is discussed in detail in the next chapter. See UDHR (1948), art 25(1); ICESR (1966), art 11(1).

towards its progressive realisation.[131] In this section, the scope, status, and mechanism for enforcing the right to an adequate standard of living in Ghana comes into focus. This is done bearing in mind the provision ofArticle 36(2)(a) of the Ghana Constitution. The argument here is that realising this right requires adopting a holistic approach encompassing health, housing, food, water, sanitation, employment, and social security.

Under Ghana's Constitution, directive principles of State policy like the right to an adequate standard of living are non-justiciable.[132] While the courts cannot enforce this right, the right remains a guide for the Government of Ghana to provide policy.[133] Despite the non-justiciable nature of the right to an adequate standard of living in Ghana, there are mechanisms in the country to ensure enforcement of the principle to a certain degree. However, it has been noted that these mechanisms are categorised into weak and strong mechanisms.[134]

The weak enforcement mechanisms in Ghana include the following:

- Advocacy and social activism on the part of members of the Ghanaian public. For example, citizens can organise advocacy campaigns, demonstration, media engagement among others, to compel the Government of Ghana to adopt policies and allocate resources toward realising the right.[135]
- The Legislative arm in Ghana or the Parliament, having the responsibility for State policy and budgets, can hold the Executive accountable for implementing the right to an adequate standard of living in the country. Parliament can achieve this via a variety of means including questions, debates, committees and law-making.[136] It is incumbent on the opposition to put the ruling party on the spotlight as well.
- Furthermore, political parties can be made to commit to the right in their manifestos. During election, the voting public can vote out a government that is not responsive to the principles as stated in the Constitution.[137]

Some of the strong enforcement methods put forward include the following:

- Linking directive principles of State policy to justiciable rights. This way, courts can creatively expand the scope of the latter to include the former.

131 Etse Sikanku, 'Notes on the Justiciability of Constitutional Directive Principles' (2016) 2(1) *CNLU Law Journal* 98,99.

132 Constitution of the Republic of Ghana (note 129).

133 See the case of *New Patriotic Party v Attorney-General* [1996-1997] SCGLR 729.

134 Frans Viljoen, *International Human Rights Law in Africa* (2nd ed) (Oxford: Oxford University Press, 2012) 246.

135 Joseph Amaliba and Kojo Pumpuni Asante, '"God Bless Our Homeland Ghana": The Constitutional Promise to Ensure "An Adequate Means of Livelihood" and "Suitable Employment"' (2016) 2 *CNLU Law Journal* 199-221.

136 See Parliament of Ghana <www.parliament.gh> accessed 15 July 2023.

137 E Gyimah-Boadi, 'Confronting the Legacy of Human Rights Abuse in Africa: Lessons from Ghana' (2003) 1 *African Studies Bulletin* 54-58.

- The citizens can also use international channels such as the ECOWAS regional court and the African Commission to hold the government accountable based on regional treaties recognising the right.
- Amending Ghana's Constitution to make the right to an adequate standard of living is also a strategy that can be explored in order to give the courts in Ghana the jurisdiction to enforce socio-economic rights such as the right to an adequate standard of living.

The above notwithstanding, it is important to consider how to track the efforts of the public authority in Ghana to ensure that citizens enjoy good quality of life in the country. To assess this, one has to examine what the government is doing, especially in the following critical areas:

- Pursuing pro-poor programmes like LEAP cash transfers and school feeding.
- Implementing poverty reduction strategies such as the Ghana Shared Growth Development Agenda.[138]
- Increasing the minimum wage levels for formal sector workers.
- Providing subsidised utilities and food items.

However, major gaps have been noted in terms of the high poverty rate in the country.[139] Ghana has a weak social security system for informal sector workers who usually lack pensions or health insurance. Furthermore, inadequate housing, water and sanitation, especially in rural areas and urban slums, remain a challenge for Ghana. Also, it is worth noting that there is a lack of decent employment opportunities in the formal sector, with environment pollution from illegal mining causing challenges to health and livelihoods.[140]

The non-justiciable right to an adequate standard of living is a vial socio-economic right in Ghana's Constitution that sets directive policy goals for the State. While its non-justiciability poses challenges for enforcement, Ghanaians are not devoid of options to compel State action through civic activism, legislative engagement, media advocacy, and electoral politics. Additionally, indirect legal enforcement via justiciable rights provides avenues for judicial enforcement. There is the need for constitutional reform to strengthen this right. Overall, the right places important moral, political, and legal responsibilities on the State to continuously improve living conditions and provide

138 Government of Ghana, 'Ghana Shared Growth and Development Agenda (2010-2013)' available at <www.un-page.org/ghana> accessed 15 July 2023.

139 The World Bank, 'The World Bank in Ghana' available at <www.worldbank.org/ghana> accessed 15 July 2023.

140 Seth A Appiah *et al*, 'Causes of Poverty in Sub-Saharan Africa: A Review of Contemporary Studies' (2021) 11(7) *Cogent Social Sciences*

gainful livelihoods for the people of Ghana through holistic and rights-based development policies.

Kenya

Kenya's 2010 Constitution contains an expansive Bill of Rights, including economic and social rights. One such right is the directive principle on the 'right to be free from hunger, and to have adequate food of acceptable quality' under Article 43(1)(c).[141] This corresponds with the international treaties already discussed above. While this right is not enforceable in the courts in Kenya, this right creates State obligations for the Government of Kenya.

Under the Kenya Constitution, there is no imposed obligation on the State to take legislative, policy, and other measures towards achieving progressive realisation of the right to an adequate standard of living.[142]

Some of the weak enforcement mechanisms for enforcing the right to an adequate standard of living in Kenya include advocacy and activism, legislative action, electoral policies, and the role of oversight bodies such as the Kenya National Human Rights and Equality Commission.[143] Again, regarding strong enforcement measures, public interest litigation, international bodies such as the African Court and Commission and Constitutional amendment may be applied.

Notably, the Kenyan Government has taken some measures in the past to implement this right. These include, and are not limited to, pro-poor initiatives/food subsidies, slum upgrading programmes (low-cost housing schemes, expanding access to healthcare, education, water and sanitation, raising the minimum wage, and implementing development plans like Vision 2030).

Major gaps in Kenya include the high poverty rate of almost 40 percent, undernutrition, acute shortage of affordable housing, water and sanitation especially in informal settlements, weak assistance for the poor and vulnerable groups, and environmental threats from practices such as charcoal burning and waste dumping.[144]

In sum, the right to an adequate standard of living is non-justiciable in Kenya. However, it remains a vital human right directing State policy on social and economic development. Citizens can rely on civic activism, legislative engagement, media, national institutions, regional bodies, and creative public interest litigation to compel State action. Interestingly, however, reducing poverty and fulfilling this right requires adopting a comprehensive,

141 Constitution of Kenya (2010), art 43(1)(c).
142 Ibid, art 21(2).
143 See Kenya Human Rights Commission, <wwknchr.org> accessed 15 July 2023.
144 Githu Muigai, 'Non-Justiciable Rights: The Elusive Search for a Constitutional Basis' (2011) *International Journal of Human Rights* 115.

well-resourced, and rights-based approach focusing on the most marginalised populations and all dimensions related to an adequate living standard.

South Africa

The South African Constitution of 1996 contains an extensive Bill of Rights covering both civil-political rights and socio-economic rights. While most socio-economic rights are fully justiciable in South Africa, the right to an adequate standard of living under section 27(2) is designated as non-justiciable.[145]

In the South African context, while the rights to housing, healthcare, education, and social security are fully justiciable under section 26 and 27(1), the right to sufficient food and water is designated non-justiciable under section 27(2).[146] The rationale lies in institutional competence considerations, as courts face inherent limitations in making determinations on the reasonableness of State action to realise socio-economic rights.[147] Such decisions have budgetary and policy implications across multiple sectors.[148]

The South African Government has taken measures to fulfil this right including:

- Implementing social assistance programmes like social grants, food parcels, and school nutrition.[149]
- Adopting pro-poor fiscal policies, labour laws, land reform, etc.[150]
- Expanding access to housing, water, sanitation, healthcare, and education.[151]
- Raising minimum wage levels.[152]

The above notwithstanding, there are gaps in the poverty rate, undernutrition, acute shortage of affordable housing, weak social assistance for unemployed youth, and environmental threats from mining and air pollution.

Thus, while commendable progress has been made since apartheid, holistic State action across health, housing, water, environment, food security, and social assistance sectors is still required to fully realise the right to an adequate standard of living for all in South Africa.

145 Constitution of the Republic of South Africa (1996), s 27(2).
146 See *Government of the Republic of South Africa v Grootboom* [2000] ZACC 19.
147 Eric C Christiansen, 'Adjudicating Non-Justiciable Rights: Socio-Economic Rights and the South African Constitutional Court' (2007) 38 *Columbia Human Rights Law Review* 321.
148 Sandra Lienbenberg, 'Socio-Economic Rights Adjudication Under a Transformative Constitution' (2013) 24(2) *European journal of International Law* 739-744.
149 Romi Gondwe, 'The Right to Social Assistance: Realisation, Implementation and Enforcement Challenges' (SAHRC 2019).
150 UN Committee on Economic, Social and Cultural Rights, 'Concluding observations on the initial report of South Africa' (2018) UN Doc E/C.12/ZAF/CO/1.
151 Department of Water and Sanitation, 'Strategic Plan 2020-2025' (2020).
152 Department of Employment and Labour, 'National Minimum Wage' available at <www.employment.gov.za> accessed 15 July 2023.

In summary, realising the non-justiciable constitutional right to an adequate living standard is vital for human dignity and development in South Africa. While direct legal enforcement avenues are restricted, citizens can still employ extensive civic and political advocacy along with regional mechanisms to hold the State accountable and push for progressive fulfilment of this right. A comprehensive rights-based approach encompassing health, housing, water, food, social security, and environment aspects is imperative.

Uganda

The 1995 Constitution of Uganda contains a broad range of human rights including non-justiciable socio-economic rights. One such right is the right to an adequate standard of living under Objective XIV, which is not directly enforceable in the courts in Uganda.[153] However, the State still bears a duty to take measures towards its progressive realisation.

Under the 1995 Constitution, while civil and political rights are justiciable in Uganda, socio-economic rights like standard of living are expressly designated as non-justiciable in Objective XIV.[154] Courts cannot directly enforce these provisions by striking down laws or awarding remedies.[155] While framed narrowly under Objective XIV, the right to an adequate standard of living was clearly intended to have a comprehensive scope covering multiple facets of human welfare. This is confirmed by the constitutional inclusion of related objectives like healthcare, housing, food security, and education, among others.[156] Ugandan courts have also interpreted it expansively based on human dignity.[157]

Notably, the Ugandan government has undertaken measures aimed at implementing this right in the following ways:

- Implementing universal primary education and social assistance for the elderly and disabled.[158]
- National development plans like the Vision 2040.[159]
- Pro-poor programmes like cash transfers, school feeding, immunisation drives, etc.[160]

153 Constitution of the Republic of Uganda (1995) Objective XIV.
154 Ibid.
155 See *Uganda Association of Women Lawyers v Attorney General (Constitutional Petition No. 2 of 2003)* [2004] UGCC 1.
156 Jude Rwemisisi, 'The Enforceability of Socio-Economic Rights Under the 1995 Constitution of Uganda' (2018) 2 *HURIPEC.*
157 See *Centre for Health, Human Rights and Development (CEHURD) & 3 Others v Attorney General (Constitutional Petition No. 16 of 2011)* [2012] UGCC 4.
158 Ministry of Gender, Labour and Social Development, 'Uganda Social Protection Public Expenditure Review' (2019).
159 Government of Uganda, 'Uganda Vision 2040' (2007).
160 Ministry of Gender, Labour and Social Development, op cit (note158).

Be that as it may, there are still notable gaps in ensuring that the right to an adequate standard of living is fulfilled in Uganda. Some of these include:

- Poverty rate remains very high at over 20 percent.[161]
- Undernutrition is rampant, with stunted growth in 29 percent of children under the age of five.[162]
- Shortages of affordable housing, water, and sanitation services.[163]
- Inadequate social assistance for the poor, youth, and unemployed.[164]
- Environmental damage from activities like deforestation.[165]
- Lack of decent work opportunities in the formal sector.[166]

The case of Uganda calls for more holistic State action across health, housing, water, food, environment, social security, education, and employment sectors to progressively achieve the constitutional objective of adequate standard of living for all in Uganda.

Gambia

The Constitution of Gambia 1997 contains provisions on political, civil, and socio-economic rights, including the non-justiciable right to an adequate standard of living.[167] This right corresponds with international standards set out in instruments such as at the Universal Declaration of Human Rights (UDHR).[168] While not directly enforceable in Gambian courts, the State is still obligated to take measures towards progressive realisation.

The Government of Gambia has taken measures aimed at implementing the right to an adequate standard of living as follows:

- Establishing the Social Development Fund to finance programmes targeting poverty.[169]
- Implementing education, health, and infrastructure policies to improve access to services.[170]

161 Uganda Bureau of Statistics, 'Uganda Poverty Assessment Report 2016' (2018).
162 Ibid.
163 Ministry of Lands, Housing and Urban Development, 'Uganda Housing Sector Profile' (2016).
164 Development Initiatives, 'Uganda: Social Protection Expenditure and Performance Review and Social Budget Analysis' (2020).
165 National Environment Management Authority, 'State of Environment Report for Uganda 2014' (2014).
166 Ibrahim Mwesige, 'The Minimum wage-Setting Policy in a Low-Income Country: The Case of Uganda' (2021) 15(4) *Review of Economics and Political Economy* 665.
167 Constitution of the Republic of The Gambia 1997, s17(2)d).
168 Universal Dclaration of Human Rights 1949, art 25(1).
169 See Social Development Fund Act 2015.
170 Ministry of Finance and Economic Affairs, 'The Gambia National Development Plan 2018-2021' (2018).

- Providing subsidies on basic food items and agricultural inputs.[171]
- Providing subsidies on petrol.[172]
- Rural electrification and village water supply projects.[173]
- Slum upgrades and low-cost housing schemes.[174]

However, major gaps persist in fulfilling the right to an adequate standard of living. The gaps include and are not limited to:

- High poverty rate which is nearly at 48 percent.
- Widespread undernutrition, especially among children.[175]
- Shortages of affordable housing, water, and sanitation, especially in rural areas.[176]
- High youth unemployment.[177]
- Inadequate protection for poor and vulnerable groups.[178]
- Environmental threats from activities such as timber extraction.[179]

Thus, while commendable efforts have been made, holistic State action across health, housing, water, food security, environment, employment, and social welfare sectors is still required to fully realise the right to an adequate standard of living for all in The Gambia.

Namibia

The Constitution of Namibia 1990 contains an extensive Bill of Rights, including non-justiciable socio-economic rights. One such right is the right to an adequate standard of living under Article 95, which is not directly enforceable in courts.[180] While the right to an adequate standard of living is not enforceable in the courts in Namibia, the government has a duty to ensure that there is a progressive realisation of the right.

171 Essa Janneh, 'Barrow Government Spent over D673M on Bread, Flour Subsidies' *The Standard Newspaper* (Banjul, 10 May 2020.
172 Buba Gagiga, 'President Barrow Says Gov't Spent Over D1.6 Billion on Fuel Subsidy in 2022' available at < President Barrow Says Gov't Spent Over D1.6 Billion On Fuel Subsidy In 2022 – Kerr Fatou Online Media House> accessed 25 July 2023.
173 Mamadou Dem, 'Gambia: Electricity and Rural Infrastructure' (FAO, 15 September 2015).
174 Omar Touray, 'Government Rolls out New Housing Models for Civil Servants' The Gambia Echo (Serrekunda, 1 February 2022).
175 UNICEF, 'Situation Analysis of Children in The Gambia' (2018).
176 Ministry of Lands and Regional Government, 'National Housing Policy' (2010).
177 International Monetary Fund, 'The Gambia' (2019).
178 Social Development Fund Act 2015.
179 Ministry of Environment, Climate Change and Natural Resources, 'State of the Environment Report 2018' (2019).
180 Constitution of Namibia 1990, art 95.

The Namibian government has undertaken some measures aimed at implementing the right to an adequate standard of living. These include:

- Implementing social grants for the elderly, orphans, and veterans.[181]
- National development plans like Vision 2030 focusing on poverty reduction.[182]
- Rural development and land reform initiatives.[183]
- Slum upgrades and low-cost housing schemes.[184]
- Increasing budget allocations for health, education, and social welfare.[185]

Despite the above strides, there remain huge gaps that need to be closed, especially as it concerns the following:

- High poverty rate, currently at 28 percent.[186]
- Widespread undernutrition among children.
- Shortage of over 80,000 housing units, exacerbated by rapid urbanisation.[187]
- Inadequate access to sanitation, especially in rural areas.[188]
- High youth unemployment.[189]
- Environmental threats from mining and deforestation.[190]

There is, therefore, the need to employ a comprehensive State action across health, housing, water, food security, social welfare, employment, and environmental sectors to achieve the constitutional directive on standard of living in Namibia.

Somalia

Unfortunately, little can be written about enforcing the right to an adequate standard of living in Somalia. This reason is because Somalia does not currently have a national constitution outlining fundamental rights and directive principles. The country has faced long-running conflict and instability which has impeded the adoption of a permanent constitution. Some key challenges include the following:

181 Namibia National Gender Policy 2010-2020 (Office of the President 2010).
182 Namibia Vision 2030 (2004).
183 National Resettlement Policy (2001).
184 GRN/EU, 'Development of Affordable Building Technologies
185 Deloitte, 'Namibia's Budget for FY2019/20' (2019).
186 The World Bank, 'The World Bank in Namibia' (2021) available at < https://www.worldbank.org/en/country/namibia/overview> accessed 25 July 2023.
187 National Housing Enterprise, 'Mass Housing Development Programme' (2018).
188 Ministry of Agriculture, Water and Forestry, 'Mass Housing development Programme' (2018).
189 IMF Country Report No. 18/384 (IMF 2018).
190 State of Environment Report on Waste Management and Pollution Control 2014.

- Somalia is still in the process of establishing functioning governing institutions and legal frameworks after years of unrest and civil war.
- There is no universally agreed upon national constitution. The Provisional Constitution of 2012 which contain some human rights provisions is still considered provisional.
- The rights and directive principles contained in the Provisional Constitution are not comprehensive and the document has legitimacy issues.
- There is limited legal precedent or jurisprudence on enforcing socio-economic rights in Somalia.
- Ongoing conflict and humanitarian crises have made socio-economic conditions very dire, with high poverty and inadequate access to basic services for large sections of the population.
- Institutional weaknesses in bodies like parliament, the judiciary, and the human rights commission impede enforcement right of rights.

Togo

The Constitution of Togo 1992 contains provisions on civil liberties along with non-justiciable directive principles on socio-economic rights. One such right is the right to an adequate standard of living under Article 34, which is not directly enforceable in courts.[191] Notwithstanding, the State of Togo still bears responsibility for taking measures towards its progressive realisation.

The Togolese government has undertaken some measures aimed at implementing this right. Some of these measures include the following:

- Implementing social assistance programmes like cash transfers for the vulnerable.[192]
- National development plans focusing on poverty reduction.[193]
- Investments to expand access to education, healthcare, water, electricity, etc.[194]
- Agriculture and rural infrastructure policies.[195]

Despite the efforts of the government, there are still major gaps in fulfilling the right to an adequate standard of living in the following areas:

- High poverty rate which is close to 50 percent.[196]

191 Constitution de la République Togolaise 1992, art 34.
192 Teresa Cavero and Cecile Cherrier, 'Etude de cas sur les programmes de filets sociaux adptatifs au Togo' (World Bank 2017).
193 'Plan national de développement (PND) 2018-2022' (République Togolaise 2018)..
194 Banque Africaine de Développement, 'Profil de gouvernance-pays: Togo' (2018).
195 Ministère de l'Agriculture de l'Elevage et de l'Hydraulique, 'Politique de développement agricole du Togo' (2010).
196 Banque Africaine de Développement, op cit (note 194).

- Undernutrition is widespread, with stunting in 27 percent of children under the age of five.[197]
- Shortages of affordable housing, water and sanitation, especially in rural areas.[198]
- Weak social protection coverage for poor and vulnerable groups.[199]
- High unemployment around 15 percent, concentrated among youth.[200]
- Environmental threats from activities like mining and poaching.[201]

Like most SSA countries, Togo needs holistic State action across health, water, housing, food security, social services, employment, and environment sectors to achieve the constitutional directive on standard of living.

Sierra Leone

The Constitution of Sierra Leone 1991 contains an extensive Bill of Rights including non-justiciable socio-economic rights. One of such rights is the right to an adequate standard of living under section 8(3)(b), which is not directly enforceable by the courts.[202] However, the Government of Sierra Leone still bears the duty to take measures towards its progressive realisation.

In Sierra Leone, there is a growing call for citizens to be able to compel State action on the right to an adequate standard of living.[203] There have been some efforts on the part of the government towards implementing the right to an adequate standard of living. These include:

- The implementation of social protection programmes like cash transfers.[204]
- National development plans like the Agenda for Prosperity 2013-2018.[205]
- Investments to expand access to education, healthcare, electricity, and water.[206]
- Programmes for youth employment and micro credit.[207]

197 Enquête par grappes à indicateurs multiples au Togo 2017, Rapport Final (Ministère du Plan et du Dévéloppment 2018).
198 Cécile Bastien, 'Politique nationale de l'habitat et de développement urbainau Togo' (Ministère de l'Urbanisme 2016).
199 Teresa Cavero and Cécile Cherrier, op cit (note 192).
200 Banque Africaine de Développement, op cit (note 194).
201 '5ème Rapport national sur la diversité biologique – Togo' (Ministère de l'Environnement et des Ressources Forestières 2014).
202 The Constitution of Sierra Leone 1991, s 8(3)(b).
203 Sandra Liebenberg, *Socio-Economic Rights: Adjudication under a Transformative Constitution* (Juta 2010).
204 DFID, 'DFID Sierra Leone Operational Plan 2011-2016' (2011).
205 The Agenda for Prosperity: Road to Middle Income Status (2013).
206 Ministry of Education, 'Education Sector Plan 2018-2020' (2017).
207 Bert Ingelaere and others, 'What's at Stake in the 2018 Elections in Sierra Leone?' (African Arguments, 6 March 2018) <https://africanarguments.org/2018/03/06/sierra-leone-2018-elections-whats-at-stake/> accessed 15 February 2023.

Again, however, major gaps persist in fulfilling the right to an adequate standard of living in the following areas:

- High poverty rate of over 50 percent.[208]
- Undernutrition remains widespread, with stunting in 28 percent of children under the age of five.[209]
- Shortage of around 100,000 housing units.[210]
- Weak social assistance or poor, persons with disabilities and the unemployed.[211]
- Over 70 percent youth unemployment.[212]
- Environmental threats from activities like mining and deforestation.[213]

Sierra Leone is in dire need of developing a holistic approach to fulfilling the right to an adequate standard of living, especially as it concerns health, housing, water, food security, social services, employment, and environmental sectors to achieve the constitutional directive on standard of living.

Conclusion

The right to an adequate standard of living is a vital multifaceted socio-economic right aimed at upholding human dignity and enabling equitable national development, especially for a region like SSA. As examined in this chapter, the right encompasses the interlinked rights to adequate food, housing, water, health, education, sanitation, decent work, and social security for individual and community well-being.

While originally conceived as a non-justiciable directive policy principle in most Sub-Saharan constitutions, recent jurisprudence and scholarship show a clear trend towards strengthening the justiciability and enforcement of this right in the region.[214] Realising the right requires adopting an integrative approach interlinking rights to health, water, housing, food, and other associated entitlements that holistically shape human welfare.[215]

The African Charter on Human and Peoples' Rights (African Charter) reinforces the interdependence of different facets of an adequate standard of

208 The World Ban, 'Sierra Leone' (2019) <https://data.worldbank.org/country/sierra-leone> accessed 15 February 2023.

209 Sierra Leone 2015 Population and Housing Census (Statistics Sierra Leone 2016).

210 National Social Security and Insurance Trust, 'Housing Policy' (2015).

211 Rights Way International, 'Analysis of the Legal Protection of Economic, Social and Cultural Rights in Sierra Leone' (2020).

212 Bert Ingelaere and others, op cit (note 207).

213 Environmental Protection Agency, 'National Environmental Policy of Sierra Leone' (2003).

214 Katharine G Young, 'The Minimum Core of Economic and Social Rights: A Concept in Search of Content' (2008) 33 *Yale J Int'l L* 113.

215 Magdalena Sepúlveda, The Nature of Obligations under the International Covenant on Economic, Social and Cultural Rights (Intersentia 2003) 187.

living by guaranteeing rights to health, work, food, and overall satisfactory environment.[216] Similarly, UN treaties like the ICESCR establish the indivisibility of the right to an adequate living standard with other socio-economic rights.[217] International bodies like the UN Committee on Economic, Social and Cultural Rights have outlined the core minimum obligations of States to ensure basic levels of health, shelter, food and social welfare.[218]

Governments in SSA bear a duty to take deliberate, concrete, and targeted steps towards the full realisation of the right to an adequate standard of living for all people under their jurisdiction. This requires prioritising and affirmatively assisting vulnerable, disadvantaged, and marginalised groups through social policies, welfare systems, and special measures.[219] It also requires ensuring equitable resource allocation and service delivery between rural and urban areas.

Strategies for realising this right include expanding social security coverage and benefits, instituting nutritional support and food subsidy schemes, constructing low-cost housing, enhancing affordable access to healthcare, water, sanitation, education and skills-training, generating decent employment, and protecting livelihoods against environmental threats.[220] While historical challenges like limited resources constrain implementation, governments must demonstrate that they are making maximum use of available resources and steadily enhancing resource mobilisation and financing through equitable fiscal and budgetary policies.[221]

Creatively strengthening the justiciability and enforcement of the right is imperative, notwithstanding original constitutional classifications as non-justiciable principles. Recent court judgements on countries like South Africa, Kenya, Uganda, Ghana, and Nigeria demonstrate the possibility of indirect enforcement by upholding linked justiciable rights or creatively interpreting socio-economic rights provisions.[222] Extensive civic advocacy and activism can also effectively compel State action on realising this right.[223]

216 African Charter on Human and Peoples' Rights (1981), arts 15-16 & 24.

217 International Covenant on Economic, Social and Cultural Rights (1966), arts 11-12.

218 UN Committee on Economic, Social and Cultural Rights, General Comment No. 3: The Nature of States Parties' Obligations (1990) UN Doc E/1991/23, paras 10-11.

219 Ruth Hall 'A Political Economy of Land Reform in South Africa' (2013) 31 *Rev. Afr. Pol. Econ.* 213.

220 Food and Agriculture Organization of the United Nations, 'The Right to Food in Africa' (Addis Ababa 2016).

221 Navi Pillay, 'Economic, Social and Cultural Rights' in Mashood Baderin and Manisuli Ssenyonjo (eds), *International Human Rights Law: Six Decades after the UDHR and Beyond* (Routledge 2010).

222 See Government of south Africa v Grootboom (2001) 1 SA 46 (CC); Satrosay Ravalomanana v Madagascar (2017) 2 AfCLR 9 (AfCHPR 2017).

223 Patricia Kameri-Mbote and Collins Odote, "Courts as Champions of Sustainable Development: Lessons from East Africa" (2015) 10(1) *Law, Environment and Development Journal* 31

Regional human rights bodies like the African Commission and Court have a critical role to play in considering complaints, directing remedial action, and recommending requisite policy and legislative measures to guarantee the right.[224] International human rights treaty bodies also periodically review States' progressive realisation of the right and suggest interventions. While justiciability strengthens enforcement, implementing this right ultimately requires sufficient political will, legislation, policies, programmes, and resource allocation by the executive and legislature.

Upholding the right to an adequate standard of living is essential for human development, social justice, and stability in SSA. The region continues to face massive deficits in food security, housing, healthcare, water, sanitation, and essential welfare services which severely undermine human dignity potentials.[225] Comprehensively guaranteeing adequate standards of health, nutrition, shelter, water, education, and overall human well-being for all persons and communities is vital for the socio-economic empowerment and capabilities of Africa's people. It requires strenghtnening the integrative implementation, enforceability, monitoring, and justiciability of this multifaceted right across the region.

Realising this right necessitates adopting some context-specific strategies in SSA such as:

- Prioritising public investments in smallholder agriculture, which forms the economic mainstay of most countries. This includes ensuring land access to farmers, agricultural extension services, rural infrastructure development, crop insurance, and so on.[226]
- Ensuring an equitable balance between expanding modern water systems and making affordable basic services accessible to rural communities and urban slums currently lacking connections.[227]
- Leveraging traditional communal land ownership systems alongside formal title deeds to enhance tenure security for all.[228]
- Harnessing international development partnerships to finance programmes targeting poverty and food security.[229]
- Formalising the informal sector and expanding social security coverage for workers outside formal employment through cooperative schemes, etc.[230]

224 Frans Viljoen, International Human Rights Law in Africa (2nd edn) (OUP 2012) 385.

225 Dan Banik, 'Poverty and Elusive Development in Sub-Saharan Africa' (2021) 59 *Africa Spectrum* 120.

226 African Union, 'Malabo Declaration on Accelerated Agricultural Growth' (2014).

227 Lyla Mehta and Synne Movik, 'Liquid Reforms: Post-privatisation Realities in Cape Town and Delhi' (2014) 56(2) *Geoforum* 26.

228 Ben Cousins, 'Potential and Pitfalls of "Communal" Land Tenure Reform' (2009) 129 ODI Opinions.

229 Katrin Glatzel, 'International Partnerships for Sustainable Development Goals' in Louis Meuleman (ed), Metagovernance for Sustainability (outledge 2019).

230 International Labour Organization, "The Informal Economy in Africa" (2002).

- Instituting social protection floors to guarantee minimum essential levels of social services and income security for disadvantaged groups.[231]
- Enhancing access to justice to claim these rights, including legal aid for the poor and awareness campaigns in local languages.[232]

The COVID-19 pandemic has reinforced the indivisibility of health and socio-economic rights, as crises can rapidly erase development gains.[233] Going forward, guaranteeing the right to an adequate standard of living should be an urgent priority across SSA to tackle abject poverty, deprivation, and inequality. It promises to strengthen human capabilities, foster social justice and stability, and unlock the region's human development potential.

However, there some common obstacles across the region impeding the full realisation of the right to an adequate standard of living which need to be addressed, including the below topics.

Financial and Resource Constraints

Many governments have faced historical constraints in mobilising sufficient public resources to invest adequately in health, education, housing, water, sanitation, and social welfare schemes.[234] While budgets have expanded in the last few decades, they remain insufficient compared to the scale of needs and backlogs accumulated from colonial underinvestment in African societies.[235]

231 Augustine Edobor Arimoro, 'Are They Not Nigerians? The Obligation of the State to End Discriminatory Practices against Persons with Disabilities' (2019) 19(2) *International Journal of Discrimination and the Law* 89-109; Augustine Edobor Arimoro, 'Nigeria's Legislation against Discrimination of Persons with Disabilities: An Assessment' in S Ndlovu and PN Nyoni (eds) *Social, Educational,, and Cultural Perspectives of Disabilities in the Global South* (IGI Global, 2021) 55-67; Augustine Arimoro, 'Persons with Intellectual Disability and Access to Justice in Nigeria: Challenges and the Way Forward' (2019) 5(2) Hasanuddin Law Review 180-198; Olivier De Schutter, 'The Right of Everyone to Enjoy the Benefits of Scientific Progress and the Right to Food: From Conflict to Complementarity' (2011)

232 International Development Law Organization, 'Accessing Justice: Models, Strategies and Best Practices on Women's Empowerment' (2013).

233 Gian Luca Burci, 'The Outbreak of COVID-19 Coronavirus: are the International Health Regulations fit for purpose?' (2020) EJIL Talk!<www.ejiltalk.org/the-outbreak-of-covid-19-coronavirus-are-the-international-health-regulations-fit-for-purpose/> accessed 27 February 2020; Augustine Edobor Arimoro, 'Private Sector Investment in Infrastructure in Sub-Saharan Africa Post COVID-19: The Role of Law' (2022) 27(2) *Public Works Management & Policy* 108-126.

234 21 Nairobi Statement of Principles on Sustainable Development Finance for Food Security and Nutrition (2017).

235 Jacques Enaudeau, 'The roots of the deepening water crisis in Cape Town' The Conversation (6 February 2018) <https://theconversation.com/the-roots-of-the-deepening-water-crisis-in-cape-town-91415> accessed 27 February 2023.

External debt burdens and macroeconomic shocks have also limited fiscal space for greater public spending in many countries.[236]

Governance and Institutional Weakness

Institutional deficiencies including lack of transparency, accountability, and local participation in budgeting processes undermine effective public expenditure and service delivery.[237] Weaknesses in sectors like health, education, utilities, etc., lead to poor outcomes despite spending. Corruption by public officials further dampens resource availability and distributional equity.[238] Misappropriation of aid funds has also been a concern.

Policy and Coordination Gaps

Many countries lack comprehensive rights-based policies, legislation, and integrated strategies to realise the various facets of an adequate standard of living in a coordinated way.[239] There are gaps in areas such as social housing, water and sanitation, social security, employment, climate change, adaptation, etc. Lack of disaggregated data also hinders evidence-based policy making.

Discrimination and Inequalities

Despite constitutional guarantees, women, informal workers, rural inhabitants, slum dwellers, persons with disabilities, and elderly persons face systemic discrimination in accessing essential services, land, credit, and livelihoods.[240] Vertical inequalities between regions and social groups constrain egalitarian development.[241] Entrenched power structures that enable elite capture of resources further impede economic justice.

236 Mary-Anne Hitt, 'The hidden costs of debt and deficit – Africa needs progressive tax reform to mobilise resources' (Oxfam International, 12 October 2021) <https://www.oxfam.org/en/blogs/hidden-costs-debt-and-deficit-africa-needs-progressive-tax-reform-mobilise-resources> accessed 27 February 2023.

237 Transparency International, 'Corruption in Africa: A Threat to Justice and Sustainable Development' (2021).

238 Nic Cheeseman, 'Everyday corruption and the political corruption of everyday life: Corruption, citizenship and public services in Africa' (2021) 15(1) The *Journal of Development Studies* 815.

239 Makoma Lekalakala, 'Realising the Right to Water in South Africa: Going Beyond Justiciability' in Malcolm Langford and others (eds), Social Rights Judgments and the Politics of Compliance: Making it Stick (Cambridge University Press 2017).

240 Commission for Africa, 'Our Common Interest' (Report, 2005).

241 UN Sustainable Development Group, 'Leaving No One Behind: The Imperative of Inclusive Development' (Report, 2016).

Environmental Threats

Land degradation, deforestation, extractive industries, wildlife depletion, and pollution undermine rural livelihoods and the ecological foundations that communities depend on.[242] Climate change worsens on these pressures. Lack of climate resilience strategies also threatens progress.

Therefore, while the right to an adequate standard of living has been constitutionally recognised in most SSA countries, there are structural and systemic barriers impeding its comprehensive realisation for all sections of the population. Overcoming these challenges requires not just legal and judicial efforts, but also transformative policies and programmes by governments backed by sufficient political commitment, public resources, and civic pressures.

In conclusion, guaranteeing the constitutional right to an adequate standard of living remains a pressing imperative and unfinished socio-economic priority across SSA. It will necessitate strengthening legal frameworks, social policies, institutional competence, resource mobilisation, good governance, environmental sustainability, and inclusive development. But given its vital significance for social justice and national progress, upholding this multifaceted right warrants the utmost attention from African governments, civil society, regional bodies, and international partners in the coming years.

Bibliography

Africa Progress Panel, 'Power, People, Planet: Seizing Africa's Energy and Climate Opportunities' (2015) available at https://www.esi-africa.com/reports/africa-progress-panel-2015-report-power-people-planet/ accessed 9 December 2024.

African Development Bank 'Documents de stratégie pays' (2024) available at https://www.afdb.org/en/documents/strategy-documents> accessed 9 December 2024.

Ahmad N, 'Human Right to Water Under International Law Regime: An Overview' (2020) 46(3) *Commonwealth Law Bulletin* 415–439 https://doi.org/10.1080/03050718.2020.1770618.

Amaliba J and Asante KP, '"God Bless Our Homeland Ghana": The Constitutional Promise to Ensure "An Adequate Means of Livelihood" and "Suitable Employment"' (2016) 2 *CNLU Law Journal* 199–221.

Arimoro A, 'Book Review: Implementing the Sustainable Development Goals in Nigeria (Routledge 2022)' (2022) 13(1) *Journal of Sustainable Development Law and Policy* 200–206.

Arimoro A, 'The Corona Virus (COVID-19) Pandemic and the Challenge of Healthcare Infrastructure in Nigeria: What Role for Public-Private Partnerships?' (2020) 3(5) *Theoretical and Applied Law* 18–33.

Arimoro A, 'Persons with Intellectual Disability and Access to Justice in Nigeria: Challenges and the Way Forward' (2019) 5(2) *Hasanuddin Law Review* 180–198.

242 Africa Progress Panel, 'Power, People, Planet: Seizing Africa's Energy and Climate Opportunities' (2015).

Arimoro A and Musa H, 'Towards Sustainable Water Resource Management in Rural Nigeria: The Role of Communities' (2020) 11(1) *The Journal of Sustainable Development Law and Policy* 1–17 https://doi.org/10.4314/jsdlp.v11i1.2.

Arimoro AE, 'Are They Not Nigerians? The Obligation of the State to End Discriminatory Practices against Persons with Disabilities' (2019) 19(2) *International Journal of Discrimination and the Law* 89–109.

Arimoro AE, 'Beyond Economics! The (Evolving) Role of Law in the Eradication of Extreme Poverty' (2023) *Journal of Human Rights and Social Work* https://doi.org/10.1007/s41134-023-00247-2.

Arimoro AE, 'Nigeria's Legislation against Discrimination of Persons with Disabilities: An Assessment' in S Ndlovu and PN Nyoni (eds), *Social, Educational, and Cultural Perspectives of Disabilities in the Global South* (IGI Global 2021) 55–67.

Arimoro AE, 'Private Sector Investment in Infrastructure in Sub-Saharan Africa Post COVID-19: The Role of Law' (2022) 27(2) *Public Works Management & Policy* 108–126.

Arimoro AE and Elgujja AA, 'Public-Private Partnership and the Achievement of Sustainable Development Goals: The Roel of Subnational Governments' in AB Kagu and NE Attah (eds), *Perspectives on Governance and Accountability* (Centre for Research and Capacity Development on Humanitarian Studies, Yobe State University 2019).

Banik D, 'Poverty and Elusive Development in Sub-Saharan Africa' (2021) 59 *Africa Spectrum* 120.

Banque Africaine de Développement, 'Profil de gouvernance-pays: Togo' (2018).

Bhorat H, Kanbur R and Stanwix B, 'Minimum Wages in Sub-Saharan Africa: A Primer' (2017) 32(1) *Research Observer* 21–74.

Boyle K, 'Models of Incorporation and Justiciability for Economic, Social and Cultural Rights' (2018) available at <https://www.scottishhumanrights.com/media/1809/models_of_incorporation_escr_vfinal_nov18.pdf> accessed 3 July 2023.

Cargas S, 'Fortifying the Future of Human Rights with Human Rights Education' (2019) 18(3) *Journal of Human Rights* 293–307.

Cavero T and Cherrier C, *Etude de cas sur les programmes de filets sociaux adptatifs au Togo* (World Bank 2017).

Chaman Law Firm, 'What Are Non-Justiciable Constitutional Provisions?' (2022) available at <https://www.chamanlawfirm.com/what-are-non-justiciable-constitutional-provisions> accessed 3 July 2023.

Cheeseman N, 'Everyday Corruption and the Political Corruption of Everyday Life: Corruption, Citizenship and Public Services in Africa' (2021) 15(1) *The Journal of Development Studies* 815.

Cheteni P and Mazenda A, 'Economic Impact of Government Intervention in Response to Covid-19 in Selected sub-Saharan African Countries' (2023) 40(2) *Development Southern Africa* 406–420.

Christiansen EC, 'Adjudicating Non-Justiciable Rights: Socio-Economic Rights and the South African Constitutional Court' (2007) 38 *Columbia Human Rights Law Review* 321.

Cohen M, 'The Right to Food' (March 17, 2016) in *Max Planck Encyclopedia of Comparative Constitutional Law* (Oxford University Press 2017)available at SSRN: https://ssrn.com/abstract=2969884

Commission for Africa, 'Our Common Interest' (Report 2005).

Cousins B, 'Potential and Pitfalls of "Communal" Land Tenure Reform' (2009) 129 *ODI Opinions*.availale at https://www.oicrf.org/documents/40950/43224/Potential+and+pitfalls+of+communal+land+tenure+reform+experience+in+Africa+and+implications+for+South+Africa.pdf/3759d3a6-8a0d-c9a2-738f-d27f0f3e0cc0?t=1510182547414

Crave M, *The International Covenant on Economic, Social, and Cultural Rights, A Perspective on its Development* (Clarendon Press and Oxford University Press 1995).

Davies H, *Human Rights Law* (5th edn, Oxford University Press 2021)

de Schutter O, 'Countries Tackling Hunger with a Right to Food Approach' *Briefing Note* 1 May 2010 available at <https://www2.ohchr.org/english/issues/food/docs/Briefing_Note_01_May_2010_EN.pdf> accessed 25 June 2023.

De Schutter O, The Right of Everyone to Enjoy the Benefits of Scientific Progress and the Right to Food: From Conflict to Complementarity (2011) *Human Rights Quarterly*, 33(2), 304-350. https://doi.org/10.1353/hrq.2011.0020

Deloitte, 'Namibia's Budget for FY2019/20' (2019).https://www.deloitte.com/na/en/services/tax/perspectives/deloitte-namibia-namibian-budget-guide-2022.html

Dem M, *Gambia: Electricity and Rural Infrastructure* (FAO, 15 September 2015).

Department of Employment and Labour, 'National Minimum Wage' available at <www.employment.gov.za> accessed 15 July 2023.

Department of Water and Sanitation, 'Strategic Plan 2020–2025' (2020).https://www.dws.gov.za/documents/Other/Strategic%20Plan/2021/Strategic%20Plan%202020-21%20to%202024-25_23Mar2020.pdf accessed 24 October 2024

Edih U and Ganagana B, 'Justiciable or Non-Justiciable Rights: A Debate on Socio-Economic and Political Rights in Nigeria' (2020) 8(4) *Global Journal of Politics and Law Research* 78–85.

Eide A and Eide WB, *International Human Rights Law* (4th edn, Oxford University Press 2022).

Enabulele AO and Ewere AO, 'Can the Economic Community of West African States Community Court of Justice Enforce the African Charter Replicas of the Non-Justiciable Chapter II Human Rights Provisions of the Nigerian Constitution against Nigeria?' (2012) 1 *International Human Rights Law Review* 312–337.

Enaudeau J, 'The Roots of the Deepening Water Crisis in Cape Town' *The Conversation* (6 February 2018) <https://theconversation.com/the-roots-of-the-deepening-water-crisis-in-cape-town-91415> accessed 27 February 2023.

Enquête par grappes à indicateurs multiples au Togo 2017, Rapport Final (Ministère du Plan et du Développment 2018).

Environmental Protection Agency, *National Environmental Policy of Sierra Leone* (Environmental Protection Agency 2003).

Evans T, 'A Human Right to Health?' (2002) 23(2) *Third World Quarterly* 97–215.

Ferraz OLM, 'Covd-19 and Inequality: The Importance of Social Rights' (2021) 32(1) *Kings Law Journal* 109–121.

Food and Agriculture Organization of the United Nations, *The Right to Food in Africa* (Addis Ababa 2016).

Gagiga B, 'President Barrow Says Gov't Spent Over D1.6 Billion on Fuel Subsidy in 2022' available at <President Barrow Says Gov't Spent Over D1.6 Billion On Fuel Subsidy In 2022 – Kerr Fatou Online Media House> accessed 25 July 2023.

Gian Luca Burci, 'The Outbreak of COVID-19 Coronavirus: Are the International Health Regulations Fit for Purpose?' (2020) *EJIL Talk!* available at <www.ejiltalk.org/the-outbreak-of-covid-19-coronavirus-are-the-international-health-regulations-fit-for-purpose/> accessed 27 February 2020.

Gondwe R, *The Right to Social Assistance: Realisation, Implementation and Enforcement Challenges* (SAHRC 2019).

Government of Ghana, 'Ghana Shared Growth and Development Agenda (2010–2013)' available at <www.un-page.org/ghana> accessed 15 July 2023.

Gyimah-Boadi E, 'Confronting the Legacy of Human Rights Abuse in Africa: Lessons from Ghana' (2003) 1 *African Studies Bulletin* 54–58.

Hall R, 'A Political Economy of Land Reform in South Africa' (2013) 31 *Review of African Political Economy* 213.

Harris LM, Rodina L and Morinville C, 'Revisiting the Human Right to Water from an Environmental Justice Lens' (2015) 3(4) *Politics, Groups, and Identities* 660–665 https://doi.org/10.1080/21565503.2015.1080619.

Hartman C, 'The Case for a Right to Housing' (1998) 9(2) *Housing Policy Debate* 223–246 https://doi.org/10.1080/10511482.1998.9521292.

Hepner TR and Smith-Cannoy H, 'Introduction to Human Rights on the Edge: The Future of International Human Rights Law and Practice' (2022) 21(2) *Journal of Human Rights* 118–122.

Hitt M, *The Hidden Costs of Debt and Deficit – Africa Needs Progressive Tax Reform to Mobilise Resources* (Oxfam International, 12 October 2021) <https://www.oxfam.org/en/blogs/hidden-costs-debt-and-deficit-africa-needs-progressive-tax-reform-mobilise-resources> accessed 27 February 2023.

Ibrahim Mwesige, 'The Minimum wage-Setting Policy in a Low-Income Country: The Case of Uganda' (2021) 15(4) *Review of Economics and Political Economy* 665.

Ingelaere B and others, *What's at Stake in the 2018 Elections in Sierra Leone?* (African Arguments, 6 March 2018) available at <https://africanarguments.org/2018/03/06/sierra-leone-2018-elections-whats-at-stake/> accessed 15 February 2023.

International Development Law Organization, *Accessing Justice: Models, Strategies and Best Practices on Women's Empowerment* (International Development Law Organization 2013).

International Labour Organization, *The Informal Economy in Africa* (International Labour Organization 2002).

International Monetary Fund, *The Gambia* (International Monetary Fund 2019).

Janneh E, 'Barrow Government Spent over D673M on Bread, Flour Subsidies' *The Standard Newspaper* (Banjul 10 May 2020).

Jukes K, 'There is a Human Right to Health, and this is How it Works' (2016) available at <https://eachother.org.uk/is-there-a-right-to-health/> accessed 27 June 2023.

Kameri-Mbote P and Odote C, 'Courts as Champions of Sustainable Development: Lessons from East Africa' (2015) 10(1) *Law, Environment and Development Journal* 31.

Katharine G Young, 'The Minimum Core of Economic and Social Rights: A Concept in Search of Content' (2008) 33 *Yale Journal of International Law* 113.

Khamene'I SA, 'Rules Regarding Looking, Touching and Examining' (2023) available at <https://www.al-islam.org/islamic-rulings-medical-issues-sayyid-ali-khamenei/rules-regarding-looking-touching-and-examining> accessed 27 June 2023.

Lekalakala M, 'Realising the Right to Water in South Africa: Going Beyond Justiciability' in M Langford and others (eds), *Social Rights Judgments and the Politics of Compliance: Making it Stick* (Cambridge University Press 2017).
Lienbenberg S, 'Socio-Economic Rights Adjudication Under a Transformative Constitution' (2013) 24(2) *European Journal of International Law* 739–744.
Macrotrends, 'Sub-Saharan Africa Healthcare Spending 2000–2023' (2023) available at <https://www.macrotrends.net/countries/SSF/sub-saharan-africa-/healthcare-spending> accessed 27 June 2023.
McCall-Smith K, 'Incorporation of International Human Rights Briefing Series: The Right to an Adequate Standard of Living' (2021) available at <https://hrcscotland.org/wp-content/uploads/2021/11/Final-Right-to-Adequate-Standard-of-Living-Briefing-Nov-2021.pdf> accessed 11 June 2023.
Mehta Land Movik S, 'Liquid Reforms: Post-privatisation Realities in Cape Town and Delhi' (2014) 56(2) *Geoforum* 26.
Mekonnen EE and Amede AK, 'Food Insecurity and Unemployment Crises under COVID-19: Evidence from sub-Saharan Africa' (2022) 8(1) *Cogent Social Sciences* https://doi.org/10.1080/23311886.2022.2045721.
Ministry of Agriculture, Water and Forestry, *Mass Housing development Programme* (Ministry of Agriculture, Water and Forestry 2018).
Ministry of Education, *Education Sector Plan 2018–2020* (Ministry of Education 2017).
Ministry of Environment, *Climate Change and Natural Resources, 'State of the Environment Report 2018'* (Ministry of Environment 2019).
Ministry of Finance and Economic Affairs, *The Gambia National Development Plan 2018–2021* (Ministry of Finance and Economic Affairs 2018).
Ministry of Gender, Labour and Social Development, *Uganda Social Protection Public Expenditure Review* (Ministry of Gender, Labour and Social Development 2019).
Ministry of Lands, Housing and Urban Development, *Uganda Housing Sector Profile* (Ministry of Lands, Housing and Urban Development 2016).
Ministry of Lands and Regional Government, *National Housing Policy* (Ministry of Lands and Regional Government 2010).
Mobosi IA, 'Health Burdens amid COVID-19 Pandemic: A Stark Barrier to Labour Productivity in Africa' (2022) *Health Care for Women International* available at <https://doi.org/10.1080/07399332.2022.2089146> accessed 11 June 2023.
Mpinga EK and Chastonay P, 'Satisfaction of Patients: A Right to Health Indicator?' (2011) 100 (1–2) *Health Policy* 144–150 https://doi.org/10.1016/j.healthpol.2010.11.001.
Muigai G, 'Non-Justiciable Rights: The Elusive Search for a Constitutional Basis' (2011) *International Journal of Human Rights* 115.
Namatovu R and Larsen MM, 'Responding to COVID-19: Insights from African Firms' (2021) 7(1) *African Journal of Management* 104–120.
Namibia National Gender Policy 2010–2020 (Office of the President 2010).
National Environment Management Authority, *State of Environment Report for Uganda 2014* (National Environment Management Authority 2014).
National Housing Enterprise, *Mass Housing Development Programme* (National Housing Enterprise 2018).
Nnaeme CC, '"The Community Comes to Life': How Social Grants Enable Participation in the Local Economy and Possible Effect on Post-COVID-19 Recovery in Soweto South Africa' (2022) 49(3) *Forum for Development Studies* 493–510.

OCHR, Fact Sheet No. 16 (Rev. 1): The Committee on Economic, Social and Cultural Rights.

Office of the High Commissioner, United Nations Human Rights, 'The Right to Adequate Housing in Human Rights Law' *Fact Sheet* 21 available at <https://www.ohchr.org/sites/default/files/Documents/Publications/FS21_rev_1_Housing_en.pdf> accessed 27 June 2023.

Oguz SP, 'Right to Water: Politics and Struggles Concerning Water' (2017) 2(1) *Research and Policy on Turkey* 25–37 https://doi.org/10.1080/23760818.2016.1272265.

Pamukcu K, 'The Right to Water: An Assessment' (2005) 11(2–3) *Contemporary Politics* 157–167 https://doi.org/10.1080/13569770500275155.

Pillay N, 'Economic, Social and Cultural Rights' in M Baderin and M Ssenyonjo (eds), *International Human Rights Law: Six Decades after the UDHR and Beyond* (Routledge 2010).

Rose S, Suri J, Brooks M and Ryan PG, 'COVID-19 and Citizen Science: Lessons Learned from Southern Africa' (2020) 91(2) *Journal of African Ornithology* 188–191.

C Mbazira 'Enforcement of economic, social and cultural rights in Uganda A brief overview' (2009) available at https://journals.co.za/doi/pdf/10.10520/EJC33306 accessed 24 October 2024.

Sandra Liebenberg, *Socio-Economic Rights: Adjudication under a Transformative Constitution* (Juta 2010).

Sepúlveda M, *The Nature of Obligations under the International Covenant on Economic, Social and Cultural Rights* (Intersentia 2003) 187.

Sikanku E, 'Notes on the Justiciability of Constitutional Directive Principles' (2016) 2(1) *CNLU Law Journal* 98–99.

Smith RKM, *International Human Rights Law* (10th edn, Oxford University Press 2021).

Stadler SL and Collins D, 'Assessing Housing First Programs from a Right to Housing Perspective' (2021) (38) *Housing Studies* https://doi.org/10.1080/02673037.2021.1982873.

Sucheran R, 'The COVID-19 Pandemic and Guesthouses in South Africa: Economic Impacts and Recovery Measures' (2021) 39(1) *Development Southern Africa* 35–50.

Suzuki N, Ogawa T and Inaba N, 'The Right to Adequate Housing: Evictions of the Homeless and the Elderly Caused by the 2020 Summer Olympics in Tokyo' (2018) 37(1) *Leisure Studies* 89–96 https://doi.org/10.1080/02614367.2017.1355408.

The World Bank, 'Current health Expenditure of SSA States' (2023) available at <https://data.worldbank.org/indicator/SH.XPD.CHEX.GD.ZS> accessed 27 June 2023.

The World Bank, 'Sierra Leone' (2019) available at <https://data.worldbank.org/country/sierra-leone> accessed 15 February 2023.

The World Bank, 'The World Bank in Ghana' available at <www.worldbank.org/ghana> accessed 15 July 2023.

The World Bank, 'World Water Day' (2023) available at <https://blogs.worldbank.org/opendata/world-water-day-two-billion-people-still-lack-access-safely-managed-water> accessed 26 June 2023.

Touray O, 'Government Rolls out New Housing Models for Civil Servants The Gambia Echo' *Serrekunda* 1 February 2022.

Transparency International, *Corruption in Africa: A Threat to Justice and Sustainable Development* (Transparency International 2021).

Tusting LS et al, 'Housing and Child Health in Sub-Saharan Africa: A Cross Sectional Analysis' (2020) *PLoS Medicine* available at <https://journals.plos.org/plosmedicine/article?id=10.1371/journal.pmed.1003055> accessed 27 June 2023.

Tusting LS et al, 'Mapping Changes in Housing in Sub-Saharan Africa from 2000 to 2015' (2019) 568 *Nature* 391–394 https://doi.org/10.1038/s41586-019-1050-5.

Uganda Bureau of Statistics, *Uganda Poverty Assessment Report 2016* (Uganda Bureau of Statistics 2018).

UN Committee on Economic, Social and Cultural Rights (CESCR), 'Concluding observations on the initial report of South Africa' (2018) UN Doc E/C.12/ZAF/CO/1.

UN Committee on Economic, Social and Cultural Rights (CESCR), General Comment No. 9: The Domestic Application of the Covenant, 3 December 1998, E/C.12/1998/24.

UN Sustainable Development Group, 'Leaving No One Behind: The Imperative of Inclusive Development' (Report 2016).

UNICEF, *Situation Analysis of Children in The Gambia* (UNICEF 2018).

United Nations, 'The Right to Adequate Food' – Fact Sheet No. 34 (2010) available at <https://www.ohchr.org/sites/default/files/Documents/Publications/FactSheet34en.pdf> accessed 13 June 2023.

United Nations, 'The Right to Health' *Fact Sheet* 31 available at <https://www.ohchr.org/sites/default/files/Documents/Publications/Factsheet31.pdf> accessed 27 June 2023.

United Nations Statistics Division, 'Make Cities and Human Settlements Inclusive, Safe, Resilient and Sustainable' (2019) available at <https://unstats.un.org/sdgs/report/2019/goal-11/> accessed 27 June 2023.

Viljoen F, *International Human Rights Law in Africa* (2nd edn, Oxford University Press 2012) 246.

We Are Water Foundation, 'What Do We Mean When We Talk About Access to Water' (2021) available at <https://www.wearewater.org/en/what-do-we-mean-when-we-talk-about-access-to-water_346091#:~:text=%E2%80%9CAccess%E2%80%9D%20refers%20to%20the%20existence,%2C%20health%20centers%2C%20and%20workplaces> accessed 26 June 2023.

World Health Organization, 'Health Is a Fundamental Human Right' (2017) available at <https://www.who.int/news-room/commentaries/detail/health-is-a-fundamental-human-right> accessed 27 June 2023.

World Health Organization, 'Right to Health 2018' (2018) available at <https://www.emro.who.int/images/stories/palestine/documents/who_right_to_health_2018_web-final.pdf?ua=1> accessed 27 June 2023.

Yosra Saidi et al, 'Economic Growth and Extreme Poverty in Sub-Saharan African Countries: Non-Linearity and Governance Threshold Effect' (2024) 15 *Journal of the Knowledge Economy* 7819-7851 available at https://link.springer.com/article/10.1007/s13132-023-01421-7 accessed 9 December 2024.

Yung B and Lee F, 'Right to Housing in Hong Kong: Perspectives from the Hong Kong Community' (2012) 29(4) *Housing, Theory and Society* 401–419 https://doi.org/10.1080/14036096.2012.655382.

3 Legal Framework

Introduction

This chapter examines the legal frameworks for the right to an adequate standard of living in the context of Sub-SaharanSaharan Africa (SSA). The right to an adequate standard of living is recognised under international law and international human rights norms. The right is fundamental to human dignity, well-being, and development.[1] Further, the right is a *sine qua non* for enabling equitable development.[2] However, in SSA, entrenched poverty and deprivation continue to deny millions of the citizens access to adequate food, shelter, healthcare, water, sanitation, and social security.[3] As such, strengthening the legal frameworks concerning the right to an adequate standard of living is imperative to ensure substantive protections and accountability.

This chapter undertakes a socio-legal analysis of the international and domestic legal instruments establishing State obligations regarding the right to an adequate standard of living in SSA.[4] It aims to elucidate the protections and enforcement mechanisms codified in global and regional treaties as well as in domestic constitutions, legislation, and policies across countries. Through comparative examination, it will identify strengths, gaps, and good practices to inform legal and policy reforms towards full realisation of this right.

The introductory section lays the conceptual foundations, noting the multifaceted nature covering food, housing, healthcare, education, decent work, social security, water, sanitation, and environment. Thereafter, key global treaties like the ICESCR, regional instruments like the African Charter, and the role of bodies like CESCR and African Commission are

1 UN Committee on Economic, Social and Cultural Rights, 'General Comment No. 12: The Right to Adequate Food (Art 11)' (1999) UN Doc E/C.12/1999/5.

2 Ibid.

3 United Nations Human Rights Office of the High Commission, 'Special Rapporteur on Extreme Poverty and Human Rights' (2018) available at < https://www.ohchr.org/en/special-procedures/sr-poverty> accessed 1 August 2023.

4 See generally, Obiora Chinedu Okafor, 'Critical Third World Approaches to International Law (TAWAIL): Theory, Methodology or Both?' (2008) 10 *International Community Law Review* 371-378.

DOI: 10.4324/9781032628974-3

discussed. The typologies of constitutional provisions recognising the right across the region are then examined, contrasting justiciable and non-justiciable approaches.

Domestic legislative, policy, and institutional frameworks are analysed next. The discussion focuses on sectoral laws concerning components like food, housing, social security, healthcare, and education. Gaps like inadequate coverage of informal workers and weaknesses in enforcement are highlighted. Thereafter, varying country approaches are compared based on the degree of constitutional recognition and justiciability.

The conclusion summarises persistent deficits such as resource constraints, limited political commitment, and systemic inequalities that constrain legal effectiveness. It outlines strategic priorities like increased budgets, anti-discrimination legislation, strengthened adjudication, and grievance redress systems to enhance realisation. Special attention is given to the needs of marginalised groups including women, informal workers, slum dwellers, pastoralists, and persons with disabilities.

By undertaking an in-depth assessment of legal frameworks from international to domestic levels, this chapter elucidates State obligations, good practices, and gaps concerning the right to an adequate standard of living in SSA. It highlights opportunities for cross-learning and priorities for strengthening legal protection and enforcement across countries in the region. The analysis can inform advocacy efforts by civil society as well as policy reforms by governments to uphold this vital socio-economic right.

International Human Rights Framework

In this section, the chapter discusses the international instruments that guarantee the right to an adequate standard of living within the context of SSA. These instruments include the Universal Declaration of Human Rights (UDHR), the International Covenant on Economic, Social and Cultural Rights (ICESCR), the Convention on the Rights of the Child, the Convention on the Rights of Persons with Disabilities (CRPD), as well as the United Nations Declaration on the Rights of Peasants and other People Working in Rural Areas (UNDRPPRA).

Universal Declaration of Human Rights

According to McFarland, the UDHR, which was adopted by the United Nations (UN) on 10 December 1948, serves as the 'foundation of virtually all modern human rights developments.'[5] The UDHR has a special status as

5 Sam McFarland, 'The Universal Declaration of Human Rights: A Tribute to Its Architects' (2017) 19(2) *Public Integrity (Symposium on the Social Practices of Human Rights)* at 108.

far as global human rights practice is concerned.[6] The instrument was the first international instrument to articulate the right to an adequate standard of living as a universal human right.[7] Although the UDHR was not initially legally binding, it has become an embodiment of customary international law exerting profound moral and political influence across the globe. This Sub-Saharan section examines the provisions and significance of UDHR concerning the right to an adequate standard of living in the SSA context.

Article 25 of the UDHR proclaims the right to an adequate standard of living in the following terms:

> Everyone has the right to a standard of living adequate for the health and well-being of himself and of his family, including food, clothing, housing and medical care and necessary social services, and the right to security in the event of unemployment, sickness, disability, widowhood, old age or other lack of livelihood in circumstances beyond his control.[8]

This holistic provision encompasses multiple interconnected dimensions including adequate food, clothing, housing, healthcare, necessary social services, and social security. The inclusion of a right to social security is particularly significant, as it recognises the need to specially protect the most marginalised and vulnerable sections unable to work and earn due to reasons like unemployment, disability, old age, or other contingencies beyond their control.[9]

The right is framed as a universal entitlement of 'everyone', emphasising its applicability to all human beings regardless of nationality, race, gender, or socioeconomic status. The phrase 'himself and of his family' indicates protections covering dependents like children and older persons under one's care. This underscores how realising the right to an adequate standard of living for an individual is integrally linked to fulfilling the same for their household and community.[10]

The reference to circumstances 'beyond his control' clarifies that the State bears the responsibility to provide special assistance where people are unable to meet their needs due to systemic barriers or exigencies outside their control. This affirms that poverty, deprivation, and vulnerability resulting from structural factors or discrimination warrant State support.[11]

6 Joe Hoover, 'Rereading the Universal Declaration of Human Rights: Plurality and Contestation, Not Consensus' (2013) 12(2) *Journal of Human Rights* 217-241.

7 Peter Bailey, 'The Right to an Adequate Standard of Living: New Issues for Australian Law' (1997) 4(1) *Australian Journal of Human Rights* 25-50.

8 Universal Declaration of Human Right 1948, Art 25.

9 Ibid.

10 M Magdalena Sepúlveda Carmona, *The Nature of the Obligations under the International Covenant on Economic, Social and Cultural Rights* (Antwerpen; New York: Intersentia, 2003).

11 Maastricht Guidelines on Violations of Economic, Social and Cultural Rights (26 January 1997) available at < https://www.hlrn.org/img/documents/Maastricht%20Guidelines.pdf> accessed 1 August 2023.

In addition, Article 22 of the UDHR upholds the right to social security. Further, rights to just remuneration for work, reasonable limitation of working hours, and ability to form trade unions enshrined in Articles 23 and 24 complement standard of living protections.[12] Taken together, these provisions outline a comprehensive foundation for realising the multidimensional right to adequate living standards under the UDHR.

The UDHR provisions carried tremendous significance for SSA peoples and nations, considering that nearly all countries in the region were under oppressive systems of colonialism and racial discrimination when it was adopted in 1948.[13]

The UDHR affirmation of fundamental economic and social rights like adequate living standards challenged the systemic exploitation, dispossession, and deprivation inflicted on African peoples under colonialism and apartheid. It repudiated racial discrimination and affirmed these rights as universal entitlements of all human beings regardless of race, class, gender, or cultural background.[14]

In the aftermath of independence starting from the late 1950s, the human rights principles embodied in the UDHR came to inspire many post-colonial African constitutions, bills of rights, and social policy frameworks. For instance, Ghana's 1969 Constitution incorporated verbatim sections of the UDHR text, while countries like Senegal and Tanzania constitutionally embedded social rights drawing from the UDHR.[15]

However, the lived reality of entrenched poverty and gross inequality across many parts of SSA underscores the enduring challenge of fully translating these constitutionally enshrined rights into tangible change in ordinary people's lives. According to the World Bank, over 40 percent of SSA's population still live below the international poverty line.[16]

Weak rule of law, lack of democratic accountability, corruption, and governance deficits further constrain social rights implementation for the poor despite constitutional guarantees.[17] The failure to close glaring inequalities

12 UDHR (note 8).

13 Franck Kuwonu, 'Africa's Freedom Struggles and the Universal Declaration of Human Rights' (2019) available at < https://www.un.org/africarenewal/magazine/december-2018-march-2019/africa%E2%80%99s-freedom-struggles-and-universal-declaration-human-rights> accessed 1 August 2023. See also, R Murray Thomas, 'The Universal Declaration of Human Rights and Sub-Saharan Africa: A Post-Colonial Reading' (2011) 26 *UCLA Journal of International Law and Foreign Affairs* 101.

14 Makau Mutua, 'The Complexity of Universalism in Human Rights' in A Sajo (eds), *Human Rights with Modesty: The Problem of Universalism* (Dordrecht: Springer, 2004).

15 Constitution of Ghana (1969); Constitution of the Republic of Senegal (1963); Interim Constitution of Tanzania (1965).

16 The World Bank, 'Macro Poverty Outlook for Sub-Saharan Africa' (2022) available at < https://www.worldbank.org/en/publication/macro-poverty-outlook/mpo_ssa> accessed 1 August 2023.

17 Dan Banik, 'Legal Empowerment as Conceptual and Operational Tool in Poverty Eradication' (2009) 1(1) *Hague Journal on the Rule of Law* 117-131.

based on race, gender, ethnicity, religion, class, and geographic region exemplify the gaps that persist between *de jure* and *de facto* human rights in the region.[18]

Nevertheless, the UDHR lays down an important moral and legal foundation for continuously advocating the universal right to an adequate standard of living in the SSA context. Its principles helped catalyse post-colonial rights-based constitutions and social policy efforts across newly independent African countries. The UDHR continues to inspire human rights activism and serve as a benchmark for national human rights commissions advocating against poverty and systemic discrimination across the region.[19]

The 2030 Sustainable Development Agenda, with its emphasis on eradicating poverty, reducing inequalities, and ensuring universal access to adequate food, water, healthcare, education, housing, and social protection for all, builds on the UDHR's transformative legacy.[20] However, fully realising the multidimensional right to an adequate standard of living for everyone as envisaged under Article 25 of the UDHR still remains an unfinished task in SSA as in most of the world. It necessitates strengthening social rights justiciability, anti-discrimination legal frameworks, resource allocation and democratic accountability across the region. The universal human right to dignity through an adequate standard of living must be claimed with renewed urgency by the region's impoverished and marginalised populations.

International Covenant on Economic, Social and Cultural Rights

The International Covenant on Economic, Social and Cultural Rights (ICESCR), adopted in 1966 and in force since 1976, is the seminal global treaty enshrining the right to an adequate standard of living as a legally binding human right. This section examines the significance and influence of the ICESCR in relation to upholding the right to an adequate standard of living in the SSA context.

Article 11 of the ICESCR recognises 'the right of everyone to an adequate standard of living for himself and his family, including adequate food, clothing and housing and to the continuous improvement of living conditions.'[21]

18 Manisuli Ssenyonjo, *Economic, Social and Cultural Rights in International Law* (2nd ed) (London: Bloomsbury Publishing, 2016).

19 George Mukundi Wachira, 'African Court on Human and Peoples' Rights: Ten Years on and Still No Justice' (2008) available at < https://primarysources.brillonline.com/browse/human-rights-documents-online/african-court-on-human-and-peoples-rights-ten-years-on-and-still-no-justice-sept-2008-36-pp;hrdhrd02090232> accessed 1 August 2023.

20 United Nations, 'Transforming Our World: The 2030 Agenda for Sustainable Development' (2015) available at < https://sdgs.un.org/publications/transforming-our-world-2030-agenda-sustainable-development-17981> accessed 1 August 2023.

21 International Covenant on Economic, Social and Cultural Rights (adopted 16 December 1966, entered into force 3 January 1976) 993 UNTS 3 Art 11 (ICESCR).

The right to an adequate standard of living specifically encompasses key dimensions including food, clothing, housing, and the continuous enhancement of overall living conditions. While the Universal Declaration of Human Rights (UDHR) was non-binding, the inclusion of this same right in a legally binding covenant strengthened its international legal force and enforceability .[22]

In addition, Article 11 upholds 'the fundamental right of everyone to be free from hunger and obligates states to improve methods of production, conservation and distribution of food' and disseminate nutritional knowledge.[23] This provision integrates the right to adequate food as an essential component within the wider framework of an adequate standard. Articles 12 to 15 of the Covenant guarantee several other interdependent rights constituting key attributes of an adequate standard of living, including the rights to physical and mental health, education, access to water and sanitation, social security, decent work, and participation in cultural life.[24]

General Comment 19 of the ESCR Committee interprets the right to an adequate standard of living as integrally linked to the rights to food, housing, water, health, education, work, and social protection.[25] Thus, the ICESCR outlines an expansive and multidimensional legal framework for ensuring adequate living standards in a holistic manner. As a legally binding treaty under international law, the ICESCR imposes concrete obligations on States' parties to respect, protect, and fulfil economic-social rights through all appropriate means.[26] The responsibility of States to 'progressively realise' these rights to the maximum extent of their available resources are consistently coupled with an obligation to ensure at least minimum essential levels as expeditiously as possible even in contexts of resources' constraints.[27]

The UN Committee on Economic, Social and Cultural Rights (CESCR) has sought to delineate the core minimum obligations corresponding to the specific right to an adequate standard of living which include:

- Ensuring the right to adequate food, basic shelter and housing, essential medicines, and water on a non-discriminatory basis.
- Equitable access to and utilisation of such resources by all, especially marginalised groups.
- Special attention to vulnerable and disadvantaged populations.

22 Eibe Riedel and others, 'The Making of the International Bill of Human Rights' (United Nations Human Rights Office of the High Commissioner, 2006)

23 ICESCR (note 21).

24 Ibid, Art 2.

25 UN Committee on Economic, Social and Cultural Rights 'General Comment No. 19: The Right to Social Security' (2008) UN Doc E/C.12/GC/19.

26 ICESCR (note 21), art 11.

27 UN Committee on Economic, Social and Cultural Rights, 'General Comment No. 3: The Nature of States Parties' Obligations.

- Adopting strategies, policies, and programmes covering these key dimensions.[28]

Thus, while progressive realisation based on maximum available resources is recognised as a pragmatic principle under the ICESCR, State parties are still duty-bound to immediately guarantee certain 'non-derogable' minimum levels of economic-social rights fulfilment as a matter of human rights law.[29] The ICESR carries profound significance for SSA as the first international treaty to codify a legally binding right to an adequate standard of living, along with other economic-social rights. An overwhelming majority of countries in the region have ratified the Covenant, with 49 out of 54 States currently parties to it.[30]

The ICESR had a major influence on constitution-making law and policy formulation in newly independent African countries during the 1960s and 1970s. For instance, Kenya's Independence Constitution incorporated extensive economic-social rights provisions modelled directly along the lines of the ICESR framework.[31] South Africa's post-apartheid Bill of Rights and constitutional provisions on housing, healthcare, food, and water also drew inspiration from the ICESR.[32] More recently, the African Commission on Human and Peoples' Rights has involved States' obligations under the Covenant in its standing of living jurisprudence concerning issues like forced evictions.[33]

For civil society, the CESCR's authoritative interpretations provide a strong basis for rights-based advocacy on matters like social assistance, food security, land reform, healthcare, education, and housing across SSA.[34] Its norms reinforce legal empowerment efforts to render socio-economic rights justiciable before national courts. However, massive gaps remain between the comprehensive legal standard outlined in the ICESCR and the abject reality of widespread poverty and deprivation afflicting most parts of SSA. As already mentioned, World Bank estimates show that over 40 percent of the region's population still subsists below the international poverty line and face hunger, disease, inadequate housing, and lack of access to essential services like water, sanitation, and education.

This disjuncture underscores how formal ratification alone is insufficient for social rights fulfilment in the absence of accountable institutions, participatory

28 UN CESCR 'General Comment No. 12: The Right to Adequate Food (Art 11)' (1999) UN Doc E/C.12/1999/5.

29 Carmona, op cit (note 10).

30 See United Nations Treaty Collection, 'International Covenant on Economic and Social Rights' available <https://treaties.un.org> accessed 1 August 2023.

31 Constitution of Kenya (1963) chap VI.

32 Constitution of the Republic of South Africa (1996) chap 2.

33 See *Social and Economic Rights Action Centre (SERAC) and anor v Nigeria* (2001) AHRLR 60 (ACHPR 2001).

34 E Durojaye and G Mirugi-Mukundi, 'Realising Access to Medicine in International Law: Imperative Standards for the SADC Region' (2018) 18 *African Human Rights Law Journal.*

policymaking processes, and adequately resourced implementation mechanisms. Weak enforcement of economic social rights norms, despite clear ICESCR State obligations, constrain fulfilment, especially for marginalised groups.

The International Covenant on Economic, Social and Cultural Rights (ICESCR) provides an important normative foundation and legal basis for rights-based social policies across Sub-Saharan Africa. These policies aim to address poverty reduction, social protection, food security, housing, healthcare, education, and sustainable development. To strengthen the enforcement of socio-economic rights in national courts, advocates should pursue creative legal interpretations and advocacy strategies. This includes strictly enforcing core obligations and establishing robust accountability mechanisms for violations.

Moreover, the ICESCR's provisions emphasise the need for an integrated approach recognising the multidimensionality and intersectionality of the various components of an adequate living standard. The task ahead lies in evolving the treaty from a set of legally binding but abstract principles into directly actionable entitlements and equitable outcomes. Bridging implementation gaps through multisectoral strategies guided by human rights is essential for the Covenant to uplift millions across SSA from abject poverty to a life of dignity, freedom, and justice.

Convention on the Rights of the Child

According to Quennerstedt, Poland suggested to the UN Economic and Social Council that an international convention on the rights of the child should be adopted to celebrate the International Year of the Child 1979.[35] The Convention on the Rights of the Child (CRC), adopted in 1989 and near-universally ratified, contains provisions specifically upholding children's right to an adequate standard of living. This section examines the relevance and importance of the CRC framework in relation to protecting the right to adequate living standards, health, nutrition, and overall development for children in the SSA context. It is worthy of note that 'most UN member states have revised their laws and adjusted their policies and budgets to reflect the mandates of the CRC.'[36]

Article 27 of the CRC specifically enshrines children's right to a 'standard of living adequate for the child's physical, mental, spiritual, moral, and social development.'[37] While recognising the responsibilities of parents and their

35 Ann Quennerstedt, 'Balancing the Rights of the Child and the Rights of Parents in the Convention on the Rights of the Child' (2009) 8(2) *Journal of Human Rights* 162-176.

36 Elisabeth Kofler Shuman, 'Anticipating the Convention on the Rights of the Child' (2017) 93(3) *Childhood Education* at 246.

37 Convention on the Rights of the Child (adopted 20 November 1989, entered into force 2 September 1990) 1577 UNTS 3 art 27 (CRC).

guardians to provide adequate conditions for children 'within their abilities,' the provision clarifies it is ultimately the State which holds the primary obligation to take 'appropriate measures to assist parents and others responsible for the child' and 'in case of need' to 'provide material assistance and support programmes' necessary for the child's well-being and development.[38]

The CRC integrates children's right to an adequate standard of living firmly within the normative paradigm of the International Covenant on Economic, Social and Cultural Rights (ICESCR), while expanding further on the specific physical, mental, moral, and social developmental attributes required to ensure the well-being and dignity of the child.[39] The comprehensive substantive standard covers adequate nutrition, clothing, housing, water, sanitation, and developmental requisites.

Other salient CRC provisions related to the right to an adequate standard of living include Article 24, which protects children's right to the 'highest attainable standard of health,' including pre-natal and post-natal care of mothers; Article 28, which guarantees children's right to education directed at holistic development of abilities on the basis of equal opportunity; and Article 23, which safeguards disabled children's right to special care, education, training, rehabilitation, preparation for employment and 'a standard of living conducive to the child's well-being.'[40]

Article 26 of the CRC upholds children's right to benefit from social security insurance and social protection provisions from the State, 'taking into account the resources and the circumstances of the child and persons having responsibility for the maintenance of the child.'[41] Article 18 obligates the State to support working parents by providing assistance with childcare services.[42] Article 20 provides special protections for children deprived of a family environment.[43] Together these provisions establish a strong legal basis and comprehensive normative framework at the global level for realising children's right to adequate living standards and well-being.

The Convention establishes a legally binding obligation on States' parties to ensure to the 'maximum extent possible,' not just the basic survival but also the healthy growth, well-being and development of all children, including through the provision of adequate living standards and material assistance where parents, guardians, or families lack sufficient resources.[44]

The overarching principles of universality, non-discrimination, and the prioritisation of the best interests of the child always consistently underline and

38 Ibid.

39 International Covenant on Economic, Social and Cultural Rights (adopted 16 December 1966, entered into force 3 January 1976) 993 UNTS 3 arts 11-12 (ICESCR).

40 CRC, op cit (note 37) arts 23-28.

41 Ibid, art 26.

42 Ibid, art 18.

43 Ibid art 20.

44 Ibid arts 6, 27

reinforce States' duties under the CRC towards realising child rights.[45] The Committee on the Rights of the Child, which is the treaty body monitoring implementation of the Convention, has asserted that fulfilling children's socio-economic rights, including to adequate standard of living, is a fundamental 'human rights imperative, not charity.'[46]

The Convention on the Rights of the Child carries tremendous legal and moral significance for SSA, because all countries across the region are States' parties having ratified the treaty.[47] For the millions of children in SSA facing sustained poverty, deprivation, malnutrition, lack of education, forced labour, preventable diseases, and lack of access to essential services, the CRC's provisions legally mandating rights-based State obligations to ensure adequate food, clothing, housing, water, sanitation, and holistic development take on vital importance.[48] The treaty provides an authoritative basis for rights-based public budgeting and expenditure, targeted nutrition programmes, healthcare policies, social assistance and protection schemes, educational initiatives, and developmental measures that aim to tangibly benefit children and enhance their well-being.[49] The African Charter on the Rights and Welfare of the Child builds upon the CRC framework in contextualising child rights to health, adequate nutrition, shelter, and education within the African context.[50]

Several SSA governments have instituted social protection schemes, poverty reduction action plans, and socio-economic programmes targeted at children and families based on the standards and principles of the CRC, though implementation and reach remain a challenge.[51] Public interest litigation efforts have also utilised CRC obligations on States to push for greater protection and fulfilment of socio-economic entitlements for street children, orphans, and child-headed households.[52] However, despite near universal ratification and pockets of progress, alarming disparities persist between the international legal standards codified in the CRC and the actual situation on the ground confronting most of SSA's children. Undernutrition and malnutrition remain widespread affecting around 32 percent of children as per UNICEF, manifesting in stunting and wasting with severe long-term health and development consequences.[53]

45 CRC op cit (note 37) arts 2-3.

46 UN CRC 'General Comment No. 9

47 United Nations Treaty Collection, 'Convention on the Rights of the Child' available at <https://treaties.un.org> accessed 27 February 2023.

48 African Child Policy Forum, 'Budgeting for Children in Africa' (2019).

49 African Charter on the Rights and Welfare of the Child 1990, art 14.

50 Ibid.

51 Sonia Bhalotra and others, 'Social Assistance Spending and Infant Mortality in Sub-Saharan Africa: Evidence from Zimbabwe' (2021) 79 *World Development* 2.

52 See *Centre for Child Law v Minister of Home Affairs* 2005 ZAGPHC 10.

53 UNICEF, 'Child Stunting Analysis of Children in Sub-Saharan Africa' (2019).

While the CRC lays out a robust and far-reaching legal framework, operationalising and translating these treaty obligations into tangible improvements in children's well-being through accountable institutions, democratic governance, progressive legislation, evidence-based public expenditure, non-discrimination, and closing disparities remains a pressing challenge confronting Sub-Saharan African States. Nevertheless, the CRC supplies a vital morally authoritative and legally empowering tool for civil society advocacy on increasing child-focused social spending, strengthening public healthcare and nutrition programmes, enhancing food security schemes, improving access to adequate housing and sanitation facilities, and instituting effective social protection policies across SSA to uphold children's right to an adequate standard of living.

Convention on the Rights of Persons with Disabilities

The Convention on the Rights of Persons with Disabilities (CRPD) adopted in 2006 and in force since 2008, contains specific provisions upholding the right of persons with disabilities to an adequate standard of living on an equal basis with others. This section examines the significance and relevance of the CRPD framework in relation to protecting and fulfilling the right to adequate housing, food, clothing, water, social security, and overall living standards for persons with disabilities in the SSA context.

Article 28 of the CRPD specifically recognises the right of persons with disabilities to an adequate standard of living for themselves and their families, including adequate food, clothing, housing and 'continuous improvement of living conditions'.[54] It obligates States' parties to take appropriate steps to safeguard and promote the realisation of this right for persons with disabilities without discrimination. To achieve this, the CRPD mandates States to undertake measures to ensure equal access by persons with disabilities to clean water services, poverty reduction programmes, public housing, retirement benefits, and disability-related assistance, including personal assistance support for disability-related needs.[55] The provision applies to both urban and rural areas.[56]

In enshrining the right to an adequate standard of living, Article 28 of the CRPD integrates it firmly within the substantive and normative paradigm of the International Covenant on Economic, Social and Cultural Rights (ICESCR) while contextualising the application of this right for persons with disabilities by emphasising the need to ensure their equal access on an equitable basis.[57]

54 Convention on the Rights of Persons with Disabilities (adopted 13 December 2006, entered into force 3 May 2008) 2515 UNTS 3 art 28 (CRPD).

55 Ibid.

56 Ibid.

57 International Covenant on Economic, Social and Cultural Rights (adopted 16 December 1966, entered into force 3 January

In addition, Article 27 of the CRPD separately upholds the right of persons with disabilities to work and employment, including the opportunity to gain a living through freely chosen work, equal remuneration, access to the labour market, vocational and professional rehabilitation services, and protection against workplace exploitation and abuse.[58] Enjoyment of this right is essential for income security and standard of living.

Other salient CRPD provisions related to realising adequate living standards for persons with disabilities include Article 24, which guarantees the right to inclusive education at all levels without discrimination and on the basis of equal opportunity; and Article 25, which protects the right to the highest attainable standard of health without discrimination, encompassing provision of the same quality, range, and standard of free or affordable health services within the same system as other members of society.[59]

Article 20 of the Convention obligates States' parties to take effective measures to facilitate the personal mobility and independence of persons with disabilities by ensuring their access to quality mobility aids, assistive technologies, and accessible information at affordable cost, as well as forms of assistance and intermediaries like guides and readers.[60] Enjoyment of this right promotes standard of living through enabling access to places, services, and the community.

Article 9 prescribes comprehensive standards and measures for accessibility including identification and elimination of obstacles, application of universal design principles, and establishment of minimum standards for accessibility to the built environment, transportation, information, communications, and services open to the public in both urban and rural areas.[61] Accessibility in all spheres of life is imperative for equal standard of living.

Taken together, these provisions of the CRPD establish an extensive, equality-based framework cantered on inclusion, accessibility, reasonable accommodation and individual autonomy for upholding and fulfilling the right to an adequate standard of living and associated entitlements for persons with disabilities globally.

As a binding international human rights treaty, the CRPD places concrete legal obligations on States' parties to ensure the full realisation of all human rights, including the specific right to an adequate standard of living, for all persons with disabilities without any discrimination.[62]

To achieve rights on an equal basis, States are duty-bound to identify and abolish any laws, policies, programmes, infrastructure, or facilities that directly or indirectly discriminate against or exclude persons with disabilities, and take

58 CRPD (note 54) art 27.
59 Ibid arts 24-25
60 Ibid art 20.
61 Ibid art 3-4
62 Ibid art 5.

all appropriate steps to modify, adapt, redesign, reasonably accommodate, or replace them to enable universal accessibility and inclusion.[63]

The CRPD also obligates States to undertake or promote research and development, encourage international partnerships, and facilitate capacity building including through international development aid to provide affordable assistive technologies, accessibility solutions, and measures to uphold the right to an adequate standard of living for all persons with disabilities equitably.[64]

The Convention on the Rights of Persons with Disabilities carries tremendous significance for Sub-Saharan Africa, considering that 44 out of the 54 countries across the region have currently ratified the treaty, underscoring its relevance and applicability to the African context.[65] However, effective implementation of the CRPD standards through policy, legislation, and programming remains a substantial challenge across many states in the region.

In most Sub-Saharan African countries, persons with disabilities continue to face systemic barriers and extreme disadvantages across the multifaceted dimensions of poverty, hunger, inadequate housing, denial of reasonable accommodation, lack of access to equitable education and employment opportunities, exclusion from healthcare and rehabilitation services, and lack of accessibility that constrain their equal enjoyment of an adequate standard of living.[66]

Attitudinal barriers amongst the public and inadequate awareness and knowledge regarding disability accentuate stigma and prejudice, while lack of appropriately disaggregated data impedes evidence-based, targeted and inclusive policymaking, and budget expenditure across sectors that benefits persons with disabilities.[67]

Nevertheless, the coming into force of the CRPD has helped inspire regional frameworks like the Protocol to the African Charter on Human and Peoples' Rights on the Rights of Persons with Disabilities adopted in 2018, which draws from and aligns closely with the CRPD in highlighting the priorities of promoting and protecting the dignity, inclusion, accessibility, and mainstreaming of the rights of persons with disabilities across development, governance and human rights laws, policies, strategies, and programmes in the African context.[68]

63 Ibid 32.

64 Ibid.

65 United Nations Treaty Collection '

66 Judith McKenzie and others, 'Disability-inclusive Community Based Childcare Centres in Malawi' (2019) 25 *Child: Care, Health and Development* 267.

67 Marianne Schulze, Understanding the UN Convention on the Rights of Persons with Disabilities (Handicap International 2009).

68 Protocol to the African Charter on Human and Peoples' Rights on the Rights of Persons with Disabilities (2018).

Several SSA countries have enacted dedicated new disability rights and inclusion legislation or amended existing laws to align them closer with the CRPD framework, established national disability rights coordination offices or commissions, and instituted targeted disability social protection schemes and accessibility standards seeking adherence to the Convention.[69]

Disabled persons organisations (DPOs) and civil society groups have sought to utilise the CRPD reporting processes and invoke the legal obligations enshrined within it on States' parties before regional judicial and non-judicial human rights bodies to push for greater realisation of civil-political and socio-economic rights, including the right to adequate standard of living for persons with disabilities relating to issues like ending abuse in institutions, increasing accessibility to the built environment, realising inclusive education, and reasonable accommodation in the workplace.[70]

However, despite these pockets of progress, ensuring equal access to an adequate standard of living for persons with disabilities across its multiple dimensions including housing, health, food, water, education, livelihoods, rehabilitation, accessibility and inclusion remains a substantial and pressing unfulfilled challenge across most countries in the Sub-Saharan region. Targeted resources, comprehensive anti-discrimination legislation, collection and use of disaggregated data and metrics, universal promotion of accessibility and reasonable accommodation in all facilities, services and programmes, and meaningful efforts to combat stigma through awareness remain vital measures that need urgent prioritisation by States to translate the CRPD from paper to practice and tangibly uplift persons with disabilities across SSA towards fulfilment of equal rights and the highest attainable standard of living.

The UN Declaration on the Rights of Peasants and Other People Working in Rural Areas

The United Nations Declaration on the Rights of Peasants and Other People Working in Rural Areas, adopted by the UN General Assembly in 2018, contains specific provisions upholding the rights of peasants and rural populations to an adequate standard of living and development. This section examines the relevance and significance of this international Declaration in relation to protecting the livelihoods, food security, standard of living, and overall well-being of peasant farmers and rural communities in the Sub-Saharan African context.

Article 16 of the UN Declaration specifically recognises the rights of peasants and other people working in rural areas to adequate food and fundamental

69 J Awori, 'Emerging Disability Law Jurisprudence in East Africa: What is there to Learn and What are the Gaps?' (2019) 7 *African Disability Rights Yearbook* 105.

70 *Purohit and Moore v The Gambia* (2003) AHRLR 96 (ACHPR 2003).

right to be free from hunger.[71] It obligates States to ensure that peasants are free from malnutrition and enabled to develop their full human potential. Enjoyment of the right to clean water and sanitation, as well as access to adequate housing is also upheld.[72]

Article 17 of the Declaration upholds the rights of peasants to the enjoyment of the highest attainable standard of physical and mental health.[73] Articles 19 and 20 enshrine the rights of peasants to education and to take part in cultural life.[74] Article 5 obligates States to eliminate discrimination and take special measures to eradicate extreme poverty, hunger and malnutrition among peasants, especially women, children, elderly persons and persons with disabilities.[75]

Article 4 mandates states to take measures to eliminate all forms of discrimination against peasant women and to promote their empowerment in order to ensure they fully and equally enjoy their human rights, including the right to an adequate standard of living.[76]

Articles 6 and 23 of the Declaration recognise the rights of peasants to have access to, sustainably use and manage land, fisheries, forests, water and seeds as central to upholding their livelihoods and development.[77]

Taken together, these key provisions of the UN Declaration on the Rights of Peasants establish substantive standards closely aligned with those of landmark international human rights instruments like the Universal Declaration of Human Rights and the International Covenant on Economic, Social and Cultural Rights, in seeking to universally uphold the equal rights of peasants and rural populations to an adequate standard of living, development, dignity, and well-being.

The UN Declaration on the Rights of Peasants carries relevance and significance for Sub-Saharan Africa, considering that a predominantly high proportion of the population, nearly 60 percent across most countries in the region, live in rural areas and depend on smallholder, family-based peasant agriculture and associated informal work for their survival and livelihoods.[78]

Poverty, food insecurity, deprivation of adequate housing, clean water, sanitation, and essential social services remain pressing systemic issues confronting

71 United Nations Declaration on the Rights of Peasants and Other People Working in Rural Areas (2018) UN Doc A/RES/73/165, art 16.
72 Ibid.
73 Ibid art 17.
74 Ibid arts 19-20.
75 Ibid art 5.
76 Ibid art 4.
77 Ibid arts 6, 23.
78 Boaventura Monjane, 'Transforming the Politics of Food in Southern Africa, From the Local to the Global' (2018) available at <https://viacampesina.org/en/transforming-the-politics-of-food-in-southern-africa-from-the-local-to-the-global/> accessed 4 August 2023.

rural peasants and communities across many parts of SSA, necessitating urgent and targeted action by States as duty-bearers.

Within the peasantry, rural women farmers are disproportionately impacted by the consequences of intersecting inequalities arising from poverty, informal work, childcare responsibilities, lack of access to credit and agricultural resources like land, discriminatory laws and deep-rooted patriarchal norms, and face immense constraints in enjoying their right to an adequate standard of living on par with others.[79]

In this context, the UN Declaration represents a landmark global pronouncement affirming the urgent priority that needs to be accorded by states and international organisations to comprehensively upholding and fulfilling the equal entitlements and dignity of the poorest, most neglected rural populations of peasants and informal agricultural workers through targeted policies across a range of human rights, including the rights to land, productive resources, decent work, education, health, housing, water, sanitation, social security, and an adequate standard of living free from hunger and malnutrition.[80]

It obligates States to take appropriate legislative, policy, budgetary, and institutional steps at both national and international levels on priority areas like genuine agrarian and land reform, agricultural research, and extension services targeted at smallholder farmers, facilitating affordable access to rural credit, agricultural technologies, markets and value addition, social protection schemes, and climate change adaptation and mitigation measures which tangibly benefit and uplift peasant groups.[81]

A number of Sub-Saharan African countries, including South Africa, Angola, Eswatini, Lesotho, Malawi, Madagascar, Burkina Faso, Central African Republic, Chad, and Ghana, that voted in favour of the UN Declaration at the UN General Assembly, have cited the acute need to protect the livelihoods, rights, and development of peasant farmers in rural areas who face systemic marginalisation, deprivation, and poverty as a key reason motivating their support and recognition of this international instrument.[82]

Some countries in the region like Mali and Burkina Faso have also taken recent legislative initiatives to incorporate elements of the UN Declaration on the Rights of Peasants within national laws and policies, including through statutes recognising forms of collective peasant rights.[83]

79 Naomi Hassan and Patta Scott-Villiers, 'Purchasing and Protesting: Power from Below in the Global Food Crisis' (2019) 50(2) IDS *Bulletin* available at <https://bulletin.ids.ac.uk/index.php/idsbo/article/view/3037/Online%20article> accessed 4 August 2023.

80 UN Declaration on the Rights of Peasants (note 74).

81 Ibid.

82 UN General Assembly, 'General Assembly Endorses Landmark Global Compact on Refugees, adopting 53 Third Committee Resolutions, 6 Decisions Covering Range of Human Rights' (2028) UN Doc GA/12107.

83 Food and Agriculture Organization of the UN, 'Peasant Rights' (2020) available at <https://www.fao.org/plant-treaty/tools/toolbox-for-sustainable-use/details/en/c/1373893/> accessed 4 August 2023.

However, massive gaps remain between the comprehensive substantive human rights standards related to upholding the right to an adequate standard of living articulated in the UN Declaration, and the actual lived reality confronting the vast majority of rural peasantry across Sub-Saharan Africa. Hunger, malnutrition, poverty, deprivation of access to adequate housing, clean water, sanitation, health, education, and essential social services remains widespread afflicting rural populations, undermining their rights and potential.[84]

The incidence of undernourishment and stunting among children, maternal malnutrition and anaemia among women, smallholder farmer poverty and food insecurity remain particularly high across most countries in Sub-Saharan Africa reflecting policy gaps.[85] Environmental and climate change-related threats like land degradation, loss of biodiversity, water scarcity, declining soil fertility, erratic rainfall patterns, droughts, and floods further exacerbate challenges confronting rural livelihoods and standard of living.[86]

Moreover, the absence of any legally binding force or justiciability constrains the enforceability of the standards and obligations outlined in the UN Declaration on Peasants' Rights. Nevertheless, the Declaration still carries important moral force and legitimacy as representing the voice and urgent priorities of marginalised peasant constituencies globally. It can serve as a vital advocacy tool and moral basis for rights-based law and policymaking upholding the livelihoods, economic empowerment, food security, and standard of living of peasants if creatively leveraged by civil society and policymakers.

Strategic utilisation of its human rights-based standards lies in raising mass awareness of its norms among rural communities, proactively integrating its principles within national laws, development policies, strategies and programmes, and invoking the provisions before judicial and non-judicial human rights monitoring bodies like National Human Rights Institutions and the African Commission to strengthen promotion and protection of the right to an adequate standard of living for the massive peasant populace across Sub-Saharan Africa.

Role of Monitoring Bodies under International Framework to Ensure the Realisation of the Right to an Adequate Standard of Living

Under the international rights framework, various UN and regional treaty bodies have been conferred an authoritative monitoring role regarding State obligations on ensuring the realisation of the right to an adequate standard of living.

84 Ahmed Adefemi Adesete and others, 'Climate Change and Food Security in Selected Sub-Saharan African Countries' (2022) 25 *Environment, Development and Sustainability* available at <https://www.ncbi.nlm.nih.gov/pmc/articles/PMC9510474/pdf/10668_2022_Article_2681.pdf> accessed 4 August 2023.

85 Hassan and Scott-Villiers, op cit (note 79).

86 Ibid.

This section provides an in-depth discussion on the specific functions and powers of key global and regional monitoring bodies in assessing compliance, revealing implementation gaps, providing recommendations, and seeking enhanced State fulfilment of the right to adequate food, housing, clothing, water, health, and overall living conditions. It analyses their working modalities, strengths, and limitations in ensuring substantive outcomes and tangible improvements on the ground.

United Nations Committee on Economic, Social and Cultural Rights

The Committee on Economic, Social and Cultural Rights (CESCR) is the expert UN treaty body mandated with monitoring State party compliance with upholding the range of substantive protections enshrined in the International Covenant on Economic, Social and Cultural Rights. With regards to the specific rights to an adequate standard of living, the CESCR's monitoring role and activities encompass:

Periodic State Reporting and Review

- Receiving and scrutinising periodic reports submitted every five years by State parties detailing the measures they have taken, and progress made in respect of upholding the right to an adequate standard of living under Article 11 of the Covenant including the provision of adequate food, clothing, housing, and continuous improvement of overall living conditions.[87]
- The review process provides an opportunity for constructive dialogue with the State party delegation where Committee members can seek additional information and clarifications through questioning.[88] The CESCR engages in robust examination of challenges, gaps, and areas for improved implementation highlighted in the State report or civil society submissions.[89]
- At the end of the process, the CESR issues Concluding Observations summarising the key issues of concern, positive aspects, and concrete recommendations prescribing time-bound actions for the State party to undertake to address gaps and enhance enjoyment of the right to an adequate standard of living.[90]

Publishing Authoritative General Comments

- Drafting and issuing substantive general comments providing authoritative interpretation on the normative scope, elements, and State party obligations

87 International Covenant on Economic, Social and Cultural Rights (1966) art 16.
88 Office of the High Commissioner for Human Rights, 'Committee on Economic, Social and Cultural Rights' (Fact Sheet No. 16 Rev. 1).
89 International Covenant on Economic, Social and Cultural Rights, op cit (note 87).
90 Ibid art 16.

pertaining to specific rights enshrined in in the Covenant including the right to an adequate standard of living.[91]

- General Comment 4 discusses Article 11(1) on the right to adequate housing in detail, laying out dimensions like legal security of tenure, availability of services, affordability, habitability, accessibility, location, and cultural adequacy.[92] General Comment 7 focuses on forced evictions and displacements in relation to the right to housing.[93]
- General Comment 12 elaborates on the right to adequate food in Article 11, discussing issues like food availability, accessibility, and adequacy.[94] General Comment 19 links the right to social security intrinsically to realisation of an adequate standard of living.[95]
- While the general comments are non-binding, they provide authoritative guidance to States on implementation of obligations and serve as benchmarks for assessing compliance.[96]

Adjudicating Individual Complaints

- With the entry into force of the Optional Protocol in 2013, hearing complaints submitted by individuals or groups alleging violations of the right to an adequate standard of living under the Covenant and providing recommendations to governments for requisite remedial action.[97]
- For instance, the ESCR Committee found Spain's mortgage laws failed to adequately protect against homelessness and promote the right to housing with dignity. It prescribed legal amendments, debtor relief programmes, and human rights impact assessments.[98]
- While decisions are technically non-binding, they carry moral weight and persuasive authority. However, lack of enforcement mechanisms constrains follow-up implementation by States.[99]

91 Philip Alston, 'The Historical Origins of the Concept of 'General Comments' in Human Rights Law' in Laurence Boisson de Chazournes and Vera Gowlland-Debbas (eds), *The International Legal System in Quest of Equity and Universality* (Leiden: Brill) 763-776.
92 UN CESCR 'General Comment No. 4: The Right to Adequate Housing' (1991) UN Doc E/1992/23.
93 UN CESCR 'General Comment No. 7: The Right to Adequate Housing' (1997) UN Doc E/1998/22.
94 UN CESCR 'General Comment No. 12: The Right to Adequate Food (Art 11)' (1999) UN Doc E/C. 12/1999/5.
95 UN CESCR 'General Comment No. 19: The Right to social Security (Art 19)' (2007) UN Doc E/C.12/GC/19.
96 Sepúlveda Carmona, op cit (note 10).
97 Optional Protocol to the International Covenant on Economic, Social and Cultural Rights (2008) arts 1-2.
98 *IDG v Spain CESCR* (2015) UN Doc E/C.12/55/D/2/2014.
99 Malcom Langford and Evan Rosevear, 'Economic and social Rights' in DS Law, H Lau and A Schwartz (eds) *Oxford Handbook of Constitutional Law in Asia* (Oxford: Oxford University

Conducting Inquiries into Grave Systemic Violations

- Under the Optional Protocol, initiating confidential investigative enquiries in cases where it receives reliable information indicating grave or systematic violations by a State party of the right to an adequate standard of living and associated Covenant rights.[100]
- For example, the CESCR recently conducted an enquiry into Spain for forced evictions and homelessness impacting the right to adequate housing, formulating detailed recommendations.[101] However, this procedure has not yet been utilised to full potential.

Undertaking Country Visits

- Under the Optional Protocol, visiting countries by request to directly access the on-ground situation and engage with relevant stakeholders regarding the implementation of the right to an adequate standard of living and suggest required interventions.[102]
- Country visits enable more intensive investigation of systemic challenges and gaps, facilitating tailored recommendations. However, visits require State consent which is not always forthcoming regarding economic-social rights.[103]

In essence, the CESCR has been instrumental through its reporting procedures, formulation of normative standards and jurisprudence, investigative powers and country visits in developing the scope of State obligations with regards to ensuring specific attributes of adequacy, affordability, accessibility, cultural appropriateness, and habitability in relation to the right to housing, equitable non-discriminatory access to food aid and nutritional support programmes by marginalised groups; provision of social security schemes covering the most disadvantaged sections; implementing minimum core entitlements regarding livelihood, food, housing, and healthcare; and adopting comprehensive national strategies and action to uplift standards of living.[104]

Press 2020) available at < https://papers.ssrn.com/sol3/papers.cfm?abstract_id=3595167> accessed 5 August 2023.

100 Optional Protocol to the International Covenant on Economic, Social and Cultural Rights (2008) op cit (note 97) art 11.

101 Office of the High Commissioner for Human Rights, 'Statement by Professor Philip Alston, United Nations Special Rapporteur on Extreme Poverty and Human Rights, on His Visit to Spain 27 January – 7 February 2020' (2020) available at < https://www.ohchr.org/en/statements/2020/02/statement-professor-philip-alston-united-nations-special-rapporteur-extreme> accessed 5 August 2023.

102 Optional Protocol to the International Covenant on Economic, Social and Cultural Rights (2008) op cit, (note 97) arts 11.

103 International Covenant on Economic, Social and Cultural Rights, op cit, art 16.

104 Sepúlveda Carmona, op cit (note 10).

However, the CESCR's recommendations are technically non-binding with limited enforceability. Weak follow-up remains an issue with many States failing to sufficiently implement its recommendations in actual policy and programmes. Domestic incorporation and invocation of CESCR jurisprudence before national courts and authorities also remain limited, constraining tangible impacts.[105] Targeted efforts by the CESCR to increase engagement with States on implementation, coupled with strategic civil society partnerships to raise awareness and bring international recommendations into domestic rights advocacy are vital for enhancing its efficacy in securing real improvements in standard of living for marginalised communities.

UN Committee on the Rights of the Child

The Committee on the Rights of the Child (CRC Committee) is the authoritative monitoring body of the UN Convention on the Rights of the Child. Under its protective mandate, the Committee undertakes the following functions in relation to upholding children's right to survival, growth, and an adequate standard of living under the treaty:

Reviewing Periodic Reports

- Scrutinising periodic reports submitted by State parties detailing measures adopted to implement child rights to the enjoyment of an adequate standard of living, health, nutrition, social security, an adequate standard of living, and protection from exploitation as recognised under the Convention.[106]
- The review process involves close questioning and investigation of gaps, challenges, and emerging issues, even those not raised in the report, to provide recommendations for strengthening legal frameworks, policies, programmes, budget allocations, and mechanisms to facilitate realisation of children's right to an adequate standard of living.[107]

Publishing General Comments

- Publishing authoritative general comments expounding on the normative scope and content of substantive provisions in the Convention, including child rights associated with the attainment of an adequate standard of living.[108]
- General Comment 15 discusses the intrinsic interlinkages between child health and the enjoyment of other rights including an adequate standard of

105 Langford and Rosevear, opt cit (note 99).
106 Convention on the Rights of the Child (1989) art 44.
107 Nartniranjan Casinader, 'CESCR's Recommendations: An Analysis of Compliance and Implementation' (2019) 13(2) *Trade, Law and Development* 364.
108 Convention on the Rights of the Child, art 45.

living, nutrition, housing, water, sanitation, and an environment free from harm.[109]

Adjudicating Individual Complaints

- With the Optional Protocol on Communications entering force in 2014, reviewing individuals' complaints submitted by or on behalf of children alleging violations by States of rights interconnected with adequate living standards and prescribing appropriate remedies and reparations.[110]
- For example, the CRC previously found Denmark failed to provide adequate housing support for a homeless 17-year-old, in violation of Article 27 on standard of living.[111] While decisions are recommendatory, they carry interpretative value.

Conducting Enquiries into Grave Systemic Issues

- Under the Optional Protocol, proactively initiating enquiries regarding grave or systematic violations of children's rights to health, nutrition, housing, and social services that fundamentally impact their survival and development.
- For instance, the CRC previously investigated issues like unprecedented levels of infant mortality in Myanmar and the dire situation of homeless street children in Brazil impacted by denial of basic socio-economic rights.[112]

Through its reporting procedure, jurisprudence, and investigative processes, the CRC Committee has provided comprehensive guidance and specific recommendations to States on issues like prioritising children's well-being in national and household budgeting processes; implementing social protection floors to ensure basic income security for deprived children; enhancing availability, accessibility, and affordability of public healthcare and nutrition support; guaranteeing minimum core entitlements connected to child rights to food, shelter, and clean water; instituting mandatory standards for habitability, sanitation, and hygienic conditions in housing including informal settlements; enhancing access to safe drinking water and sanitation in schools, healthcare facilities, public institutions, and households; and collecting robust disaggregated data to map gaps for targeted interventions.[113]

109 Gerison Lansdown, 'The reporting process under the Convention on the Rights of the Child' in A Alen and others (eds), A commentary on the United Nations Convention on the Rights of the Child (Martinus Nijhoff Publishers 2006).

110 Optional Protocol No. 3 to the Convention on the Rights of the Child (2011) art 12.

111 *LH v Denmark CRC* (2016) UN Doc CRC/C/77/D/3/2016.27 Optional Protocol No 3 to the Convention on the Rights of the Child art 13.

112 UN CRC, 'Report on the Session' (2012) UN Doc CRC/C/58; UN CRC, 'Report on the Session' (2009) UN Doc CRC/C/46.

113 Benyam Dawit Mezmur, 'The African Children's Charter versus the UN Convention on the Rights of the Child: A Zero-Sum Game?' (2008) 23 SAPL 1.

However, follow-up on concluding observations remains inconsistent and civil society partnerships to strengthen national level implementation is vital. Resource and capacity constraints also adversely affect the functioning of the Committee. Mainstreaming child rights into local and national development planning and increasing visibility of the CRC's jurisprudence before domestic courts can boost its impact in securing better realisation of an adequate standard of living for children.[114]

UN Committee on the Rights of Persons with Disabilities

The CPRD Committee is the expert monitoring body of the 2006 UN Disability Rights Convention. Under its mandate, key functions undertaken by the Committee encompass:

Reviewing Periodic State Reports

- Reviewing periodic State party reports monitoring implementation of the right to social protection, adequate standard of living, access to public housing, retirement benefits, and individualised disability support services without discrimination under Article 28.[115]
- The constructive dialogue process during review enables the Committee to thoroughly investigate gaps in legal protections, accessibility of facilities and services, availability of reasonable accommodation, housing inadequacies, design universal protection, and priority accorded to marginalised groups of persons with disabilities.[116]

Publishing General Comments

- Drafting authoritative general comments elucidating the normative scope of treaty provisions, such as General Comment 5 discussing State obligations regarding equality and non-discrimination in relation to Convention rights.[117]
- General Comment 6 focuses on women and girls with disabilities, addressing accessibility and inclusion imperatives connected to standard of living.[118] General Comment 7 discusses State duties regarding inclusive education and its intrinsic links with future employment, livelihoods, and living standards for persons with disabilities.[119]

114 UNICEF, 'Twenty-Five Years of the Convention on the Rights of the Child' (2015).
115 Convention on the Rights of Persons with Disabilities (2006) art 35.
116 Theresia Degener, 'Disability in a Human Rights Context' (2016) 5 *Laws* 35.
117 UN CRPD 'General Comment No. 5 (2017) on living independently and being included in the community' UN Doc CRPD/C/GC/5.
118 UN CRPD 'General Comment No. 6 (2018) on equality and non-discrimination' UN Doc CRPD/C/GC/6.
119 UN CRPD 'General Comment No. 7 (2018) on the participation of persons with disabilities, including children with disabilities, through their representative organizations, in the implementation and monitoring of the Convention' UN Doc CRPD/C/GC/7.

Adjudicating Individual Communications

- With the Optional Protocol in force since 2008, adjudicating individual complaints alleging violations of the right to adequate standard of living and associated rights and providing recommendations to governments on measures of reparation, rehabilitation, and structural improvements.[120]
- For example, the CRPD Committee in 2021 found France failed to fulfil accessible and affordable housing rights of an elderly woman with disabilities, disregarding her choice to live independently, and prescribed policy reforms.[121]

Conducting Enquiries on Grave Issues

- Under Article 6, proactively investigating grave or systematic violations of the Convention through country visits and reporting. While underutilised presently, this can be deployed to probe systemic denials of adequate housing and living standards.[122]

The CRPD has called for targeted action by States on implementing reasonable accomodation across all spheres of life including housing design, urban development and building norms; enhancing accessibility in the provision of services like water, sanitation, transportation, and assistive technologies; instituting rights-based universal social protection systems; collecting disaggregated data to map needs and gaps; adopting comprehensive national disability rights strategies and harmonising laws in line with the Convention to uphold standard of living.[123]

However, the persistence of multiple barriers including inaccessible physical environments, pervasive discrimination, lack of accomodation in policies, and resource constraints point to substantial implementation gaps warranting strengthened monitoring procedures, network building across government departments, and partnerships with representative organisations of persons with disabilities to ensure substantive right outcomes.[124]

African Commission and Court on Human and Peoples' Rights

At the regional level, the African Commission and Court on Human and Peoples' Rights are the principal monitoring bodies of the African Charter on

120 Optional Protocol to the Convention on the Rights of Persons with Disabilities (2006) art 1.
121 *H.M. v. France CPRD Committee* (2021) UN Doc CRPD/C/23/D/42/2017.
122 Convention on the Rights of Persons with Disabilities (note 115) art 6.
123 Marianne Schulze, *Understanding the UN Convention on the Rights of Persons with Disabilities* (3rd ed) (New York: Handicap International 2010).
124 Anna Lawson, 'The European Union and the Convention on the Rights of Persons with Disabilities: Complexities, Challenges and Opportunities' in Valentina Della Fina, Rachele Cera and Giuseppe Palmisano (eds), *The United Nations Convention on the Rights of Persons with Disabilities* (Gewerbestrasse: Springer 2016) 61-76.

Human and Peoples' Rights and allied instruments.[125] Their protective mandate encompasses:

Reviewing Periodic State Reports

- Considering periodic reports submitted by State parties on legislative, policy, programmatic, and other measures adopted to realise rights intrinsically linked to the attainment of adequate standards of living under the Charter including rights to dignity, health, family protection, vulnerable groups' welfare and development.[126]
- The reporting process provides opportunities to investigate gaps, constructive challenges, and emerging concerns and issue recommendations for enhanced implementation, even though State compliance has been consistent.[127]

Adjudicating Complaints on Standard of Living Issues

- Adjudicating individual and group communications submitted by victims alleging violations of Charter rights associated with adequate living standards like dignity, family welfare, access to housing, forced evictions, women, and child rights.[128]
- For instance, the African Court held Tanzania violated the right to dignity by denying land rights to a pastoralist indigenous community.[129] The Commission found Nigeria violated obligations by failing to regulate oil activities threatening health and livelihoods.[130] While technically advisory, decisions carry moral authority and governments face pressure to comply.

Undertaking Investigative and Fact-Finding Missions

- Proactively commission investigative, fact-finding, and information-gathering missions in countries to probe into situations of systemic rights violations connected to standard of living including massive internal displacement, gross inequality, poverty, and deprivation.[131]

125 African Charter on Human and Peoples' Rights (1981) arts 30, 45, 46 & 62.
126 Evelyn A Ankumah, *The African Commission on Human and Peoples' Rights* (The Hague: Martinus Nijhoff Publishers 1996).
127 Frans Viljoen and Lirette Louw, 'State Compliance with the Recommendations of the African Commission on Human and Peoples' Rights 1994–2004' (2007) 101 *AJIL* 1
128 Ibid.
129 *African Commission on Human and Peoples' Rights v Kenya* (2017) 2 AfCLR 9.
130 *Social and Economic Rights Action Center (SERAC) and Another v Nigeria* (2001) AHRLR 60
131 Rachel Murray and Debra Long, 'Implementation of the Findings of the African Commission on Human and Peoples' Rights' (2015) *CUP* 115.

- These enable on-site assessment of violations, facilitating recommendations. However, undertaking visits require consent which poses challenges. Only a few visits have addressed socio-economic rights issue thus far.[132]

Publishing Thematic Guidelines

- Developing promotional guidelines and principles incorporating elements of the right to an adequate standard of living like health, food, nutrition, housing, and social security which assist in interpreting Charter-based State duties.[133]
- For instance, the Principles on the Implementation of Socio-Economic Rights detail obligations like ensuring minimum core entitlements, prioritising vulnerable groups and allocating maximum resources.[134]

The African system has helped develop standards and jurisprudence against practices like forced evictions, address protection gaps for groups like internally displaced persons, refugees, women and children, and focused attention on issues like preventable diseases, maternal mortality, and realising access to anti-retroviral treatment which are crucial to uplifting standards of living.[135] However, major challenges exist around State reporting non-compliance, restrictive standing requirements constraining victim access, weak implementation of recommendation, and inadequate follow-up.[136] Addressing these limitations by fostering broader alliances between monitoring bodies and national civil society, enhancing domestic visibility of international recommendations, strategic public interest litigation invoking treaty obligations, and ardently pressing for political and legislative reforms is imperative to convert universal human rights principles into living realities.

Domestic Frameworks for Right to an Adequate Standard of Living in Selected Countries in Sub-Saharan Africa

The right to an adequate standard of living is a fundamental human right enshrined in various international human rights instruments, including the Universal Declaration of Human Rights (UDHR) and the International Covenant on Economic, Social and Cultural Rights (ICESCR). This right

132 Chidi Odinkalu, 'The Role of Case and Complaints Procedures in the Reform of the African Regional Human Rights System' (2001) 1 AHRLJ 225.
133 African Commission on Human and Peoples' Rights, 'Principles and Guidelines on the Implementation of Economic, Social and Cultural Rights in the African Charter on Human and Peoples' Rights' (2011).
134 Ibid.
135 Viljoen and Louw, op cit (note 127).
136 Nsongurua J Udombana, 'So Far, So Fair: The Local Remedies Rule in the Jurisprudence of the African Commission on Human and Peoples' Rights' (2003) 97 *AJIL* 1.

encompasses several interrelated components, such as the right to adequate food, clothing, housing, and the continuous improvement of living conditions.[137]

In Sub-Saharan Africa (SSA), where poverty, inequality, and economic disparities persist, ensuring an adequate standard of living for all citizens remains a significant challenge. Despite the region's rich natural resources and economic potential, a substantial portion of the population still grapples with severe deprivation, lacking access to basic necessities like food, clean water, and shelter.[138] This section aims to explore the domestic legal frameworks for the right to an adequate standard of living in selected SSA countries, including Nigeria, Ghana, South Africa, Kenya, Uganda, Ethiopia, Malawi, Togo, Ivory Coast, Zambia, and Zimbabwe. By examining the constitutional provisions, national legislation, and judicial interpretations, this study seeks to understand the extent to which these countries have incorporated and implemented this fundamental right within their domestic legal systems.

Nigeria

The Constitution of the Federal Republic of Nigeria, adopted in 1999 (as amended), does not explicitly recognise the right to an adequate standard of living as a justiciable right.[139] However, Chapter II of the Constitution, referred to as the Fundamental Objectives and Directive Principles of State Policy, provides guidance on economic, social, and cultural rights, including the provision of adequate shelter, food, and a reasonable living wage for all citizens.[140]

It is noteworthy that Nigeria has enacted various laws and policies at promoting aspects of the right to an adequate standard of living. For example, the National Housing Policy of 2012 seeks to ensure access to affordable housing for all Nigerians.[141] Further, the country's National Food and Nutrition Policy of 2016 addresses issues related to food security and nutrition.[142] Similarly, Nigeria's Social Safety Nets Programmes aims to provide social assistance to

137 Zhihang Zheng, 'The Right to an Adequate Standard of Living' in J Yao (ed) *The Legal Issues of the Emerging Rights* (Springer, 2024) DOI: 10.1007/978-981-97-0499-6_9.

138 The World Bank Group, 'Macro Poverty Outlook for Sub-Saharan Africa' (2023) available at < https://www.worldbank.org/en/publication/macro-poverty-outlook/mpo_ssa> accessed 6 April 2024.

139 Rhuks Ako, Ngozi Stewart and Eghosa O Ekhator, 'Overcoming the (Non)justiciable Conundrum: The Doctrine of Harmonious Construction and the Interpretation of the Right to a Healthy Environment in Nigeria' in A Diver and J Miller (eds) *Justiciability of Human Rights Law in Domestic Jurisdictions* (Springer 2015) DOI: 10.1007/978-3-319-

140 Constitution of the Federal Republic of Nigeria, Chapter II.

141 National Housing Policy (Federal Republic of Nigeria 2012).

142 National Policy on Food and Nutrition in Nigeria (Federal Ministry of Health 2016).

vulnerable groups, including cash transfers and conditional cash transfers.[143] Despite these efforts, the realisation of the right to an adequate standard of living in Nigeria remains a significant challenge, with substantial portions of the population living in poverty and lacking access to basic necessities.

Ghana

The Constitution of the Republic of Ghana, adopted in 1992, recognises the right to an adequate standard of living in several provisions. For example, Article 34 of the Constitution of the Republic of Ghana affirms the right to good healthcare and the right to work under satisfactory and safe working conditions.[144] Article 37 of the Ghana Constitution addresses the right to adequate housing and the provision of affordable and adequate housing for all Ghanaians.[145]

The Republic of Ghana has enacted several laws and policies to give effect to these Constitutional rights. For example, the National Housing Policy of 2015 aims to ensure access to adequate and affordable housing for all Ghanaians.[146] The implementation of the policy, however, has been criticised given the fact that 'successive governments have not deviated from the colonial logic of piecemeal intervention.'[147] The argument is that the focus should be on implementing a wholesale effort to solve the problem by providing housing for those that need it.[148] Again, increasingly in Ghana, high-end houses are being built with less provision of low-cost or affordable housing.[149] The Ghana government has not considered multifamily housing which should ordinarily suit the Ghanaian communal lifestyle.[150]

Furthermore, the country's National Health Insurance Scheme (NHIS), which was established by the National Health Insurance Act of 2003, seeks to promote access to affordable housing. According to Alhassan et al, the NHIS contributed to improved healthcare delivery in Ghana.[151] They opine that the

143 See The World Bank, 'Nigeria's Social Safety Nets: Realities and Reinforcements' (2021) available at < https://documents.worldbank.org/en/publication/documents-reports/documentdetail/813221467989481643/nigeria-national-social-safety-nets-project> accessed 6 April 2024.

144 Constitution of the Republic of Ghana 1992, Article 34.

145 Constitution of the Republic of Ghana 1992, Article 37.

146 National Housing Policy (Republic of Ghana 2015).

147 Irene Appeaning Addo and Chika C Mba, 'Geneologies of Ghana's Housing Crisis: The Role of Colonial Interventions and Neoliberal Reforms' (2021) 22(2) *International Journal of Housing Policy* 299-313 at 309 DOI: 10.1080/19491247.2021.1999127.

148 Ibid.

149 Ibid.

150 Ibid.

151 Robert Kaba Alhassan, Edward Nketiah-Amponsah and Daniel Kojo Arhinful, 'A Review of the National Health Insurance Scheme in Ghana: What Are the Sustainability Threats and Prospects?' (2016) 11(11) *Plos One* DOI: 10.1371/journal.pone.0165151.

NHIS continues to 'play a critical role towards attaining universal health coverage in Ghana.'[152] Some of the lofty policies under Ghana's NHIS policy include free health insurance for pregnant women in 2008 and the exemption of payment of premiums for people under 18 years and senior citizens from 70 years and above.[153] However, it is noted that poor infrastructure has hampered the benefits of the scheme as there is a huge deficit of medical facilities and personnel to cater to Ghana's healthcare needs.[154]

Ghana's National Social Protection Policy of 2015 provides a framework for social protection programmes, including cash transfers and livelihood support initiatives.[155] Ghana introduced reforms to the contributory social insurance system and limited social assistance schemes during the tenure of President John Kuffor.[156] The lofty reforms continued, with modest expansion of social assistance under the Mills and Mahama administrations.[157] Unfortunately however, it appears from the argument of Grebe, that the reforms were motivated for electoral patronage rather than to ensure that a welfare system is entrenched to support the ordinary people of Ghana.[158]

Finally, unlike Nigeria, the justiciability of the legal provisions of socio-economic rights has been sufficiently addressed. For example, the courts in Ghana recognise the constitutional provision of the right education based on specific constitutional provisions.[159]

South Africa

The Constitution of the Republic of South Africa, adopted in 1996, enshrines the right to an adequate standard of living in several provisions. Section 26 guarantees the right to adequate housing, while section 27 recognises the rights to healthcare, food, water, and social security. Section 27 provides as follows:

Everyone has the right to have access to:

(a) Healthcare services, including reproductive healthcare;
(b) Sufficient food and water; and

152 Ibid.
153 Ibid.
154 Ibid.
155 National Social Protection Policy (Republic of Ghana 2015).
156 Eduard Grebe, 'The Politics of Social Protection in Ghana: Policy Reform in a Competitive African Democracy (2000-2014)' (2017) available at < https://www.researchgate.net/publication/317999283_The_Politics_of_Social_Protection_in_Ghana_Policy_Reform_in_a_Competitive_African_Democracy_2000-2014> accessed 8 Aprill 2024.
157 Ibid.
158 Ibid.
159 Francisw Kofi Korankye-Sakyi, Solomon Faakye and Peter A Atupare, 'Critical Reflections on the Justiciability of the Right to Education in Ghana' (2022) 22 *African Human Rights Journal* 161-186 DOI: 10.17159/1996-2096/2022/v22n1a7.

(c) Social security, including, if they are unable to support themselves and their dependents, appropriate social assistance.[160]

The Constitution declared in unequivocal terms that the State must take reasonable legislative measures, within its available resources, to achieve the progressive realisation of each of these rights.[161] In the same vein, the Constitution of South Africa provides that no one may be refused emergency treatment.[162] Furthermore, section 28 specifically addresses the rights of children, including the right to basic nutrition, shelter, and social services.[163]

South Africa has enacted various pieces of legislation to give effect to these constitutional rights. The Housing Act 1997 and the Social Housing Act of 2008 aim to facilitate access to adequate housing for all South Africans, particularly those in disadvantaged communities.[164] The National Health Act of 2003 seeks to promote the right to healthcare services, while the Social Assistance Act of 2004 provides a legal framework for social grants and social assistance programmes.[165]

It is worthy of note that the Constitutional Court of South Africa has played a pivotal role in interpreting and enforcing the right to an adequate standard of living. In the landmark case of *Government of the Republic of South Africa and Others v Grootboom and Others,*[166] the Constitutional Court, for the first time in any country, enforced the constitutionality of socio-economic right, giving legitimacy to the so-called second-generation rights.[167] The case 'delimited the obligations of the South African government to fulfil the right to adequate housing as guaranteed in the South African Constitution, and it also set an international precedent for other governments to deliver socio-economic rights enshrined in their constitutions.'[168]

Kenya

The Constitution of Kenya, promulgated in 2010, enshrines the right to an adequate standard of living in several provisions. Article 43 recognises the rights to adequate housing, reasonable standards of sanitation, freedom from

160 Constitution of the Republic of South Africa 1996.
161 Constitution of the Republic of South Africa 1996, section 27(2).
162 Constitution of the Republic of South Africa 1996, section 27(3).
163 Constitution of the Republic of South Africa 1996, section 28.
164 Housing Act 1997; Social Housing Act 2008.
165 National Health Act 2003; Social Assistance Act 2004.
166 (CCT11/00) [2000] ZACC 19.
167 Tadamun, 'The Landmark Case of Grootboom versus the Republic of South Africa' (2014) available at < https://www.tadamun.co/the-landmark-case-of-grootboom-versus-the-republic-of-south-africa/?lang=en> accessed 8 April 2024.
168 Ibid.

hunger, and clean and safe water in adequate quantities.[169] Additionally, Article 53 specifically addresses the rights of children, including the right to basic nutrition, shelter, and healthcare services.[170]

Kenya has enacted various laws to give effect to these constitutional rights. The Housing Act of 2012 provides a framework for the development of affordable housing and the promotion of housing standards.[171] The Water Act of 2016 aims to ensure access to clean and safe water for all Kenyans, while the Food and Nutrition Security Policy of 2012 addresses issues related to food security and nutrition.[172]

The Kenyan High Court in *JM v Attorney General and 6 Others,* found violations of rights to health, dignity, and personal integrity in a maternal healthcare case.[173] In that case, the court found that the Kenyan 'government violated JM's constitutional and international human rights by seriously mistreating her and not providing her with mandated free quality maternal healthcare when she gave birth in a public hospital in August 2013.'[174]

Uganda

The Constitution of the Republic of Uganda, adopted in 1995, recognises the right to an adequate standard of living through various provisions. Article 8A affirms the State's commitment to ensuring food security and nutrition for all Ugandans.[175] Article 34 recognises the rights to adequate housing, clean and safe water, and decent shelter.[176] Additionally, Article 39 specifically addresses the rights of children, including the right to basic nutrition, shelter, and medical services.[177]

Uganda has enacted several laws and policies to give effect to these constitutional rights. The National Housing Policy of 2016 aims to promote access to adequate and affordable housing for all Ugandans.[178] The Food and Nutrition Policy of 2003 and the Uganda Nutrition Action Plan 2011-2016 address issues related to food security and nutrition.[179] The Social Assistance

169 Constitution of Kenya 2010, art 43.
170 Constitution of Kenya 2010, art 53.
171 Housing Act 2012.
172 Water Act 2016; Food and Nutrition Security Policy (Republic of Kenya 2012).
173 See Case Law Database available at < https://www.escr-net.org/caselaw/2019/jm-v-attorney-general-and-6-others> accessed 8 April 2024.
174 Ibid.
175 Constitution of the Republic of Uganda 1995, art 8A.
176 Constitution of the Republic of Uganda 1995, art 34.
177 Constitution of the Republic of Uganda 1995, art 39.
178 Constitution of the Republic of Uganda 1995, art 8A.
179 Food and Nutrition Policy (Republic of Uganda 2003); Uganda Nutrition Action Plan 2011-2016.

Grants for Empowerment (SAGE) programme provides cash transfers and other forms of assistance to vulnerable groups.[180]

Notably, the Ugandan judiciary has played a role in interpreting and enforcing the right to an adequate standard of living. In the case of *Centre for Food and Adequate Living Rights (CEFROHT) v Attorney General*,[181] the High Court of Uganda affirmed the justiciability of economic, social, and cultural rights, including the right to adequate food and nutrition.[182]

Ethiopia

The Constitution of the Federal Democratic Republic of Ethiopia, adopted in 1994, recognises the right to an adequate standard of living in several provisions of the Constitution. Article 41 affirms the rights to education, health, and housing.[183] Article 90 specifically addresses the rights of children, including the right to life, a name and nationality, and access to basic services such as healthcare and education.[184] Furthermore, Ethiopia has enacted various laws and policies aimed at promoting aspects of the right to an adequate standard of living. The National Housing Development Programme, launched in 2005, aims to facilitate access to affordable housing for low-income households.[185] The National Nutrition Programme of 2008–2013 and the National Nutrition Programme of 2016–2020 address issues related to food security and nutrition.[186] The Productive Safety Net Programme provides cash and food transfer to vulnerable households, as well as public works employment opportunities.[187]

180 Nekesa Winny Akullo, 'Social Assistance Grants for Empowerment (SAGE) Programme in Uganda' (2017) available at < https://socialprotection.org/discover/blog/social-assistance-grants-empowerment-sage-programme-uganda> accessed 8 April 2024

181 Reference No. 39 of 2020 available at <https://www.eacj.org/?cases=reference-no-39-of-2019-centre-for-food-and-adequate-living-rights-cefroht-3-others-v-the-attorney-general-of-the-republic-of-uganda-the-attorney-general-of-united-republic-of-tanzania-and-the> accessed 10 April 2024.

182 Centre for Food and Adequate Living Rights (CEFROHT) v Attorney General Misc. Cause No. 211 of 2019.

183 Constitution of the Federal Democratic Republic of Ethiopia 1994, art. 41.

184 Constitution of the Federal Democratic Republic of Ethiopia 19994, art 90.

185 The World Bank, 'Urban Land Supply and Affordable Housing Study Synthesis Report' (2017) available at <https://documents1.worldbank.org/curated/en/549221572382742218/pdf/Unlocking-Ethiopias-Urban-Land-and-Housing-Markets-Synthesis-Report.pdf.> accessed 10 April 2024.

186 National Nutrition Programme 2008-2013 (Federal Democratic Republic of Ethiopia); National Nutrition Programme 2016-2020 (Federal Democratic Republic of Ethiopia).

187 Socialprotection.org, 'Productive Safety Net Programme, PSNP5' (2023) available at <https://socialprotection.org/discover/programmes/productive-safety-net-programme-psnp5> accessed 10 April 2024.

Despite these efforts, the realisation of the right to an adequate standard of living in Ethiopia remains a significant challenge, with a substantial portion of the population living in poverty and lacking access to basic necessities.

Malawi

The Constitution of Malawi, adopted in 1994, recognises the right to an adequate standard of living through various provisions. Section 13 affirms the right to development, which includes the right to an adequate standard of living.[188] Section 30 specifically addresses the right to adequate food and nutrition, while section 31 recognises the right to adequate housing and sanitation.[189]

Malawi has enacted several laws to give effect to these constitutional rights. The Malawi Housing Corporation Act of 1964 aims to promote the provision of adequate housing for all Malawians.[190] The Food and Nutrition Policy of 2005 and the National Nutrition Policy and Strategic Plan of 2007–2012 addresses issues related to food security and nutrition.[191]

The Malawian judiciary has played a role in interpreting and enforcing the right to an adequate standard of living. In the case of *Malawi Congress Party and Others v Attorney General and Others*,[192] the High Court of Malawi affirmed the justiciability of economic, social, and cultural rights, including the right to adequate housing and sanitation.

Togo

The Constitution of Republic of Togo, adopted in 1992 and amended in 2007, does not explicitly recognise the right to an adequate standard of living as a justiciable right. However, Article 34 affirms the State's commitment to ensuring the right to health and access to healthcare services for all citizens.[193] Togo has enacted several laws and policies aimed at promoting aspects of the right to an adequate standard of living. The National Housing Policy of 2010 aims to facilitate access to adequate and affordable housing for all Togolese citizens.[194] The National Food Security and Nutrition Policy of 2012–2025 addresses issues related to food security and nutrition.[195] The National

188 Constitution of Malawi 1994, s 13.
189 Constitution of Malawi 1994, ss 30-31.
190 Malawi Housing Corporation Act 1964.
191 Food and Nutrition Security Policy (Malawi 2005); National Nutrition policy and Strategic Plan 2007-2012 (Republic of Malawi).
192 [2012] MWHC 31.
193 Constitution of the Togolese Republic 1992 (rev 2007), art 34.
194 National Housing Policy (Republic of Togo 2010).
195 National Food Security and Nutrition Policy 2012-2025 (Republic of Togo).

Social Protection Policy of 2013 provides a framework for social protection programmes, including cash transfers and livelihood support initiatives.[196]

Despite these efforts, the realisation of the right to an adequate standard of living in Togo remains a significant challenge, with a substantial portion of the population living in poverty and lacking access to basic necessities.

Ivory Coast

The Constitution of the Republic of Cote d'Ivoire, adopted in 2016, recognises the right to an adequate standard of living in several provisions. Article 7 affirms the right to decent housing and access to public services.[197] Article 13 specifically addresses the rights of children, including the right to health, education, and protection from violence and exploitation.[198]

Ivory Coast has enacted several laws and policies aimed at promoting aspects of the right to an adequate standard of living. The National Housing Policy of 2014 seeks to facilitate access to adequate and affordable housing for all Ivorians.[199] The National Food Security and Nutrition Policy of 2012–2025 addresses issues related to food security and nutrition.[200] The National Social Protection Strategy of 2013–2023 provides a framework for social protection programmes, including cash transfers and livelihood support initiatives.[201]

Despite these efforts, the realisation of the right to an adequate standard of living in Ivory Coast remains a significant challenge, with a substantial portion of the population living in poverty and lacking access to basic necessities.

Zambia

The Constitution of the Republic of Zambia, amended in 2016, recognises the right to an adequate standard of living through various provisions. Article 112 affirms the right to decent shelter and access to basic services such as clean water and sanitation.[202] Article 113 specifically addresses the rights of children, including the right to basic nutrition, shelter, and healthcare services.[203]

Zambia has enacted several laws and policies aimed at promoting aspects of the right to an adequate standard of living. The National Housing Policy of 2012 seeks to facilitate access to adequate and affordable housing for all Zambians.[204] The National Food and Nutrition Policy of 2011 addresses issues

196 National Social Protection Policy 2013 (Republic of Togo).
197 Constitution of the Republic of Cote d'Ivoire 2016, art 7.
198 Constitution of the Republic of Cote d'Ivoire 2016, art 13.
199 National Housing Policy (Republic of Cote d'Ivoire 2014)
200 National Food and Nutrition Policy 2012-2025 (Republic of Cote d'Ivoire).
201 National Social Protection Strategy 2013-2023 (Republic of Cote d'Ivoire).
202 Constitution of the Republic of Zambia 1991 (rev 2016), art 112.
203 Constitution of the Republic of Zambia 1991 (rev 2016), art 113.
204 National Housing Policy (Republic of Zambia 2012).

related to food security and nutrition.[205] The Social Cash Transfer Programme provides cash transfers to vulnerable households, including those affected by poverty, disability, and HIV/AIDS.[206]

Despite these efforts, the realisation of the right to an adequate standard of living in Zambia remains a significant challenge, with a substantial portion of the population living in poverty and lacking access to basic necessities.

Zimbabwe

The Constitution of Zimbabwe, adopted in 2013, recognises the right to an adequate standard of living in several provisions. Section 77 affirms the right to food and water, while section 81 recognises the rights of children, including the right to basic nutrition, shelter, and healthcare services.[207] Section 19 specifically addresses the rights of children, including the right to basic nutrition, shelter, and healthcare services.[208]

Zimbabwe has enacted various laws and policies aimed at promoting aspects of the right to an adequate standard of living. The National Housing Policy of 2012 seeks to facilitate access to adequate and affordable housing for Zimbabweans.[209] The Food and Nutrition Security Policy of 2012–2025 addresses issues related to food security and nutrition.[210] The Harmonised Social Cash Transfer Programme provides cash transfers to vulnerable households, including those affected by poverty, disability, and chronic illness.

Despite these efforts, the realisation of the right to an adequate standard of living in Zimbabwe remains a significant challenge, exacerbated by economic instability, political turmoil, and recurring draughts and natural disasters.

Understanding the Challenges of the Domestic Frameworks

Despite the constitutional and legislative frameworks in place, the realisation of the right to an adequate standard of living in SSA continues to face significant challenges. These include:

- Poverty and inequality: High levels of poverty and income inequality persist in many SSA countries, limiting access to basic necessities for a significant portion of the population.
- Resource constraints: Limited financial and human resources, coupled with competing development priorities, often hinder the effective implementation

205 National Food and Nutrition Policy (Republic of Zambia 2011).
206 The World Bank, 'Understanding Poverty' available at < https://www.worldbank.org/en/topic> accessed 10 April 2024.
207 Constitution of Zimbabwe 2013, ss 77, 81.
208 Constitution of Zimbabwe 2013, s 19.
209 National Housing Policy (Republic of Zimbabwe 2012).
210 Food and Security Policy (Republic of Zimbabwe 2012-2025).

of policies and programmes aimed at promoting an adequate standard of living.
- Rapid urbanisation and informal settlements: Rapid urbanisation and the proliferation of informal settlements have exacerbated housing and sanitation challenges, particularly in urban areas.
- Weak institutional capacity and corruption: Weak governance structures, limited institutional capacity, and corruption can undermine effective implementation and enforcement of laws and policies related to the right to an adequate standard of living.
- Climate change and environmental degradation: Climate change and environmental degradation pose threats to food security, water availability, and housing conditions, further exacerbating challenges of achieving an adequate standard of living.
- Conflict and insecurity: Ongoing conflicts, civil unrest, and insecurity in some SSA countries have disrupted agricultural production, displaced populations, and hindered the delivery of essential services, thereby undermining the realisation of the right to an adequate standard of living.
- Gender inequality and discrimination: Women and girls in many SSA countries faces discrimination and unequal access to resources, education, and economic opportunities, which can exacerbate poverty and hinder their ability to achieve an adequate standard of living.

Conclusion

The right to an adequate standard of living is a fundamental human right that remains elusive for many individuals and communities in SSA. While several countries in the region have incorporated this right into their domestic legal frameworks, significant challenges persist in its effective implementation and realisation.

This chapter reviewed the international and domestic legal frameworks for implementing the right to an adequate standard of living in SSA. It is noted that while there are international norms and instruments that can be relied upon to form the basis for the implementation of the right to an adequate standard of living in SSA, it is not all countries in SSA that recognise the right as justiciable. Again, even in countries where the right is considered as a justiciable right, there are several challenges to ensuring that the right is upheld by the State.

Ultimately, the realisation of the right to an adequate standard of living is not only a moral and legal obligation but also a crucial step towards achieving sustainable development, social stability, and human dignity in the region. By prioritising this fundamental right, SSA countries can unlock their full potential and create a more just and equitable society for present and future generations.

The right to an adequate standard of living is a multidimensional concept that encompasses various interconnected components, including the rights to adequate food, housing, water and sanitation, and continuous improvement of living conditions. The UN Committee on Economic, Social and Cultural Rights has provided authoritative interpretations and guidance on these components through its General Comments.

The right to adequate food implies access to nutritious and culturally acceptable food that meets dietary needs and food preferences, as well as the means to acquire such food in a dignified manner. The right to adequate housing encompasses security of tenure, availability, habitability, accessibility, location, and cultural adequacy. The right to water requires access to safe, sufficient, affordable, and physically accessible water for personal and domestic use. Additionally, the United Nations High Commissioner for Refugees (UNHCR) and UN-Water have addressed issues related to land, property, and access to water for vulnerable populations.

The realisation of the right to an adequate standard of living is closely linked to the achievement of the Sustainable Development Goals (SDGs), particularly SDG 1 (No poverty), SDG 2 (Zero hunger), SDG 3 (Good health and well-being), SDG 6 (Clean water and sanitation), and SDG 11 (Sustainable cities and communities).

At the regional level, the African Commission on Human and Peoples' Rights has adopted the 'Principles and Guidelines on the Implementation of Economic, Social and Cultural Rights in the African Charter on Human and Peoples' Rights,' which provide guidance to African States on the implementation of these rights, including the right to an adequate standard of living. Furthermore, the African Union's Agenda 2063 emphasises the importance of promoting inclusive growth and sustainable development, which are essential for achieving an adequate standard of living for all Africans.

References

Addo IA and Mba CC, 'Geneologies of Ghana's Housing Crisis: The Role of Colonial Interventions and Neoliberal Reforms' (2021) 22(2) *International Journal of Housing Policy* 299–313 at 309 https://doi.org/10.1080/19491247.2021.1999127.

Adesete AA and others, 'Climate Change and Food Security in Selected Sub-Saharan African Countries' (2022) 25 *Environment, Development and Sustainability* available at <https://www.ncbi.nlm.nih.gov/pmc/articles/PMC9510474/pdf/10668_2022_Article_2681.pdf> accessed 4 August 2023.

African Charter on Human and Peoples' Rights (1981) arts 30, 45, 46 & 62.

African Commission on Human and Peoples' Rights, 'Principles and Guidelines on the Implementation of Economic, Social and Cultural Rights in the African Charter on Human and Peoples' Rights' (2011).

African Commission on Human and Peoples' Rights v Kenya (2017) 2 AfCLR 9.

Ako R, Stewart N and Ekhator EO, 'Overcoming the (Non)justiciable Conundrum: The Doctrine of Harmonious Construction and the Interpretation of the Right to a Healthy Environment in Nigeria' in A Diver and J Miller (eds), *Justiciability of*

Human Rights Law in Domestic Jurisdictions (Springer 2015) https://doi.org/10.1007/978-3-319-24016-9_6.
Akullo NW, 'Social Assistance Grants for Empowerment (SAGE) Programme in Uganda' (2017) available at <https://socialprotection.org/discover/blog/social-assistance-grants-empowerment-sage-programme-uganda> accessed 8 April 2024
Alhassan RK, Nketiah-Amponsah E and Arhinful DK, 'A Review of the National Health Insurance Scheme in Ghana: What Are the Sustainability Threats and Prospects?' (2016) 11(11) *PLoS One* https://doi.org/10.1371/journal.pone.0165151.
Alston P, 'The Historical Origins of the Concept of "General Comments" in Human Rights Law' in Laurence Boisson de Chazournes and Vera Gowlland-Debbas (eds), *The International Legal System in Quest of Equity and Universality* (Brill 2002) 763–776.
Ankumah EA, *The African Commission on Human and Peoples' Rights* (Martinus Nijhoff Publishers 1996).
Awori J, 'Emerging Disability Law Jurisprudence in East Africa: What is there to Learn and What are the Gaps?' (2019) 7 *African Disability Rights Yearbook* 105.
Bailey P, 'The Right to an Adequate Standard of Living: New Issues for Australian Law' (1997) 4(1) *Australian Journal of Human Rights* 25–50.
Banik D, 'Legal Empowerment as Conceptual and Operational Tool in Poverty Eradication' (2009) 1(1) *Hague Journal on the Rule of Law* 117–131.
Bhalotra S and others, 'Social Assistance Spending and Infant Mortality in Sub-Saharan Africa: Evidence from Zimbabwe' (2021) 79 *World Development* 2.
Casinader N, 'CESCR's Recommendations: An Analysis of Compliance and Implementation' (2019) 13(2) *Trade, Law and Development* 364.
Constitution of Corte d'Ivoire 2016.
Constitution of Kenya 2010.
Constitution of Malawi 1994.
Constitution of the Federal Republic of Nigeria 1999.
Constitution of the Republic of Ghana 1992
Constitution of the Republic of South Africa 1996.
Constitution of the Republic of Uganda 1995.
Convention on the Rights of Persons with Disabilities (2006) art 35.
Convention on the Rights of the Child (adopted 20 November 1989, entered into force 2 September 1990) 1577 UNTS 3 art 27 (CRC).
Constitution of the Togolese Republic 1992.
Degener T, 'Disability in a Human Rights Context' (2016) 5 *Laws* 35.
Durojaye E and Mirugi-Mukundi G, 'Realising Access to Medicine in International Law: Imperative Standards for the SADC Region' (2018) 18 *African Human Rights Law Journal.* 219-244
Food and Agriculture Organization of the UN, 'Peasant Rights' (2020) available at <https://www.fao.org/plant-treaty/tools/toolbox-for-sustainable-use/details/en/c/1373893/> accessed 4 August 2023.
Grebe E, 'The Politics of Social Protection in Ghana: Policy Reform in a Competitive African Democracy (2000–2014)' (2017) available at <https://www.researchgate.net/publication/317999283_The_Politics_of_Social_Protection_in_Ghana_Policy_Reform_in_a_Competitive_African_Democracy_2000-2014> accessed 8 Aprill 2024.
Hassan N and Scott-Villiers P, 'Purchasing and Protesting: Power from Below in the Global Food Crisis' (2019) 50(2) *IDS Bulletin* available at <https://bulletin.ids

.ac.uk/index.php/idsbo/article/view/3037/Online%20article> accessed 4 August 2023.

H.M. v. *France CPRD Committee* (2021) UN Doc CRPD/C/23/D/42/2017.

Hoover J, 'Rereading the Universal Declaration of Human Rights: Plurality and Contestation, Not Consensus' (2013) 12(2) *Journal of Human Rights* 217–241.

International Covenant on Economic, Social and Cultural Rights (adopted 16 December 1966, entered into force 3 January 1976) 993 UNTS 3 Art 11 (ICESCR).

Korankye-Sakyi FK, Faakye S and Atupare PA, 'Critical Reflections on the Justiciability of the Right to Education in Ghana' (2022) 22 *African Human Rights Journal* 161–186 https://doi.org/10.17159/1996-2096/2022/v22n1a7.

Kuwonu F, 'Africa's Freedom Struggles and the Universal Declaration of Human Rights' (2019) available at <https://www.un.org/africarenewal/magazine/december-2018-march-2019/africa%E2%80%99s-freedom-struggles-and-universal-declaration-human-rights> accessed 1 August 2023.

Lansdown G, 'The Reporting Process under the Convention on the Rights of the Child' in A Alen and Others (eds), *A commentary on the United Nations Convention on the Rights of the Child* (Martinus Nijhoff Publishers 2006).

Lawson A, 'The European Union and the Convention on the Rights of Persons with Disabilities: Complexities, Challenges and Opportunities' in Valentina Della Fina, Rachele Cera and Giuseppe Palmisano (eds), *The United Nations Convention on the Rights of Persons with Disabilities* (Springer 2016) 61–76.

Maastricht Guidelines on Violations of Economic, Social and Cultural Rights (26 January 1997) available at <https://www.hlrn.org/img/documents/Maastricht%20Guidelines.pdf> accessed 1 August 2023.

Malcom Langford and Evan Rosevear, 'Economic and social Rights' in DS Law, H Lau and A Schwartz (eds), *Oxford Handbook of Constitutional Law in Asia* (Oxford University Press 2020) available at <https://papers.ssrn.com/sol3/papers.cfm?abstract_id=3595167> accessed 5 August 2023.

McFarland S, 'The Universal Declaration of Human Rights: A Tribute to Its Architects' (2017) 19(2) *Public Integrity (Symposium on the Social Practices of Human Rights)* at 108.

Mezmur BD, 'The African Children's Charter versus the UN Convention on the Rights of the Child: A Zero-Sum Game?' (2008) 23 *SAPL* 1.

Monjane B, 'Transforming the Politics of Food in Southern Africa, From the Local to the Global' (2018) available at <https://viacampesina.org/en/transforming-the-politics-of-food-in-southern-africa-from-the-local-to-the-global/> accessed 4 August 2023.

Murray R and Long D, 'Implementation of the Findings of the African Commission on Human and Peoples' Rights' (2015)Cambridge University Press *CUP* 115.

Mutua M, 'The Complexity of Universalism in Human Rights' in A Sajo (ed), *Human Rights with Modesty: The Problem of Universalism* (Springer 2004).

National Housing Policy (Federal Republic of Nigeria 2012).

National Housing Policy (Republic of Ghana 2015).

National Policy on Food and Nutrition in Nigeria (Federal Ministry of Health 2016).

National Social Protection Policy (Republic of Ghana 2015).

Odinkalu C, 'The Role of Case and Complaints Procedures in the Reform of the African Regional Human Rights System' (2001) 1 *AHRLJ* 225.

Office of the High Commissioner for Human Rights, 'Statement by Professor Philip Alston, United Nations Special Rapporteur on Extreme Poverty and Human Rights, on His Visit to Spain 27 January – 7 February 2020' (2020) available at <https://www.ohchr.org/en/statements/2020/02/statement-professor-philip-alston-united-nations-special-rapporteur-extreme> accessed 5 August 2023.

Okafor OC, 'Critical Third World Approaches to International Law (TAWAIL): Theory, Methodology or Both?' (2008) 10 *International Community Law Review* 371–378.

Optional Protocol to the Convention on the Rights of Persons with Disabilities (2006) art 1.

Optional Protocol to the International Covenant on Economic, Social and Cultural Rights (2008) op cit (note 97) art 11.

Protocol to the African Charter on Human and Peoples' Rights on the Rights of Persons with Disabilities (2018).

Purohit and Moore v The Gambia (2003) AHRLR 96 (ACHPR 2003).

Quennerstedt A, 'Balancing the Rights of the Child and the Rights of Parents in the Convention on the Rights of the Child' (2009) 8(2) *Journal of Human Rights* 162–176.

Riedel E and others, *The Making of the International Bill of Human Rights* (United Nations Human Rights Office of the High Commissioner 2006).

Schulze M, *Understanding the UN Convention on the Rights of Persons with Disabilities* (3rd edn, Handicap International 2010).

Sepúlveda Carmona MM, *The Nature of the Obligations under the International Covenant on Economic, Social and Cultural Rights* (Intersentia 2003).

Shuman EK, 'Anticipating the Convention on the Rights of the Child' (2017) 93(3) *Childhood Education* at 246.

Social and Economic Rights Action Centre (SERAC) and anor v Nigeria (2001) AHRLR 60 (ACHPR 2001).

Ssenyonjo M, *Economic, Social and Cultural Rights in International Law* (2nd edn, Bloomsbury Publishing 2016).

Tadamun, 'The Landmark Case of Grootboom versus the Republic of South Africa' (2014) available at <https://www.tadamun.co/the-landmark-case-of-grootboom-versus-the-republic-of-south-africa/?lang=en> accessed 8 April 2024.

The World Bank, 'Macro Poverty Outlook for Sub-Saharan Africa' (2022) available at <https://www.worldbank.org/en/publication/macro-poverty-outlook/mpo_ssa> accessed 1 August 2023.

The World Bank, 'Nigeria's Social Safety Nets: Realities and Reinforcements' (2021) available at <https://documents.worldbank.org/en/publication/documents-reports/documentdetail/813221467989481643/nigeria-national-social-safety-nets-project> accessed 6 April 2024.

The World Bank Group, 'Macro Poverty Outlook for Sub-Saharan Africa' (2023) available at <https://www.worldbank.org/en/publication/macro-poverty-outlook/mpo_ssa> accessed 6 April 2024.

Thomas RM, 'The Universal Declaration of Human Rights and Sub-Saharan Africa: A Post-Colonial Reading' (2011) 26 *UCLA Journal of International Law and Foreign Affairs* 101.

Udombana NJ, 'So Far, So Fair: The Local Remedies Rule in the Jurisprudence of the African Commission on Human and Peoples' Rights' (2003) 97 *AJIL* 1.

UN Committee on Economic, Social and Cultural Rights, 'General Comment No. 3: The Nature of States Parties' Obligations (1990).available at https://www.refworld.org/legal/general/cescr/1990/en/5613 accessed 24 October 2024

UN Committee on Economic, Social and Cultural Rights, 'General Comment No. 12: The Right to Adequate Food (Art 11)' (1999) UN Doc E/C.12/1999/5.

UN Committee on Economic, Social and Cultural Rights 'General Comment No. 19: The Right to Social Security' (2008) UN Doc E/C.12/GC/19.

UN CRPD 'General Comment No. 5 (2017) on Living Independently and Being Included in the Community' UN Doc CRPD/C/GC/5.

UN CRPD 'General Comment No. 6 (2018) on Equality and Non-discrimination' UN Doc CRPD/C/GC/6.

UN CRPD 'General Comment No. 7 (2018) on the Participation of Persons with Disabilities, Including Children with Disabilities, Through their Representative Organizations, in the Implementation and Monitoring of the Convention' UN Doc CRPD/C/GC/7.

UN General Assembly, 'General Assembly Endorses Landmark Global Compact on Refugees, Adopting 53 Third Committee Resolutions, 6 Decisions Covering Range of Human Rights' (2028) UN Doc GA/12107.

UNICEF, *Twenty-Five Years of the Convention on the Rights of the Child* (UNICEF 2015).

United Nations Declaration on the Rights of Peasants and Other People Working in Rural Areas (2018) UN Doc A/RES/73/165, art 16.

United Nations Human Rights Office of the High Commission, 'Special Rapporteur on Extreme Poverty and Human Rights' (2018) available at <https://www.ohchr.org/en/special-procedures/sr-poverty> accessed 1 August 2023.

United Nations Treaty Collection, 'International Covenant on Economic and Social Rights' available at <https://treaties.un.org> accessed 1 August 2023.

United Nations, 'Transforming Our World: The 2030 Agenda for Sustainable Development' (2015) available at <https://sdgs.un.org/publications/transforming-our-world-2030-agenda-sustainable-development-17981> accessed 1 August 2023.

Universal Declaration of Human Right 1948, Art 25.

Viljoen F and Louw L, 'State Compliance with the Recommendations of the African Commission on Human and Peoples' Rights 1994–2004' (2007) 101 *AJIL* 1

Wachira GM, 'African Court on Human and Peoples' Rights: Ten Years on and Still No Justice' (2008) available at <https://primarysources.brillonline.com/browse/human-rights-documents-online/african-court-on-human-and-peoples-rights-ten-years-on-and-still-no-justice-sept-2008-36-pp;hrdhrd02090232> accessed 1 August 2023.

Zheng Z, 'The Right to an Adequate Standard of Living' in J Yao (ed), *The Legal Issues of the Emerging Rights* (Springer 2024) https://doi.org/10.1007/978-981-97-0499-6_9.

4 Poverty and Inequality

Introduction

Poverty and inequality remain persistent and deeply entrenched challenges in the Sub-Saharan African (SSA) region, undermining the realisation of the right to an adequate standard of living for millions of individuals.[1] Despite the significant economic growth and development efforts in recent decades, a substantial portion of the population in SSA continue to grapple with multidimensional poverty, characterised by deprivations in various aspects of human well-being, including income, health, education, and living standards.[2]

The legacy of colonialism and the subsequent challenges of nation building have indeed left indelible marks on the region's economic, political, and social landscape.[3] The colonial era was characterised by the exploitation of natural resources and the subjugation of indigenous populations, laying the foundation for economic disparities and social fragmentation. The imposition of arbitrary borders by colonial powers often divided ethnic and cultural groups, sowing seeds for future conflicts and tensions. Additionally, the extractive nature of colonial economies fostered a dependence on primary commodity exports and hindered the development of diversified and self-sustaining economic structures. The aftermath of decolonisation presented immense challenges for the newly independent nations of SSA. The transition to self-governance was often marred by power struggles, ethnic tensions, and the lack of institutional capacity to govern effectively. This vacuum of governance

1 Augustin Kwasi Fosu, 'Growth, Inequality and Poverty in Sub-Saharan Africa: Recent Progress in a Global Context' (2015) 43(1) *Oxford Development Studies* 44-59 DOI: 10.108-/13600818.2014.964195.

2 Sabina Alkire, Christoph Jindra, Gisela Robles Aguilar and Ana Vaz, 'Multidimensional Poverty Reduction Among Countries in Sub-Saharan Africa' (2017) 46(2) *Forum for Social Economics* 178-191 DOI: 10.1080/07360932.2017.1310123.

3 Ian EA Yeboah, 'Capitalism and Sub-Saharan African Human Capital' (2016) 16(1) *African Identities* 67-86 DOI: 10.1080/14725843.2017.1332983.

DOI: 10.4324/9781032628974-4

created an environment ripe for political instability, authoritarianism, and conflict, which continue to plague certain regions of SSA to the present time.[4]

Protracted armed conflicts and civil wars have had devastating consequences for the region, disrupting economic activities, displacing populations, and diverting resources away from essential services and infrastructure development. The destruction of physical and human capital during conflicts has left lasting scars, making it challenging for affecting countries to recover and rebuild.[5] Furthermore, the presence of conflict has deterred foreign investment and hindered regional economic integration, perpetuating cycles of underdevelopment.[6]

Weak governance structures, corruption, and the lack of accountability have also contributed significantly to the entrenchment of poverty and inequality in SSA. Ineffective public institutions, coupled with the mismanagement of resources and the diversion of funds for personal gain, have undermined the delivery of essential services and the implementation of policies aimed at promoting inclusive growth and social development.[7]

The persistence of poverty and inequality in SSA is further exacerbated by the region's vulnerability to external shocks, such as fluctuations in global commodity prices, climate change, and global economic downturns.[8] Many SSA economies are heavily reliant on primary commodity exports, making them susceptible to price volatility and global market fluctuations. Additionally, the impacts of climate change, including droughts, floods, and environmental degradation, have disproportionately affected the region, threatening livelihoods and food security, particularly among rural and marginalised communities.

Addressing these deeply entrenched challenges requires multifaceted approaches that involve strengthening governance structures, promoting inclusive political processes, and fostering regional cooperation and economic integration. Investments in human capital, infrastructure, and diversified economic development are crucial for breaking the cycle of poverty and inequality. Also, efforts to promote peace, stability, and conflict resolution are

4 Rob Gordon, 'Moritz Bonn, Southern Africa and the Critique of Colonialism' (2013) 45(2) *African Historical Review* 1-30 DOI: 10.1080/17532523.2013.857089.

5 Samuel Ayofemi O Adeyeye et al, 'Africa and the Nexus of Poverty, Malnutrition and Diseases' (2023) 63(5) *Critical Reviews in Food Science and Nutrition* 641-656 DOI: 10.1080/10408398.2021.1952160.

6 Adil H Suliman and Andre Varella Mollick, 'Human Capital Development, War and Foreign Direct Investment in Sub-Saharan Africa' (2009) 37(1) *Oxford Development Studies* 47-61 DOI: 10.1080/13600810802660828.

7 Poppy Sofia Koeswayo, Sofik Handoyo and Dede Abdul Hasyir, 'Investigating the Relationship between Public Governance and the Corruption Perception Index' (2024) 10(1) *Cogent Social Sciences* DOI: 10.1080/23311886.2024.2342513.

8 Alice N Sindzingre, 'The Ambivalent Impact of Commodities: Structural Change or Status Quo in Sub-Saharan Africa?' (2013) 20(1) *South African Journal of International Affairs* 23-55 DOI: 10.1080/10220461.2013.780327.

essential for creating an enabling environment for sustainable development in the region.

Understanding the causes and effects of poverty in SSA is crucial in the search for a lasting solution to the attendant problems these issues pose for the region. Following from this, this chapter undertakes a comprehensive examination of the causes and effects of poverty and inequality within SSA, shedding light on the intricate web of factors that perpetuate these socio-economic disparities and their far-reaching implications for human well-being. By delving into these complex issues, the chapter aims to contribute to a deeper understanding of the challenges faced by the region in realisation of the right to an adequate standard of living, as enshrined in various international human rights instruments, including the Universal Declaration of Human Rights (UDHR) and the International Covenant on Economic, Social and Cultural Rights (ICESCR).[9] The main areas for consideration in this chapter include the causes of poverty and inequality in SSA, the effects of poverty and inequality on the right to an adequate standard of living as well as the efforts by the various governments in the region to address the problems of poverty and inequality in the region.

Causes of Poverty and Inequality in Sub-Saharan Africa

Under this heading, various factors that are responsible for poverty in SSA are considered. They include structural factors, economic factors as well as social factors.

Structural Factors

The persistence of poverty and inequality in SSA can be attributed to a multitude of interrelated structural factors that have their roots in the region's historical trajectories and socio-political contexts. One of the most significant structural factors is the legacy of colonialism, which has profoundly shaped the economic, political, and social structures of many SSA countries.[10] Although there are arguments to show that while other regions of the world were affected by colonialism but have since left (Sub-Saharan) Africa behind,[11] this writer argues that the colonialism with respect to Africa has resulted in

9 Please refer to Chapter 3 for a comprehensive discussion on the legal framework for the realisation of the right to an adequate standard of living in SSA.

10 Gareth Austin, 'The Economics of Colonialism in Africa,' in Celestin Monga and Justin Yifu Lin (eds), *The Oxford Handbook of Africa and Economics: Volume 1: Context and Concepts* (2015; online edn, Oxford Academic, 5 Oct 2015), https://doi.org/10.1093/oxfordhb/9780199687114.013.4, accessed 13 May 2024.

11 Leander Heldring and James A Robinson, 'Colonialism and Economic Development in Africa' (2012) Working Paper 18566 National Bureau of Economic Research.

different outcomes due to the forced grouping of different nations. In most cases, these forced unions have resulted in unending conflicts and mistrusts.

Economic Factors

Economic factors have indeed played a pivotal role in shaping the landscape of poverty and inequality in SSA. The region's heavy reliance on primary commodity exports, coupled with limited economic diversification and industrialisation, has rendered many economies vulnerable to external shocks and global fluctuations.

The dependence on a narrow range of export commodities, such as oil, minerals, and agricultural products, has been a long-standing challenge for many SSA countries. According to a report by the United Nations Conference on Trade and Development (UNTAD), the share of primary commodities in total merchandise exports for SSA countries averaged around 70 percent in 2019.[12] This reliance on primary commodities has several implications for poverty and inequality:

- Vulnerability to price volatility: Fluctuations in global commodity prices can have significant impacts on export earnings, government revenues, and overall economic performance. A study by the International Monetary Fund (IMF) found that a 10 percent decline in commodity prices can lead to a reduction in real GDP growth of up to 0.6 percentage points in commodity-exporting countries.[13] When prices decline, it can lead to economic downturns, reduced government spending, and a contraction in employment opportunities, disproportionately affecting the poor and exacerbating income inequalities.
- Limited economic diversification: The focus on primary commodity exports has often come at the expense of diversifying into other sectors, such as manufacturing and services. This lack of economic diversification limits the creation of employment opportunities, particularly in higher-valued-added sectors, and perpetuates poverty by concentrating economic activities in low-productivity sectors. Research by the World Bank has highlighted the positive relationship between economic diversification and poverty reduction, emphasising the importance of promoting structural transformation in SSA economies.[14]

12 UNCTAD, 'State of Commodity Dependence 2021' (2022) UNCTAD/DITC/COM/2021/2.

13 IMF, 'Commodity Price Shocks and Imperfect Pass-Through: A Panel Event Study' (IMF Working Paper 22/121, 2022).

14 The World Bank, 'Accelerating Poverty Reduction n Africa' (2019) available at < https://documents.worldbank.org/en/publication/documents-reports/documentdetail/985381570682302500/accelerating-poverty-reduction-in-africa> accessed 13 May 2024.

The unsustainable management of natural resources is another point for consideration. The manner in which natural resources such as land, water, and mineral resources are managed in SSA has contributed to environmental degradation. This has undermined the livelihoods of rural communities that heavily depend on these resources. A report by the United Nations Environmental Programme (UNEP) highlighted the severe consequences of land degradation, deforestation, and water scarcity for rural communities in SSA, exacerbating food insecurity, poverty, and displacement.[15]

The unequal distribution of land and limited access to productive assets have further impacted rural poverty and inequality, particularly among smallholder farmers and pastoralists. According to study by the Food and Agriculture Organisation (FAO), secure land rights and access to productive assets are crucial for reducing rural poverty and promoting inclusive economic growth in SSA.[16]

Furthermore, the adoption of structural adjustment programmes (SAPs) by many SSA countries in the 1980s and 1990s, as prescribed by the international financial institutions like the International Monetary Fund (IMF) and the World Bank, has also had a significant implication for poverty and inequality. These programmes aimed to promote economic stability and growth through austerity measures, such as public spending cuts, privatisation of state-owned enterprises, and trade liberalisation.

While the intentions behind these policies were to promote economic efficiency and attract foreign investment, their implementation often had adverse effects on the poor and vulnerable segments of society. A study by the United Nations Development Programme (UNDP) found that SAPs led to a significant increase in poverty levels in many SSA countries, as public spending cuts eroded access to essential services like education, healthcare, and social safety nets.[17]

Trade liberalisation policies, while intended to promote economic integration and export-led growth, also exposed domestic industries to intense competition from cheaper imports, leading to job losses and the erosion of livelihoods in certain sectors. The impacts of these policies were particularly severe in urban areas, where job losses and the erosion of real wages contributed to the growth of urban poverty and the expansion of informal settlements.[18]

15 UNEP, 'Responding to Climate Change' (2024) available at < https://www.unep.org/regions/africa/regional-initiatives/responding-climate-change> accessed 13 May 2024.

16 Vanya Slavchevska et al, 'Beyon Ownership: Women's and Men's Land Rights in Sub-Saharan Africa' (2021) 49(1) *Oxford Development Studies* 2-22 DOI: 10.1080/13600818.2020.1818714.

17 UNDP, 'Structural Adjustment and Poverty in Sub-Saharan Africa' (UNDP, 1998) available at < https://digitallibrary.un.org/record/101597> accessed 19 May 2024.

18 Martha Chen et al, 'Urban Livelihoods: Reframing Theory and Policy' (2016) 28(2) *Environment and Urbanisation* DOI: 10.1177/0956247816662405.

Furthermore, the economic policies prescribed by SAPs often failed to address the structural inequalities and power dynamics that perpetuated poverty and inequality in SSA. The emphasis on market-driven solutions and the withdrawal of state intervention often overlooked the needs of marginalised groups and the importance of addressing deep-rooted social and political factors that contributed to poverty and inequality. As noted by researchers at the Institute of Development Studies (IDS), a one-size-fits-all approach to economic policy reform proved ineffective in addressing the complex and context-specific challenges faced by SSA countries.[19]

Looking ahead, addressing poverty and inequality in SSA requires a multi-faceted approach that promotes economic diversification, sustainable natural resource management, inclusive growth strategies, and strengthened social safety nets. This includes investing in human capital development, supporting small and medium enterprises, fostering regional economic integration, and promoting good governance and accountability in the management of natural resources.

Additionally, it is crucial to address the structural inequalities and power dynamics that perpetuate poverty and inequality, such as unequal access to productive assets, gender disparities, and the marginalisation of certain groups. Policies that promote inclusive economic opportunities, secure land rights, and empowerment of vulnerable groups are essential for breaking the inter-generational cycles of poverty and inequality.[20]

Overall, the economic challenges faced by SSA countries are complex and deeply rooted in historical trajectories, socio-political contexts, and global economic dynamics. Addressing these challenges requires a comprehensive and context-specific approach that combines economic reforms, social policies, and efforts to promote inclusive and sustainable development.

Social Factors

Social factors, intertwined with structural and economic factors, have played a crucial role in perpetuating poverty and inequality in SSA. These factors encompass various dimensions, including limited access to education, health-care disparities, employment opportunities, land rights, and gender inequalities. Addressing these multidimensional challenges is essential for promoting inclusive and sustainable development in the region.

19 Richard Longhurst, 'Introduction: Universal Development – Research and Practice' (2017) available at < https://bulletin.ids.ac.uk/index.php/idsbo/article/download/2898/Online%20article?inline=1> accessed 20 May 2024.

20 The World Bank, 'Poverty and Shared Prosperity 2022: Correcting Course' (The World Bank 2022) available at < https://documents.worldbank.org/en/publication/documents-reports/documentdetail/099750110062235316/idu07dfa30ac034520434108ecd0db3a26cd8be6> accessed 20 May 2024.

Limited Access to Education

Access to education remains a significant challenge in many SSA countries, with substantial disparities existing between urban and rural areas, as well as across socio-economic strata. Limited access to education, coupled with inadequate investment in educational infrastructure and resources, has perpetuated intergenerational cycles of poverty and inequality.[21] Children from low-income households often face barriers to accessing education, including the inability to afford school fees, the need to engage in child labour, and long distances to travel to educational facilities.

According to a report by the United Nations Educational, Scientific and Cultural Organisation (UNESCO), in 2020, around 98 million children and youth in SSA were out of school, with significant disparities between rural and urban areas, as well as between socio-economic groups.[22] These disparities in access to education have far reaching consequences, limiting individuals' opportunities for gainful employment, hindering social mobility, and constraining the region's overall economic and social development.

Furthermore, the quality of education in many SSA countries remains a concern, with inadequate teacher training, outdated curricula, and insufficient learning materials hindering the acquisition of relevant skills and knowledge necessary for economic and social mobility. A study by the World Bank found that in many SSA countries, a significant proportion of students lack proficiency in basic reading and mathematical skills, even after several years of schooling.[23] These educational quality deficits do not only limit individuals' prospects for gainful employment and income generation but also perpetuate societal inequalities and hinder the region's overall socio-economic development.

Healthcare Disparities

Access to quality healthcare remains a significant challenge in SSA, with profound implications for poverty and inequality. Inadequate healthcare infrastructure, shortages of medical personnel, and the high cost of medical services have disproportionately impacted marginalised and low-income communities. These disparities have contributed to higher rates of preventable diseases, malnutrition, and premature deaths, further entrenching cycles of poverty and impeding human capital development.

21 Augustine Edobor Arimoro, *Public Private Partnerships in Emerging Economies* (Routledge, 2020) 15.

22 UNESCO, 'Out-of-School Children and Youth in Sub-Saharan Africa' (2021) available at <https://www.unesco.org/gem-report/en/2022-out-school> accessed 20 May 2024.

23 The World Bank, 'Facing Forward: Schooling for Learning in Africa' (2018) available at <https://www.worldbank.org/en/region/afr/publication/facing-forward-schooling-for-learning-in-africa> accessed 20 May 2024.

According to the World Health Organization (WHO), SSA carries a disproportionate burden of disease, accounting for over 24 percent of the global disease burden, despite having only 13 percent of the world's population.[24] This high disease burden, coupled with limited access to healthcare services, has had severe consequences for economic productivity, educational attainment, and overall human development in the region.

The HIV/AIDS pandemic, which has had a devastating impact on many SSA countries, has exacerbated existing healthcare challenges and deepened socio-economic inequalities. The loss of productive members of the society and the strain on healthcare systems have undermined economic productivity and worsened poverty levels, particularly among vulnerable households and communities. A study by the United Nations Development Programme (UNDP) estimated that in some severely affected countries, the HIV/AIDS pandemic reduced GDP by as much as 2–4 percent per annum.[25]

Employment Opportunities

Limited employment opportunities, particularly in the formal sector, have perpetuated poverty and inequality in SSA. High rates of unemployment and underemployment, particularly among youth and women, have constrained income-generating opportunities and hindered social mobility. The informal sector, characterised by low wages, poor working conditions, and a lack of social protections, has become a significant source of employment for many, trapping individuals in cycles of poverty and precarious livelihoods.

According to the International Labour Organisation (ILO), the informal economy accounts for around 85.8 percent of total employment in SSA, with significant proportion of workers engaged in low-productivity, low-wage activities.[26] This high level of informality not only affects the limited opportunities in the formal sector but also perpetuates poverty and inequality by denying workers access to social protections, stable income, and opportunities for upward mobility.

Furthermore, the mismatch between the skills acquired through education and the demands of the labour market has contributed to unemployment and underemployment. This disconnect has been worsened by the limited investment in vocational and technical training programmes, hindering the

24 WHO, 'The Global Burden of Disease: 2004 Update' (2008) available at <https://www.who.int/publications/i/item/9789241563710> accessed 20 May 2024.

25 UNDP, 'UNDP Regional Report on HIV/AIDS in Sub-Saharan Africa' (2018) available at <https://www.undp.org/publications/undp-regional-report-hiv/aids-sub-saharan-africa> accessed 20 May 2024.

26 ILO, *Women and Men in the Informal Economy: A Statistical Picture* (International Labour Office 2013) available at <chrome-extension://efaidnbmnnnibpcajpcglclefindmkaj/https://webapps.ilo.org/wcmsp5/groups/public/---dgreports/---stat/documents/publication/wcms_234413.pdf> accessed 20 May 2024.

development of a skilled workforce capable of driving economic diversification and sustainable growth. A study by the African Centre for Economic Transformation (ACET) highlighted the need for SSA countries to address the skills mismatch and promote demand-driven technical and vocational education and training (TVET) programmes to support industrialisation and economic transformation.[27]

Land Rights

Land rights and access to productive land resources have been contentious issues in many SSA countries, with significant implications for poverty and inequality.[28] The legacy of colonial land policies, coupled with inefficient land tenure systems and weak governance frameworks, has perpetuated inequalities in land ownership and access. Smallholder farmers, pastoralists, and indigenous communities have often been marginalised and dispossessed of their traditional lands, undermining their livelihoods and perpetuating poverty.

Less than 20 percent of land in SSA is formally registered, with the majority of rural populations relying on customary and informal land tenure systems.[29] This lack of secure land tenure has hindered investment in sustainable agricultural practices, limited access to credit, and perpetuated conflicts and displacement, further exacerbating poverty and food insecurity in rural areas.

The expansion of large-scale commercial agriculture, mining, and infrastructure projects has further worsened land conflicts and displacement, disproportionately impacting rural communities and exacerbating their vulnerability to poverty and food insecurity. Research shows that smallholder farmers and pastoralists in SSA are particularly vulnerable to land grabbing and displacement, with adverse consequences for their livelihoods, food security, and overall well-being.[30]

Gender Disparities

Gender disparities have been a significant driver of poverty and inequality in SSA, with women facing multidimensional and intersecting forms of

27 ACET, 'Developing Skills for Economic Transformation in Africa' (2022) available at <https://acetforafrica.org/> accessed 20 May 2024.

28 Augustine Arimoro, 'Public-Private Partnership and the Right to Property in Nigeria' (2019) 19(2) African Human Rights Law journal DOI: 10.17159/1996-2096/2019/v19n2a10.

29 Frank FK Byamugisha and Nancy Dubosse, 'The Investment Case for Land Tenure Security in Sub-Saharan Africa: A Cost-Benefit Analysis' (2023) 14(S1) *Journal of Benefit Cost Analysis* 272-300 DOI: 10.1017/bca.2023.14.

30 Elena Baglioni and Peter Gibbon, 'Land Grabbing, Large and Small-Scale Farming: What Can Evidence and Policy from 20th Century Africa Contribute to the Debate?' (2013) 34(9) *Third World Quarterly* 1558-1581 DOI: 10.1080/01436597.2013.843838.

discrimination and disadvantage.[31] Cultural norms, patriarchal structures, and discriminatory legal frameworks have perpetuated unequal access to economic resources, education, and employment opportunities for women.[32]

According to the United Nations Development Programme (UNDP), women in SSA are more likely to be employed in the informal sector, earn lower wages, and have limited access to productive resources, such as land, credit, and technology.[33] These gender-based inequalities not only constrain women's economic empowerment but also perpetuate intergenerational cycles of poverty and limit the region's overall economic potential.

Women in SSA often bear a disproportionate burden of unpaid care work, limiting their participation in income-generating activities and hindering their economic empowerment. A study by the International Labour Organisation (ILO) found that women in SSA spend an average of 3.4 hours per day on unpaid work, compared to 1.8 hours for men, further worsening gender inequalities in employment and income opportunities.[34]

Effects of Poverty and Inequality on the Right to an Adequate Standard of Living in Sub-Saharan Africa

The pervasive poverty and inequality in SSA have had far-reaching implications for the realisation of the right to an adequate standard of living, as enshrined in various international human rights instruments, such as the UDHR and the ICESCR. This right encompasses several interdependent and indivisible elements, including access to food, water, housing, healthcare, education, and social security. The deprivations associated with poverty and inequality have profoundly undermined the fulfilment of these essential components, perpetuating cycles of disadvantage and marginalisation.[35]

Access to Food

Poverty and inequality have posed significant challenges to access to adequate food and nutrition in SSA. The region continues to grapple with high levels of

31 Naila Kabeer, 'Gender Equality, Economic Growth, and Women's Agency: The "Endless Variety" and "Monotonous Similarity" of Patriarchal Constraints' (2015) 22(1) *Feminist Economics* 295-321 DOI: 10.1080/13545701.2015.1090009.

32 Ibid.

33 UNDP, 'Gender Inequality Index (GII)' (2022) available at < https://hdr.undp.org/data-center/thematic-composite-indices/gender-inequality-index#/indicies/GII> accessed 20 May 2024.

34 ILO, 'Care Work and Cre Jobs for the Future of Decent Work' (2018) available at < https://www.ilo.org/publications/major-publications/care-work-and-care-jobs-future-decent-work> accessed 20 May 2024.

35 Augustine Edobor Arimoro, 'Beyond Economics! The (Evolving) Role of Law in the Eradication of Extreme Poverty' (2023) 8 *Journal of Human Rights and Social Work* 192-204 DOI: 10.1007/s41134-023-00247-2.

food security, with a significant portion of the population facing chronic hunger and malnutrition. According to the Food and Agriculture Organisation (FAO), the prevalence of undernourishment in SSA stood at 22.7 percent in 2021, the highest among all regions globally.[36]

Poverty is a major determinant of food insecurity, as low-income households often lack the financial resources to purchase nutritious and sufficient food. The lack of purchasing power, coupled with limited access to productive resources such as land and agricultural inputs, has hindered the ability of many households to produce or acquire adequate food. Furthermore, the affordability of food has been affected by factors such as climate change, conflicts, and inefficient agricultural practices, disproportionately impacting marginalised communities.

Malnutrition, particularly among children, has long-term consequences for physical and cognitive development, perpetuating intergenerational cycles of poverty and limiting future economic productivity. According to the World Health Organization (WHO), in 2020, around 58 million children under the age of five in SSA were stunted (low height for age), and 14 million children were wasted (low weight for height), reflecting severe impacts of malnutrition on child growth and development.[37] These conditions not only increase the risk of mortality and morbidity but also impair cognitive development, educational attainment, and future earning potential, further entrenching poverty and inequality.

The lack of access to adequate and nutritious food not only violates the fundamental human right to be free from hunger but also undermines the realisation of other interrelated rights, such as the rights to health and education. Malnutrition can weaken the immune system, increasing susceptibility to infectious diseases and compromising overall health outcomes. Furthermore, children suffering from hunger and malnutrition often face challenges in attending and performing well in school, hindering their educational attainment and future opportunities.

Addressing food insecurity and malnutrition in SSA requires a multifaceted approach that addresses the underlying causes of poverty and inequality, as well as the specific challenges faced by marginalised communities. Investments in sustainable and resilient agricultural practices, improved access to productive resources, and strengthening social protection systems are crucial to ensuring access to adequate and nutritious food for all.

36 FAO, IFAD, UNICEF, WFP and WHO, *The State of Food Security and Nutrition in the World 2023* (FAO, IFAD, UNICEF, WFP and WHO, Rome 2023) available at <https://openknowledge.fao.org/items/a17000a4-6f42-46cf-9eaa-06007970365d> accessed 20 May 2024.

37 WHO, '2022 Global Nutrition Report: 2022 Regional Profile for Sub-Saharan Africa' (2023).

Access to Water and Sanitation

The lack of access to safe drinking water and adequate sanitation facilities remains a significant challenge in many parts of SSA, with direct implications for health, dignity, and overall well-being. Poverty and inequality have worsened these challenges, as low income households and marginalised communities often lack the financial resources to access safe water sources or invest in proper sanitation infrastructure.

According to the World Health Organization (WHO) and UNICEF, in 2020, approximately 418 million people in SSA lacked access to basic drinking water services, and 701 million people lacked access to basic sanitation services.[38] This deprivation disproportionately affects rural areas, where only 53 percent of the population had access to basic drinking water services compared to 86 percent in the urban areas.[39]

The consequences of this deprivation are severe, contributing to the spread of waterborne diseases, increased child mortality, and perpetuating cycles of poverty and inequality. Lack of access to safe water and sanitation is a leading cause of diarrheal diseases, which are among the top killers of children under five years old in SSA.[40] These diseases not only have direct health impacts but also contribute to malnutrition, impaired cognitive development, and reduced productivity, further exacerbating poverty and undermining human development.

The lack of access to water and sanitation disproportionately impacts women and girls, who often bear the burden of collecting water from distant sources, limiting their time for education, income-generating activities, and personal development. This gender-based disparity further entrenches inequalities and hinders the realisation of other interrelated rights such as the rights to education, work, and gender equality. According to UNICEF, women and girls in SSA collectively spend an estimated 40 billion hours per year collecting water, perpetuating gender inequalities, and limiting their economic and social empowerment.[41]

Moreover, the lack of adequate sanitation facilities in schools and workplaces can discourage attendance and participation, particularly for girls and women, due to concerns for privacy, safety, and menstrual hygiene management. This can have long-term consequences for educational attainment and

38 WHO and UNICEF, '2022 Progress on Household Drinking Water, Sanitation and Hygiene' (2022) available at <https://www.unicef.org/documents/unicef-wash-annual-publication-catalogue-2022> accessed 20 May 2024.

39 Ibid.

40 WHO, 'Water, Sanitation and Hygiene' (2023) available at <https://www.who.int/data/gho/data/themes/water-sanitation-and-hygiene> accessed 20 May 2024.

41 UNICEF, 'Collecting Water is Often a Colossal Waste of Time for Women and Girls' (2016) available at <https://www.unicef.org/press-releases/unicef-collecting-water-often-colossal-waste-time-women-and-girls> accessed 20 May 2024.

overall well-being, perpetuating gender inequalities and undermining progress towards achieving the Sustainable Development Goals (SDGs).

Addressing the challenges of access to water and sanitation in SSA requires significant investments in infrastructure, as well as efforts to address the underlying drivers of poverty and inequality. Sustainable and inclusive water and sanitation management practices, coupled with increased financing and capacity building efforts, are essential to ensuring universal access to these vital services and promoting human development, gender equality, and overall well-being.

Access to Adequate Housing

The right to adequate housing, as recognised by the ICESCR, encompasses not only the physical structure but also the availability of essential service, affordability, habitability, accessibility, and security of tenure. However, in many parts of SSA, poverty and inequality have resulted in widespread inadequate housing conditions, including overcrowding, lack of basic amenities, and insecure tenure.

The rapid urbanisation in the region, coupled with insufficient investment in affordable housing and urban planning, has led to the proliferation of informal settlements and slums. According to the United Nations Human Settlement Programme (UN-Habitat), in 2020, around 50 percent of the urban population in SSA lived in slums, with significant disparities across countries and regions. The lack of adequate housing in SSA has far-reaching implications for health, safety, and human dignity. Overcrowded and substandard living conditions increase the risk of communicable diseases, while the absence of basic amenities such as clean water and sanitation facilities exacerbates public health challenges.[42] Furthermore, insecure tenure and forced evictions disproportionately affect the poor and marginalised, perpetuating cycles of poverty and social exclusion.[43]

Addressing the housing crisis in SSA requires a multifaceted approach that combines policy interventions, increased investment in affordable housing, and efforts to strengthen land tenure systems. Inclusive urban planning, slum upgrading programmes, and community-led housing initiatives have shown promise in improving living conditions for the urban poor.[44] However, sustained efforts and political will are necessary to ensure the progressive realisation of the right to adequate housing for all.

42 UN-Habitat, 'Slum Almanac 2015-2016' (2016) <https://unhabitat.org/slum-almanac-2015-2016> accessed 21 May 2024.

43 Payne G, Durand-Lasserve A and Rakodi C, 'The Limits of Land Titling and Home Ownership' (2009) 21(2) *Environment and Urbanization* 443-462.

44 Cities Alliance, 'Slum Upgrading: Lessons from Brazil' (2016) <https://www.citiesalliance.org/resources/publications/cities-alliance-knowledge/slum-upgrading-lessons-brazil> accessed 21 May 2024.

Access to Healthcare

Poverty and inequality significantly impact access to healthcare in SSA, undermining the realisation of the right to the highest attainable standard of health. Limited public health expenditure, coupled with high out-of-pocket costs, has created significant barriers to healthcare access, particularly for low-income and marginalised populations.[45] The region faces a dual burden of communicable and non-communicable diseases, with HIV/AIDS, malaria, and tuberculosis continuing to pose significant public health challenges. According to the World Health Organization, SSA accounts for more than 90 percent of global malaria deaths, with children under five being particularly vulnerable.[46]

Furthermore, the COVID-19 pandemic has exposed and exacerbated existing health inequalities in the region. Limited healthcare infrastructure, shortages of medical personnel, and inequitable access to vaccines have disproportionately affected vulnerable populations, further widening health disparities.[47]

Addressing these challenges requires increased investment in public health systems, efforts to expand universal health coverage, and targeted interventions to reach marginalised communities. Community-based healthcare initiatives and mobile health technologies have shown promise in improving healthcare access in remote and underserved areas.[48]

Access to Education

While progress has been made in expanding access to primary education in SSA, significant challenges remain in ensuring quality education and equitable access at all levels. Poverty and inequality continue to impact educational outcomes, with children from low-income households facing multiple barriers to accessing and completing education.[49]

Gender disparities in education persist, with girls often facing additional barriers such as early marriage, teenage pregnancy, and cultural norms that

45 WHO, 'The State of Health in the WHO African Region: An analysis of the status of health, health services and health systems in the context of the Sustainable Development Goals' (2018) <https://www.afro.who.int/publications/state-health-who-african-region> accessed 21 May 2024.

46 WHO, 'World Malaria Report 2021' (2021) <https://www.who.int/teams/global-malaria-programme/reports/world-malaria-report-2021> accessed 21 May 2024.

47 UNDP, 'Impact of COVID-19 in Africa' (2020) <https://www.undp.org/africa/publications/impact-covid-19-africa> accessed 21 May 2024.

48 Aranda-Jan CB, Mohutsiwa-Dibe N and Loukanova S, 'Systematic review on what works, what does not work and why of implementation of mobile health (mHealth) projects in Africa' (2014) 14(1) BMC Public Health 188.

49 UNESCO, 'Global Education Monitoring Report 2020: Inclusion and education: All means all' (2020) <https://en.unesco.org/gem-report/report/2020/inclusion> accessed 21 May 2024.

prioritise boys' education.[50] These disparities not only violate the right to education but also perpetuate gender inequalities and limit women's economic empowerment.

The quality of education remains a significant concern, with many schools lacking basic infrastructure, qualified teachers, and learning materials. According to UNESCO, only 64 percent of primary school teachers in SSA were trained to national standards in 2019.[51] This shortage of qualified teachers, coupled with overcrowded classrooms and inadequate resources, undermines learning outcomes and the development of crucial skills.

Addressing these challenges requires increased investment in education, targeted interventions to support marginalised groups, and efforts to improve the quality of teaching and learning. Initiatives such as school feeding programmes, conditional cash transfers, and gender-responsive education policies have shown promise in improving educational access and outcomes for vulnerable children.[52]

Efforts to Address Poverty and Inequality in Sub-Saharan Africa

Recognising the urgent need to address poverty and inequality, many SSA countries have implemented various policies and programmes aimed at promoting inclusive growth and social development. These efforts include the below topics.

Social Protection Programmes

Several SSA countries have expanded social protection programmes to provide a safety net for vulnerable populations. These include cash transfer programmes, public works schemes, and social insurance initiatives. For example, Kenya's Hunger Safety Net Programme provides regular cash transfers to food-insecure households in arid and semi-arid regions.[53] Similarly, Ethiopia's Productive Safety Net Programme combines cash transfers with public works projects to improve food security and build community assets.[54]

50 Plan International, 'Teenage Pregnancy in Sierra Leone' (2021) <https://plan-international.org/publications/teenage-pregnancy-sierra-leone> accessed 21 May 2024.

51 UNESCO, 'Teacher policy development guide' (2019) <https://unesdoc.unesco.org/ark:/48223/pf0000370966> accessed 21 May 2024.

52 J-PAL, 'Roll Call: Getting Children into School' (2017) <https://www.povertyactionlab.org/policy-insight/roll-call-getting-children-school> accessed 21 May 2024.

53 Government of Kenya, 'Hunger Safety Net Programme' (2022) <https://www.socialprotection.go.ke/hunger-safety-net-programme-hsnp/> accessed 21 May 2024.

54 World Bank, 'Ethiopia's Productive Safety Net Program (PSNP)' (2020) <https://www.worldbank.org/en/news/feature/2019/01/17/ethiopias-productive-safety-net-program-psnp> accessed 21 May 2024.

While these programmes have shown positive impacts on poverty reduction and human development outcomes, challenges remain in scaling up coverage and ensuring sustainable financing. Strengthening social protection systems and expanding their reach to cover informal sector workers and rural populations remain critical priorities for the region.[55]

Agricultural Development and Rural Poverty Reduction

Given the high prevalence of rural poverty in SSA, many countries have implemented agricultural development programs aimed at improving productivity, market access, and rural livelihoods. These include initiatives to promote climate-smart agriculture, expand irrigation infrastructure, and strengthen agricultural value chain.[56]

For instance, Rwanda's Crop Intensification Programme has contributed to increased agricultural productivity and food security through the provision of improved seeds, fertilisers, and extension services to smallholder farmers.[57] Similarly, Nigeria's Anchor Borrowers' Programme aims to link smallholder farmers with large-scale processors, providing access to inputs and credit.[58]

While these efforts have yielded positive results in some areas, challenges persist in addressing structural constraints such as limited access to land, credit, and markets. Promoting inclusive agricultural transformation that benefits smallholder farmers and addresses rural poverty remains a key priority for the region.[59]

Economic Diversification and Job Creation

Recognising the need to create quality employment opportunities, particularly for youth, many SSA countries have implemented policies aimed at promoting economic diversification and industrialisation. These include initiatives to develop manufacturing sectors, support small and medium enterprises (SMEs), and promote digital entrepreneurship.[60]

55 ILO, 'World Social Protection Report 2020–22: Social protection at the crossroads – in pursuit of a better future' (2021) <https://www.ilo.org/global/publications/books/WCMS_817572/lang--en/index.htm> accessed 21 May 2024.

56 AGRA, 'Africa Agriculture Status Report 2021' (2021) <https://agra.org/resource-library/africa-agriculture-status-report-2021/> accessed 21 May 2024.

57 Kathiresan A, 'Strategies for Sustainable Crop Intensification in Rwanda' (2011) Ministry of Agriculture and Animal Resources, Rwanda.

58 Central Bank of Nigeria, 'Anchor Borrowers' Programme Guidelines' (2016) <https://www.cbn.gov.ng/out/2017/dfd/anchor%20borrowers%20programme%20guidelines%20-dec%20%202016.pdf> accessed 21 May 2024.

59 IFAD, 'Rural Development Report 2021' (2021) <https://www.ifad.org/en/rural-development-report/> accessed 21 May 2024.

60 African Development Bank, 'Industrialize Africa: Strategies, Policies, Institutions, and Financing' (2017) <https://www.afdb.org/fileadmin/uploads/afdb/Documents/Generic-Documents/Industrialize_Africa_report_single.pdf> accessed 21 May 2024.

For example, Ethiopia's industrial parks strategy aims to attract foreign investment and create jobs in export-oriented manufacturing sectors.[61] Similarly, Kenya's Digital Economy Blueprint outlines strategies to promote digital skills development and support technology-driven entrepreneurship.[62]

However, challenges remain in creating sufficient formal sector jobs to absorb the growing youth population and address underemployment. Enhancing skills development, improving the business environment, and promoting labour-intensive sectors remain critical for inclusive job creation in the region.[63]

Governance Reforms and Anti-Corruption Measures

Recognising the role of weak governance and corruption in perpetuating poverty and inequality, many SSA countries have implemented reforms aimed at improving transparency, accountability, and public service delivery. These include efforts to strengthen anti-corruption institutions, improve public financial management, and enhance citizen participation in governance.[64]

For instance, Ghana's Right to Information Act, passed in 2019, aims to enhance transparency and citizens' access to public information.[65] Similarly, Rwanda's Imihigo performance contracts system has been credited with improving local government accountability and service delivery.[66]

While progress has been made in some areas, challenges persist in addressing deeply entrenched corruption and strengthening institutional capacity. Continued efforts to promote good governance, strengthen the rule of law, and enhance public sector effectiveness remain crucial for addressing poverty and inequality in the region.[67]

Conclusion

The persistent challenges of poverty and inequality in Sub-Saharan Africa continue to undermine the realisation of the right to an adequate standard

61 Oqubay A, 'Industrial Policy and Late Industrialization in Ethiopia' (2018) African Development Bank Working Paper Series No 303.

62 Government of Kenya, 'Digital Economy Blueprint' (2019) <https://www.ict.go.ke/wp-content/uploads/2019/05/Kenya-Digital-Economy-2019.pdf> accessed 21 May 2024.

63 ILO, 'World Employment and Social Outlook: Trends 2022' (2022) <https://www.ilo.org/global/research/global-reports/weso/trends2022/WCMS_834081/lang--en/index.htm> accessed 21 May 2024.

64 Mo Ibrahim Foundation, 'Ibrahim Index of African Governance' (2020) <https://mo.ibrahim.foundation/iiag> accessed 21 May 2024.

65 Government of Ghana, 'Right to Information Act, 2019 (Act 989)' (2019) <https://www.rti.gov.gh/docs/Act%20989.pdf> accessed 21 May 2024.

66 Versailles B, 'Performance contracts and social service delivery – Lessons from Rwanda' (2012) International Growth Centre Working Paper.

67 Transparency International, 'Corruption Perceptions Index 2021' (2022) <https://www.transparency.org/en/cpi/2021> accessed 21 May 2024.

of living for millions of individuals. The complex interplay of structural, economic, and social factors has perpetuated cycles of deprivation and marginalisation, hindering inclusive development and human well-being in the region.

This chapter has examined the multifaceted causes of poverty and inequality in SSA, including the legacy of colonialism, economic vulnerabilities, limited access to education and healthcare, gender disparities, and weak governance structures. These factors have profound implications for various aspects of the right to an adequate standard of living, including access to food, water, housing, healthcare, and education.

The effects of poverty and inequality on the right to an adequate standard of living are far-reaching and interconnected. Food insecurity and malnutrition undermine health outcomes and cognitive development, perpetuating intergenerational cycles of poverty. Limited access to safe water and sanitation facilities exacerbates public health challenges and disproportionately affects women and girls. Inadequate housing conditions in urban slums and rural areas compromise safety, dignity, and overall well-being. Disparities in access to quality healthcare and education further entrench social inequalities and limit opportunities for social mobility.

While many SSA countries have implemented various policies and programmes to address poverty and inequality, significant challenges remain in scaling up interventions, ensuring sustainable financing, and addressing structural constraints. Social protection programmes, agricultural development initiatives, efforts to promote economic diversification and job creation, and governance reforms have shown promise in some areas. However, sustained political will, increased investment, and comprehensive strategies are necessary to achieve meaningful and lasting progress.

Moving forward, addressing poverty and inequality in SSA requires a multifaceted approach that combines economic reforms, social policies, and efforts to strengthen governance and institutional capacity. Key priorities include:

1. Investing in human capital development through improved access to quality education, healthcare, and skills training.
2. Promoting inclusive economic growth and job creation, particularly in labour-intensive sectors and the digital economy.
3. Strengthening and expanding social protection systems to provide a comprehensive safety net for vulnerable populations.
4. Addressing gender inequalities and promoting women's economic empowerment through targeted interventions and policy reforms.
5. Enhancing agricultural productivity and rural development to improve food security and rural livelihoods.
6. Improving urban planning and infrastructure development to address the challenges of rapid urbanisation and informal settlements.

7. Strengthening governance, combating corruption, and enhancing public service delivery to ensure equitable access to resources and opportunities.
8. Promoting regional integration and cooperation to address shared challenges and leverage collective resources.

Realising the right to an adequate standard of living for all individuals in SSA requires concerted efforts from governments, civil society, the private sector, and international partners. By addressing the root causes of poverty and inequality and implementing comprehensive and context-specific strategies, the region can make significant strides towards inclusive development and the fulfilment of fundamental human rights.

References

ACET, 'Developing Skills for Economic Transformation in Africa' (2022) available at <https://acetforafrica.org/> accessed 20 May 2024.

Adeyeye SAO et al, 'Africa and the Nexus of Poverty, Malnutrition and Diseases' (2023) 63(5) *Critical Reviews in Food Science and Nutrition* 641–656 https://doi.org/10.1080/10408398.2021.1952160.

African Development Bank, 'Industrialize Africa: Strategies, Policies, Institutions, and Financing' (2017) available at <https://www.afdb.org/fileadmin/uploads/afdb/Documents/Generic-Documents/Industrialize_Africa_report_single.pdf> accessed 21 May 2024.

AGRA, 'Africa Agriculture Status Report 2021' (2021) available at <https://agra.org/resource-library/africa-agriculture-status-report-2021/> accessed 21 May 2024.

Alkire S et al, 'Multidimensional Poverty Reduction Among Countries in Sub-Saharan Africa' (2017) 46(2) *Forum for Social Economics* 178–191 https://doi.org/10.1080/07360932.2017.1310123.

Aranda-Jan CB, Mohutsiwa-Dibe N and Loukanova S, 'Systematic Review on What Works, What Does Not Work and Why of Implementation of Mobile Health (mHealth) Projects in Africa' (2014) 14(1) *BMC Public Health* 188.

Arimoro A, 'Public-Private Partnership and the Right to Property in Nigeria' (2019) 19(2) *African Human Rights Law journal* 763–778 https://doi.org/10.17159/1996-2096/2019/v19n2a10.

Arimoro AE, 'Beyond Economics! The (Evolving) Role of Law in the Eradication of Extreme Poverty' (2023) 8 *Journal of Human Rights and Social Work* 192–204 https://doi.org/10.1007/s41134-023-00247-2.

Arimoro AE, *Public Private Partnerships in Emerging Economies* (Routledge 2020) 15.

Austin G, 'The Economics of Colonialism in Africa' in Celestin Monga and Justin Yifu Lin (eds), *The Oxford Handbook of Africa and Economics: Volume 1: Context and Concepts* (online edn, Oxford Academic, 5 October 2015) https://doi.org/10.1093/oxfordhb/9780199687114.013.4 accessed 13 May 2024.

Baglioni E and Gibbon P, 'Land Grabbing, Large and Small-Scale Farming: What Can Evidence and Policy from 20th Century Africa Contribute to the Debate?' (2013) 34(9) *Third World Quarterly* 1558–1581 https://doi.org/10.1080/01436597.2013.843838.

Byamugisha FFK and Dubosse N, 'The Investment Case for Land Tenure Security in Sub-Saharan Africa: A Cost-Benefit Analysis' (2023) 14(S1) *Journal of Benefit Cost Analysis* 272–300 https://doi.org/10.1017/bca.2023.14.

Central Bank of Nigeria, '"Anchor Borrowers" Programme Guidelines' (2016) available at <https://www.cbn.gov.ng/out/2017/dfd/anchor%20borrowers%20programme%20guidelines%20-dec%20%202016.pdf> accessed 21 May 2024.

Chen M et al, 'Urban Livelihoods: Reframing Theory and Policy' (2016) 28(2) *Environment and Urbanisation* 331–342 https://doi.org/10.1177/0956247816662405.

Cities Alliance, 'Slum Upgrading: Lessons from Brazil' (2016) available at <https://www.citiesalliance.org/resources/publications/cities-alliance-knowledge/slum-upgrading-lessons-brazil> accessed 21 May 2024.

FAO, IFAD, UNICEF, WFP and WHO, *The State of Food Security and Nutrition in the World 2023* (FAO, IFAD, UNICEF, WFP and WHO, Rome 2023) available at <https://openknowledge.fao.org/items/a17000a4-6f42-46cf-9eaa-06007970365d> accessed 20 May 2024.

Fosu AK, 'Growth, Inequality and Poverty in Sub-Saharan Africa: Recent Progress in a Global Context' (2015) 43(1) *Oxford Development Studies* 44–59 https://doi.org/10.108-/13600818.2014.964195.

Gordon R and Bonn M, Southern Africa and the Critique of Colonialism' (2013) 45(2) *African Historical Review* 1–30 https://doi.org/10.1080/17532523.2013.857089.

Government of Kenya, 'Digital Economy Blueprint' (2019) available at <https://www.ict.go.ke/wp-content/uploads/2019/05/Kenya-Digital-Economy-2019.pdf> accessed 21 May 2024.

Government of Kenya, 'Hunger Safety Net Programme' (2022) available at <https://www.socialprotection.go.ke/hunger-safety-net-programme-hsnp/> accessed 21 May 2024.

Heldring L and Robinson JA, 'Colonialism and Economic Development in Africa' (2012) Working Paper 18566 National Bureau of Economic Research.

IFAD, 'Rural Development Report 2021' (2021) available at <https://www.ifad.org/en/rural-development-report/> accessed 21 May 2024.

ILO, 'Care Work and Cre Jobs for the Future of Decent Work' (2018) available at <https://www.ilo.org/publications/major-publications/care-work-and-care-jobs-future-decent-work> accessed 20 May 2024.

ILO, *Women and Men in the Informal Economy: A Statistical Picture* (International Labour Office 2013) available at <chrome-extension://efaidnbmnnnibpcajpcglclefindmkaj/https://webapps.ilo.org/wcmsp5/groups/public/---dgreports/---stat/documents/publication/wcms_234413.pdf> accessed 20 May 2024.

ILO, *World Employment and Social Outlook: Trends 2022* (International Labour Office 2022) available at <https://www.ilo.org/global/research/global-reports/weso/trends2022/WCMS_834081/lang--en/index.htm> accessed 21 May 2024.

ILO, 'World Social Protection Report 2020–22: Social Protection at the Crossroads – In Pursuit of a Better Future' (2021) available at <https://www.ilo.org/global/publications/books/WCMS_817572/lang--en/index.htm> accessed 21 May 2024.

IMF, 'Commodity Price Shocks and Imperfect Pass-Through: A Panel Event Study' (IMF Working Paper 22/121, 2022).

J-PAL, 'Roll Call: Getting Children into School' (2017) available at <https://www.povertyactionlab.org/policy-insight/roll-call-getting-children-school> accessed 21 May 2024.

Kabeer N, 'Gender Equality, Economic Growth, and Women's Agency: The "Endless Variety" and "Monotonous Similarity" of Patriarchal Constraints' (2015) 22(1) *Feminist Economics* 295–321 https://doi.org/10.1080/13545701.2015.1090009.

Kathiresan A, *Strategies for Sustainable Crop Intensification in Rwanda* (Ministry of Agriculture and Animal Resources 2011).

Koeswayo PS, Handoyo S and Hasyir DA, 'Investigating the Relationship Between Public Governance and the Corruption Perception Index' (2024) 10(1) *Cogent Social Sciences* https://doi.org/10.1080/23311886.2024.2342513.

Longhurst R, 'Introduction: Universal Development – Research and Practice' (2017) available at <https://bulletin.ids.ac.uk/index.php/idsbo/article/download/2898/Online%20article?inline=1> accessed 20 May 2024.

Mo Ibrahim Foundation, 'Ibrahim Index of African Governance' (2020) available at <https://mo.ibrahim.foundation/iiag> accessed 21 May 2024.

Oqubay A, 'Industrial Policy and Late Industrialization in Ethiopia' (2018) African Development Bank Working Paper Series No 303.

Payne G, Durand-Lasserve A and Rakodi C, 'The Limits of Land Titling and Home Ownership' (2009) 21(2) *Environment and Urbanization* 443–462.

Plan International, 'Teenage Pregnancy in Sierra Leone' (2021) available at <https://plan-international.org/publications/teenage-pregnancy-sierra-leone> accessed 21 May 2024.

Sindzingre AN, 'The Ambivalent Impact of Commodities: Structural Change or Status Quo in Sub-Saharan Africa?' (2013) 20(1) *South African Journal of International Affairs* 23–55 https://doi.org/10.1080/10220461.2013.780327.

Slavchevska V et al, 'Beyon Ownership: Women's and Men's Land Rights in Sub-Saharan Africa' (2021) 49(1) *Oxford Development Studies* 2–22 https://doi.org/10.1080/13600818.2020.1818714.

Suliman AH and Mollick AV, 'Human Capital Development, War and Foreign Direct Investment in Sub-Saharan Africa' (2009) 37(1) *Oxford Development Studies* 47–61 https://doi.org/10.1080/13600810802660828.

The World Bank, 'Accelerating Poverty Reduction in Africa' (2019) available at <https://documents.worldbank.org/en/publication/documents-reports/documentdetail/985381570682302500/accelerating-poverty-reduction-in-africa> accessed 13 May 2024.

The World Bank, 'Facing Forward: Schooling for Learning in Africa' (2018) available at <https://www.worldbank.org/en/region/afr/publication/facing-forward-schooling-for-learning-in-africa> accessed 20 May 2024.

The World Bank, *Poverty and Shared Prosperity 2022: Correcting Course* (The World Bank 2022) available at <https://documents.worldbank.org/en/publication/documents-reports/documentdetail/099750110062235316/idu07dfa30ac034520434108ecd0db3a26cd8be6> accessed 20 May 2024.

UNCTAD, 'State of Commodity Dependence 2021' (2022) UNCTAD/DITC/COM/2021/2.

UNDP, *Gender Inequality Index (GII)* (UNDP 2022) available at <https://hdr.undp.org/data-center/thematic-composite-indices/gender-inequality-index#/indicies/GII> accessed 20 May 2024.

UNDP, *Impact of COVID-19 in Africa* (UNDP 2020) available at <https://www.undp.org/africa/publications/impact-covid-19-africa> accessed 21 May 2024.

UNDP, *Structural Adjustment and Poverty in Sub-Saharan Africa* (UNDP 1998) available at <https://digitallibrary.un.org/record/101597> accessed 19 May 2024.

UNDP, *UNDP Regional Report on HIV/AIDS in Sub-Saharan Africa* (UNDP 2018) available at <https://www.undp.org/publications/undp-regional-report-hiv/aids-sub-saharan-africa> accessed 20 May 2024.

UNEP, *Responding to Climate Change* (UNEP 2024) available at <https://www.unep.org/regions/africa/regional-initiatives/responding-climate-change> accessed 13 May 2024.

UNESCO, *Global Education Monitoring Report 2020: Inclusion and Education: All Means All* (UNESCO 2020) available at <https://en.unesco.org/gem-report/report/2020/inclusion> accessed 21 May 2024.

UNESCO, *Out-of-School Children and Youth in Sub-Saharan Africa* (UNESCO 2021) available at <https://www.unesco.org/gem-report/en/2022-out-school> accessed 20 May 2024.

UNESCO, *Teacher Policy Development Guide* (UNESCO 2019) available at <https://unesdoc.unesco.org/ark:/48223/pf0000370966> accessed 21 May 2024.

UN-Habitat, 'Slum Almanac 2015-2016' (2016) available at <https://unhabitat.org/slum-almanac-2015-2016> accessed 21 May 2024.

UNICEF, *Collecting Water is Often a Colossal Waste of Time for Women and Girls* (UNICEF 2016) available at <https://www.unicef.org/press-releases/unicef-collecting-water-often-colossal-waste-time-women-and-girls> accessed 20 May 2024.

WHO, *The Global Burden of Disease: 2004 Update* (WHO 2008) available at <https://www.who.int/publications/i/item/9789241563710> accessed 20 May 2024.

WHO, *2022 Global Nutrition Report: 2022 Regional Profile for Sub-Saharan Africa* (WHO 2023).

WHO, *The State of Health in the WHO African Region: An Analysis of the Status of Health, Health Services and Health Systems in the Context of the Sustainable Development Goals* (WHO 2018) available at <https://www.afro.who.int/publications/state-health-who-african-region> accessed 21 May 2024.

WHO, *Water, Sanitation and Hygiene* (WHO 2023) available at <https://www.who.int/data/gho/data/themes/water-sanitation-and-hygiene> accessed 20 May 2024.

WHO, *World Malaria Report 2021* (WHO 2021) available at <https://www.who.int/teams/global-malaria-programme/reports/world-malaria-report-2021> accessed 21 May 2024.

WHO and UNICEF, *2022 Progress on Household Drinking Water, Sanitation and Hygiene* (WHO and UNICEF 2022) available at <https://www.unicef.org/documents/unicef-wash-annual-publication-catalogue-2022> accessed 20 May 2024.

World Bank, *Ethiopia's Productive Safety Net Program (PSNP)* (World Bank 2020) available at <https://www.worldbank.org/en/news/feature/2019/01/17/ethiopias-productive-safety-net-program-psnp> accessed 21 May 2024.

Yeboah IEA, 'Capitalism and Sub-Saharan African Human Capital' (2016) 16(1) *African Identities* 67–86 https://doi.org/10.1080/14725843.2017.1332983.

5 Access to Healthcare and Education in Sub-Saharan Africa

Introduction

Access to healthcare and education is a fundamental human right and a crucial determinant of an individual's overall well-being and quality of life. The right to an adequate standard of living, as enshrined in various international human rights instruments, encompasses the right to access essential services such as healthcare and education.[1] However, in Sub-Saharan Africa (SSA), ensuring equitable access to these services remains a significant challenge, with far-reaching implications for the realisation of the right to an adequate standard of living.

Despite progress made in recent decades, SSA continues to face multifaceted barriers that hinder adequate access to healthcare and education. These challenges are rooted in a complex interplay of socio-economic, political, and structural factors, including inadequate infrastructure, limited resources, insufficient funding, geographical remoteness, cultural and gender biases, and disparities in the distribution of services.[2] The persistence of these barriers has resulted in stark inequalities in access to healthcare and education, with marginalised and vulnerable populations often bearing the brunt of these disparities.

The implications of inadequate access to healthcare and education in SSA are far-reaching and profound. Poor health outcomes, including high rates of maternal and child mortality, communicable diseases, and malnutrition, are inextricably linked to limited access to quality healthcare services.[3] Similarly,

1 United Nations General Assembly, 'International Covenant on Economic, Social and Cultural Rights' (1966) UN Treaty Series, vol. 993, Article 11.
2 Zemenu Tadesse Tessema et al, 'Determinants of Accessing Healthcare in Sub-Saharan Africa: A Mixed-Effect Analysis of Recent Demographic and Health Surveys from 36 Countries' (2022) 12(1) *BMJ Open* DOI: https://doi.org/10.1136%2Fbmjopen-2021-054397.
3 World Health Organization, 'World Health Statistics 2022' (2022) available at < https://www.who.int/news/item/20-05-2022-world-health-statistics-2022> accessed 28 May 2024.

DOI: 10.4324/9781032628974-5

restricted access to education perpetuates a cycle of poverty and inequality, limiting opportunities for social mobility and economic empowerment.[4]

Recognising the critical importance of addressing these challenges, governments, international organisations, and civil society actors in SSA have undertaken various efforts to improve access to healthcare and education. These initiatives range from policy interventions and institutional reforms to targeted programmes and community-based initiatives.[5] However, the effectiveness and sustainability of these efforts have been uneven, underscoring the need for a comprehensive and holistic approach to tackling the multidimensional barriers to access.

This chapter aims to provide a critical examination of the challenges and complexities surrounding access to healthcare and education in SSA, within the context of the right to an adequate standard of living. By analysing the socio-economic, political, and structural barriers, exploring the implications of inadequate access, and evaluating efforts to expand access to these essential services, the chapter seeks to contribute to a nuanced understanding of these vital issues and inform strategies for advancing the realisation of the right to an adequate standard of living in the region.

Barriers to Access to Healthcare in SSA

Inadequate Healthcare Infrastructure and Resources

One of the most notable barriers to accessing healthcare in SSA is the inadequate healthcare infrastructure and limited resources. Many countries in the region face a critical shortage of healthcare facilities, medical equipment, and essential medicines, particularly in rural and remote communities.[6] The scarcity of healthcare infrastructure is compounded by the uneven distribution of available resources, with urban areas often having better access to healthcare services compared to rural and marginalised communities.[7]

4 UNESCO, 'Global Education Monitoring Report 2020: Inclusion and Education: All Means All' (UNESCO, 2020) available at < https://www.unesco.org/en/articles/global-education-monitoring-gem-report-2020> accessed 28 May 2024.

5 Kathleen Beegle and Luc Christiaensen (eds), *Accelerating Poverty Reduction in Africa* (World Bank, 2019) available at < https://elibrary.worldbank.org/doi/abs/10.1596/978-1-4648-1232-3> accessed 28 May 2024.

6 Augustine Edobor Arimoro, 'The Corona Virus (COVID-19) Pandemic and the Challenge of Healthcare Infrastructure in Nigeria: What Role for Public-Private Partnerships?' (2020) 3 *Theoretical and Applied Law* 19-35 available at < https://www.taljournal.ru/jour/article/view/55?locale=en_US> accessed 28 May 2024. See also Yohannes Kinfu et al., 'The Health Worker Shortage in Africa: Are Enough Physicians and Nurses Being Trained?' (2009) 87 *Bulletin of the World Health Organization* 225.

7 Margaret K Kruk et al, 'High Quality Health Systems in the Sustainable Development Goals Era: Time for a Revolution' (2018) 6(11) *The Lancelot Global Health* DOI: https://doi.org/10.1016/S2214-109X(18)30386-3.

The shortage of healthcare workers is another critical challenge in SSA. The region bears a disproportionate burden of the global healthcare workforce crisis, with an estimated deficit of 4.2 million healthcare workers.[8] This shortage is worsened by the uneven distribution of healthcare professionals with a concentration of skilled medical personnel in urban areas and a dearth of healthcare workers in rural and underserved communities.[9] The inadequate number and distribution of healthcare workers have severe implications for the quality of accessibility of healthcare services, leading to long waiting times, overcrowded facilities, and limited capacity to provide comprehensive care.[10]

Moreover, the lack of essential medical equipment and supplies further hampers the delivery of quality healthcare services in SSA. Many healthcare facilities in the region face chronic shortages of basic medical supplies, such as syringes, gloves, and bandages, as well as essential medicines and diagnostic tools.[11] This scarcity of resources compromises the ability of healthcare providers to effectively diagnose, treat, and manage various health conditions, leading to poor health outcomes and increased morbidity and mortality rates.[12]

The inadequate healthcare infrastructure and limited resources in SSA are rooted in a complex interplay of factors, including insufficient government spending on healthcare, competing development priorities, and weak health systems governance.[13] Addressing these challenges requires sustained investments in healthcare infrastructure, strengthening supply chain management systems, and implementing policies to attract and retain healthcare workers in underserved areas.[14] Collaborative efforts between governments, international organisations, and civil society actors are crucial in mobilising resources and

8 WHO, *Global Strategy on Human Resources for Health: Workforce 2030* (WHO, 2016) available at < https://www.who.int/publications/i/item/9789241511131> accessed 28 May 2024.

9 Mel Ainscow, 'Promoting Inclusion and Equity in Education: Lessons from International Experiences' (2020) 6(1) *Nordic Journal of Studies in Education Policy* 7-16 DOI: https://doi.org/10.1080/20020317.2020.1729587

10 Moses Mulumba et al, 'Perceptions and Experiences of Access to Public Healthcare by People with Disabilities and Older People in Uganda' (2014) 13(76) *International Journal of Equity Health* DOI: https://doi.org/10.1186/s12939-014-0076-4

11 Gilbert Kombe et al, 'The Human and Financial Resource Requirements for Scaling UP HIV/AIDS Services in Ethiopia' (2005) available at <chrome-extension://efaidnbmnnnibpcajpcglclefindmkaj/https://pdf.usaid.gov/pdf_docs/Pnadc109.pdf> accessed 28 May 2024.

12 Christopher J. L. Murray and Julio Frenk, 'Ranking 37th — Measuring the Performance of the U.S. Health Care System' (2010) 362 *New England Journal of Medicine* 98-99 DOI: 10.1056/NEJMp0910064.

13 WHO, Public Spending on Health: A Closer Look at Global Trends (WHO, 2018) available at < https://www.who.int/publications/i/item/WHO-HIS-HGF-HFWorkingPaper-18.3> accessed 28 May 2024.

14 Gilles Dussault and Maria Cristina Franceschini, 'Not Enough There, Too Many Here: Understanding Geographical Imbalances in the Distribution of the Health Workforce' (2006) 5 *Human Resources for Health* 12 DOI: https://doi.org/10.1186%2F1478-4491-4-12.

expertise to bridge the gaps in healthcare infrastructure and ensure access to quality healthcare services.[15]

Financial Barriers and Out-of-Pocket Payments

Financial barriers and out-of-pocket payments pose significant challenges to accessing healthcare in SSA. Despite efforts to expand health insurance coverage and implement universal health coverage (UHC) policies, many individuals and households in the region continue to face substantial financial barriers to accessing healthcare services.[16]

Out-of-pocket payments, which refer to direct payments made by individuals to healthcare providers at the time of service use, remain the predominant mode of healthcare financing in SSA.[17] High out-of-pocket expenditures can lead to catastrophic health spending, where households are forced to spend a significant amount of their income on healthcare, pushing them into poverty or deepening their existing poverty.[18] The financial burden of out-of-pocket payments disproportionately affects low-income and vulnerable populations, who often have to choose between seeking healthcare and meeting other essential needs such as food and education.[19]

The reliance on out-of-pocket payments in SSA is rooted in the limited coverage and inadequate funding of health insurance schemes. Many countries in the region have fragmented health insurance systems, with a mix of public, private, and community-based schemes that often cover only a small proportion of the population.[20] The limited coverage of health insurance leaves a significant proportion of the population, particularly those in the informal sector and rural areas, without financial protection against healthcare costs.[21]

15 Rifat Atun et al., 'Health-System Reform and Universal Health Coverage in Latin America' (2015) 385 *The Lancet* 1230 DOI: https://doi.org/10.1016/s0140-6736(14)61646-9.

16 Diane McIntyre et al., 'What Are the Economic Consequences for Households of Illness and of Paying for Health Care in Low- and Middle-Income Country Contexts?' (2006) 62(4) *Social Science & Medicine* 858-865 DOI: https://doi.org/10.1016/j.socscimed.2005.07.001.

17 WHO, *Global Monitoring Report on Financial Protection in Health 2019* (WHO, 2019) available at < https://www.who.int/publications/i/item/9789240003958> accessed 28 May 2024.

18 Adam Wagstaff et al., 'Progress on Catastrophic Health Spending in 133 Countries: A Retrospective Observational Study' (2018) 6(2) *The Lancet Global Health* e169-e179 DOI: https://doi.org/10.1016/s2214-109x(17)30429-1.

19 Susan C Ifeagwu et al, 'Health Financing for Universal Health Coverage in Sub-Saharan Africa: A Systematic Review' (2021) 6(8) *Global Health Research Policy* DOI: https://doi.org/10.1186%2Fs41256-021-00190-7.

20 WHO, *Strategic Purchasing for Universal Health Coverage: Key Policy Issues and Questions: A Summary from Expert and Practitioners' Discussions* (WHO, 2017) available at < https://iris.who.int/handle/10665/259423> accessed 28 May 2024.

21 Chima A Onoka, 'Promoting Universal Financial Protection: Constraints and Enabling Factors in Scaling-Up Coverage with Social Health Insurance in Nigeria' (2013) 11 *Health Research and Systems* DOI: https://doi.org/10.1186/1478-4505-11-20

Moreover, even when individuals are covered by health insurance, they may still face financial barriers due to high co-payments, deductibles, and out-of-pocket expenses.[22] Theses additional costs can deter individuals from seeking necessary healthcare services, leading to delayed or foregone care and adverse health outcomes.[23]

Addressing financial barriers and reducing out-of-pocket payments requires multipronged approaches that include expanding health insurance coverage, increasing public spending on healthcare, and implementing policies to protect vulnerable populations from catastrophic health expenditures.[24] Governments in SSA need to prioritise investments in UHC and develop sustainable health financing mechanisms that pool resources and promote risk-sharing across the population.[25] Additionally, targeted interventions, such as fee waivers, subsidies, and conditional cash transfers, can help alleviate the financial burden on low-income and marginalised groups, ensuring that no one is left behind in essential healthcare services.[26]

Socio-Cultural Barriers and Gender Disparities

Socio-cultural barriers and gender disparities play a significant role in shaping access to healthcare in SSA. These barriers are deeply rooted in social norms, cultural beliefs, and traditional practices that influence health-seeking behaviours and perpetuate inequalities in access to healthcare services.[27]

Gender disparities in access tohealthcare are pronounced particularly in SSA, with women and girls often facing greater barriers compared to men and boys. Gender norms and power dynamics within households and communities can limit women's autonomy in making decisions about their health and

22 John E. Ataguba, 'Reassessing Catastrophic Health-Care Payments with a Nigerian Case Study' (2012) 10 *Health Economics, Policy and Law* 309-326 DOI: https://doi.org/10.1017/s1744133110000356.

23 Prakash Babu Kodali, 'Achieving Universal Health Coverage in Low -and -Middle-Income Countries: Challenges for Policy Post-Pandemic and Beyond' (2023) 16 *Risk Management Healthcare Policy* 607-621 DOI: https://doi.org/10.2147%2FRMHP.S366759.

24 Ellen Van de Poel et al., 'Can Vouchers Deliver? An Evaluation of Subsidies for Maternal Health Care in Cambodia' (2014) 92 Bulletin of the World Health Organization 331.

25 Sarit Rout, 'State Led Innovations for Achieving Universal Health Coverage in a Low Resource Setting Odisha, India: Opportunities and Challenges' (2021) 8(5) International Journal of Community Medicine and Public Health 2338-2345 DOI: http://dx.doi.org/10.18203/2394-6040.ijcmph20211755.

26 G Sen and P Ostlin, 'Gender Inequality in Health: Why It Exists and How We Can Change It' (2008) 3(1) *Global Public Health* 1-12 DOI: https://doi.org/10.1080/17441690801900795.

27 Eleanor E MacPherson et al, 'Gender Equity and Sexual Reproductive Health in Eastern and Southern Africa: A Critical Overview of the Literature' (2014) 7(1) *Global Health Action* DOI: https://doi.org/10.3402/gha.v7.23717.

seeking healthcare services.[28] Women may face restrictions on their mobility, requiring permission from male family members to visit healthcare facilities, which can delay or prevent them from receiving timely care.[29] Additionally, the disproportionate burden of unpaid care work and household responsibilities often falls on women, limiting their ability to prioritise their own health needs.[30]

Socio-cultural beliefs and traditional practices can also act as barriers to accessing healthcare in SSA. In some communities, there may be a preference for traditional healers and alternative forms of medicine, leading to delays in seeking formal healthcare services.[31] Stigma and discrimination associated with certain health conditions, such as HIV/AIDS and mental health disorders, can deter individuals from seeking care due to fear of social exclusion and marginalisation.[32] Moreover, cultural taboos surrounding sexual and reproductive health can hinder access to essential services, particularly for adolescents and unmarried women.[33] Language and communication barriers can further exacerbate socio-cultural barriers to accessing healthcare in SSA. Many healthcare providers may not speak the local languages or dialects, making it difficult for patients to communicate their health concerns and understand medical advice.[34] This language barrier can be particularly challenging for marginalised and indigenous communities, who may face additional discrimination and exclusion from healthcare services.[35]

28 Esther E. Anyangwe, 'Promoting Gender Equity in Access to HIV Prevention, Care and Treatment in Sub-Saharan Africa' in Fredrick Nzwili (ed), 'Where Are the Men?: Partnering with Men and Boys for Health and Gender Equity in Sub-Saharan Africa' (Hilton Publishing, 2009).

29 Audrey M Kalindi, 'Gender Inequities in Women's Access to Maternal Health Care Utilisation in Zambia: A Qualitative Analysis' (2023) *BMC Pregnancy and Childbirth* 755 DOI: https://doi.org/10.1186/s12884-023-06078-3.

30 Sujit Roy, 'Unpaid Care Work: A Critical Analysis' (2022) available at < https://www.researchgate.net/publication/366642765_Unpaid_Care_Work_A_Critical_Analysis> accessed 28 May 2024.

31 Ama de-Graft Aikins et al, 'Explanatory Models of Diabetes in Urban Poor Communities in Accra, Ghana' (2015) 20(4) *Ethn Health* 391-408 DOI: https://doi.org/10.1080/13557858.2014.921896.

32 Blessings N Kaunda-Khangamwa et al, 'Adolescents Living with HIV, Complex Needs and Resilience in Blantyre, Malawi' (2020) 17(1) *AIDS Res Ther* DOI: https://doi.org/10.1186/s12981-020-00292-1.

33 John Kuumuori Ganle, 'Why Muslim Women in Northern Ghana Do Not Use Skilled Maternal Healthcare Services at Health Facilities: A Qualitative Study' (2015) 15(10) *BMC International Health and Human Rights* DOI: 10.1186/s12914-015-0048-9.

34 Katrina L Whitaker et al, 'Addressing Language as a Barrier to Healthcare Access and Quality' (2022) 72 *British Journal of General Practice* 4-5 DOI: https://doi.org/10.3399/bjgp22X718013.

35 Kerrie Pickering, 'Indigenous Peoples and the COVID-19 Pandemic: A Systematic Scoping Review' (2023) 18(3) *Environ Res Lett* DOI: 10.1088/1748-9326/acb804.

Addressing socio-cultural barriers and gender disparities in access to healthcare requires a multifaceted approach that engages communities, challenges harmful social norms, and promotes gender equality. Interventions such as community health education programmes, culturally sensitive healthcare services, and the training of health professionals in gender-responsive care can help break down barriers.[36] Additionally, empowering women and girls through education, economic opportunities, and decision-making power can enhance their agency in seeking healthcare and advocating for their health rights.[37] Collaborative efforts between governments, civil society organisations, and community leaders are essential in fostering an enabling environment that promotes equitable access to healthcare, regardless of gender, cultural background, or social status.[38]

Barriers to Access to Education in SSA

Insufficient Educational Infrastructure and Resources

Access to education in SSA is significantly hindered by insufficient educational infrastructure and resources. Many countries in the region face a critical shortage of school facilities, classrooms, and educational materials, particularly in rural areas and marginalised communities.[39] The scarcity of educational infrastructure is compounded by the rapid population growth and increasing demand for education, putting pressure on already overstretched education systems.[40]

The shortage of qualified teachers is another major challenge in SSA. The region has the highest pupil-teacher ratios globally, with an average of 42 pupils per teacher in primary education and 24 pupils per teacher in secondary education.[41] The high pupil-teacher ratios are worsened by the uneven distribution of teachers, with a concentration of qualified educators in urban areas and a dearth of teachers in rural and remote communities.[42] The inadequate

36 R Dhatt et al, 'The Role of Women's Leadership and Gender Equity in Leadership and Health System Strengthening' (2017) 17(2) *Glob Health Epidemiol Genom* DOI: https://doi.org/10.1017/gheg.2016.22.

37 Rezwanul Haque et al, 'Women's Empowerment and Fertility Decision-Making in 53 Low and Middle Resource Countries: A Pooled Analysis of Demographic and Health Surveys' (2021) 11 *BMJ Open* DOI: https://dx.doi.org/10.1136/bmjopen-2020-045952.

38 Geordan Shannon et al, 'Gender Equality in Science, Medicine, and Global Health: Where Are We At and Why Does it Matter?' (2019) 393(10171) *The Lancet* P560-569 DOI: https://doi.org/10.1016/S0140-6736(18)33135-0.

39 World Bank, 'World Development Report 2018: Learning to Realize Education's Promise' (World Bank, 2018) available at < https://www.worldbank.org/en/publication/wdr2018> accessed 28 May 2024.

40 UNESCO Institute for Statistics, *Education in Africa* (UNESCO, 2019).

41 UNESCO Institute for Statistics, *SDG 4 Data Book: Global Education Indicators 2019* (UNESCO, 2019).

42 Kwame Akyeampong et al., 'Access to Basic Education in Ghana: The Evidence and the Issues' (CREATE Country Analytic Report, 2007).

number and distribution of teachers have severe implications for the quality of education, leading to overcrowded classrooms, limited individual attention, and reduced learning outcomes.[43]

Moreover, the lack of essential educational resources, such as textbooks, learning materials, and technology, further hampers the delivery of quality education in SSA. Many schools in the region face chronic shortages of basic educational supplies, hindering the ability of teachers to effectively deliver lessons and engage students in meaningful learning experiences.[44] The scarcity of educational resources is particularly acute in subjects such as science, technology, engineering, and mathematics (STEM), where the lack of laboratory equipment and practical learning opportunities can discourage students from pursuing these fields.[45]

The insufficient educational infrastructure and resources in SSA are rooted in a complex interplay of factors, including limited government funding for education, competing development priorities, and weak education sector governance.[46] Addressing these challenges requires sustained investments in school construction, teacher training and recruitment, and the provision of essential educational resources.[47] Collaborative efforts between governments, international organisations, and civil society actors are crucial in mobilising resources and expertise to bridge the gaps in educational infrastructure and ensure equitable access to quality education for all children in the region.[48]

Economic Barriers and Opportunity Costs

Economic barriers and opportunity costs pose significant challenges to accessing education in SSA. Despite efforts to abolish school fees and implement free primary education policies, many children and families in the region continue to face substantial economic barriers to accessing education.[49]

43 Moses Oketch and Caine Rolleston, 'Policies on Free Primary and Secondary Education in East Africa: Retrospect and Prospect' (2007) 5 *Review of Research in Education* 131.

44 Birger Fredriksen, 'Education Resource Mobilization and Use in Developing Countries: Scope for Efficiency Gains through More Strategic Use of Education Aid' (Results for Development Institute, 2011).

45 Peter Hubber and Marissa Rollnick, 'Tensions in the Teaching and Learning of Science in Developing Countries' in Mansoor Niaz and Bill Atweh (eds), 'Science Education in Developing Countries' (Springer, 2021).

46 Keith M. Lewin, 'Strategies for Sustainable Financing of Secondary Education in Sub-Saharan Africa' (World Bank, 2008).

47 Pauline Rose and Benjamin Alcott, 'How Can Education Systems Become Equitable by 2030?' (DFID Think Pieces: Learning and Equity, 2015).

48 Mathias Bashir et al., 'Facing Forward: Schooling for Learning in Africa' (World Bank, 2018).

49 Alain Mingat, Blandine Ledoux, and Ramahatra Rakotomalala, *Developing Post-Primary Education in Sub-Saharan Africa: Assessing the Financial Sustainability of Alternative Pathways* (World Bank, 2010) available at < https://openknowledge.worldbank.org/bitstream/handle/10986/2429/538780PUB0post101Official0Use0Only1.pdf> accessed 28 May 2024.

The direct costs associated with education, such as school fees, uniforms, textbooks, and transportation, can be prohibitively expensive for low-income households, forcing families to make difficult choices between sending their children to school and meeting other essential needs.[50] Even in countries where primary education is officially free, informal fees and hidden costs can still deter poor families from enrolling their children and wards in school.[51]

Moreover, the opportunity costs of education, particularly for children from economically disadvantaged backgrounds, can be a significant barrier to accessing education in SSA. In many households, children are expected to contribute to the family's income through paid work or domestic labour, making it difficult for them to attend school regularly.[52] The economic pressures faced by poor families can lead to child labour, early marriage, and other practices that negatively impact children's education and overall well-being.[53]

Gender disparities in access to education are also closely linked to economic barriers and opportunity costs. In many communities, girls are more likely to be kept out of school to perform domestic work, making it difficult for them to attend school regularly.[54] The economic constraints faced by families can perpetuate gender inequalities in education, limiting girls' opportunities for learning and future economic empowerment.[55]

Addressing economic barriers and opportunity costs requires an approach that will ensure that there is a mix of interventions, social protection measures and broader poverty reduction strategies. Governments in SSA need to prioritise investments in education and develop sustainable financing mechanisms that ensure equitable access to quality education for all children, regardless of their socio-economic background.[56] Targeted interventions, such

50 Sudhanshu Handa et al., 'Can Unconditional Cash Transfers Raise Long-Term Living Standards? Evidence from Zambia' (2018) 133 Journal of Development Economics 42-65 DOI: https://doi.org/10.1016/j.jdeveco.2018.01.008.

51 Manos Antoninis, 'Tackling the Largest Global Education Challenge? Secular and Religious Education in Northern Nigeria' (2014) 59 *World Development* 82-92 DOI: https://doi.org/10.1016/j.worlddev.2014.01.017.

52 Nicola Jones et al., *Stemming Girls' Chronic Poverty: Catalysing Development Change by Building Just Social Institutions* (Chronic Poverty Research Centre, 2010).

53 Renu Singh and Protap Mukherjee, *Comparison of the Effects of Government and Private Preschool Education on the Developmental Outcomes of Children: Evidence from Young Lives India* (Young Lives, 2017) available at < https://www.younglives.org.uk/publications/comparison-effects-government-and-private-preschool-education-developmental-outcomes> accessed 28 May 2024.

54 J Hutchinson and Kelly Kettlewell, 'Education to Employment: Complicated Transitions in a Changing World' (2015) 57(2) *Educational Research* 113-120 DOI: https://doi.org/10.1080/00131881.2015.1030848.

55 UNESCO, 'Pricing the Right to Education: The Cost of Reaching New Targets by 2030' (2015) Policy Paper 18 available at < https://unesdoc.unesco.org/ark:/48223/pf0000232197> accessed 28 May 2024.

56 Shelley Clark and Sarah Brauner-Otto, 'Divorce in Sub-Saharan Africa: Are Unions Becoming Less Stable?' (2015) 77 *Population and Development Review* 583 DOI: https://doi.org/10.1111/j.1728-4457.2015.00086.x.

as scholarships, cash transfers, and feeding programmes, can help alleviate the financial burden on low-income families and incentivise school attendance.[57]Additionally, efforts to promote gender equality in education, such as community sensitisation campaigns and girls' empowerment programmes, can help challenge social norms and practices that disadvantage girl-child education.[58]

Socio-Cultural Barriers and Marginalisation

Socio-cultural barriers and marginalisation play a significant role in shaping access to education in SSA. These barriers are deeply rooted in social norms, cultural beliefs, and traditional practices that influence attitudes towards education and perpetuate inequalities in educational opportunities.[59]

Gender norms and discriminatory practices are major socio-cultural barriers to education in SSA, particularly for girls and young women. In many communities, traditional gender roles and expectations prioritise girls' domestic responsibilities and early marriage over their education. Girls may face pressure to drop out of school to fulfil household duties, care for siblings, or enter into child marriage, limiting their opportunities for learning and personal development.[60] Moreover, the stigma surrounding teenage pregnancy and the lack of support for young mothers can further hinder girls' access to education and lead to high dropout rates.[61]

Socio-cultural beliefs and attitudes towards education can also act as barriers to accessing education in SSA.[62] In some communities, there may be a perception that formal education is less valuable than traditional knowledge and skills, leading to a lack of parental support and investment in children's education.[63] Furthermore, the perceived low returns to education, particularly

57 Rusol Adil Naji Al-Tameemi, 'Determinants of Poor Academic Performance among Undergraduate Students – A Systematic Review 4 *International Journal of Educational Research Open* DOI: https://doi.org/10.1016/j.ijedro.2023.100232.

58 Ibid.

59 Joerg Baten et al, 'Educational Gender Inequality in Sub-Saharan Africa: A Long-Term Perspective' (2021) 47(3) *Population and Development Review* 813-849 DOI: https://doi.org/10.1111/padr.12430.

60 Anita Raj, 'When the Mother is a Child: The Impact of Child Marriage on the Health and Human Rights of Girls' (2010) 95(110 *Arch Dis Child* 931-935 DOI: https://doi.org/10.1136/adc.2009.178707.

61 Faith Mkwananzi and Melanie Walker, 'Contextualizing the Role of Education in Female Employment in Sub-Saharan Africa: The Case of Kenya and South Africa' (2015) 128 International Journal of Educational Development 102511.

62 Alison Joynes and Catherine Jere, 'Teenage Pregnancy and Motherhood in Sub-Saharan Africa: A Systematic Review of Enablers' (2022) 18 *PLOS ONE* e0264722.

63 Angela W. Little, 'The Leap to Literacy: Transitions from Oral to Literate Societies' (2022) 84 *Prospects* 35.

in contexts of high unemployment and limited economic opportunities, can discourage families from prioritising their children's schooling.[64]

Linguistic and cultural diversity can also pose challenges to accessing education in SSA. Many education systems in the region are based on colonial language policies and curricula that may not reflect the diverse linguistic and cultural backgrounds of students.[65] This can lead to language barriers, cultural disconnection, and a sense of alienation among students from marginalised communities, contributing to lower educational attainment and higher dropout rates.[66]

Addressing socio-cultural barriers and marginalisation in education requires a multfaceted approach that engages communities, challenges harmful social norms, and promotes inclusive education policies. Interventions such as community sensitisation campaigns, girls' empowerment programmes, and the promotion of gender-responsive pedagogy can help break down these barriers and create an enabling environment for all children to access and thrive in education.[67] Additionally, efforts to develop culturally relevant curricula, promote mother tongue instruction, and foster inclusive learning environments can help address the needs of marginalised communities and promote equitable access to education.[68]

Efforts to Improve Access to Healthcare and Education in SSA

Policy Interventions and Institutional Reforms

Recognising the critical importance of improving access to healthcare and education in Sub-Saharan Africa (SSA), governments, international organisations, and civil society actors have undertaken various policy interventions and institutional reforms aimed at addressing the multifaceted barriers to access.[69]

64 Caine Rolleston and Zoe James, 'The Role of Schooling in Skill Development: Evidence from Young Lives in Ethiopia, India, Peru and Vietnam' (2014) UNESCO Education For All Global Monitoring Report.

65 Barbara Trudell, *The Impact of Language Policy and Practice on Children's Learning: Evidence from Eastern and Southern Africa* (UNICEF, 2016) available at < https://www.unicef.org/esa/sites/unicef.org.esa/files/2018-09/UNICEF-2016-Language-and-Learning-Full-Report.pdf> accessed 28 May 2024.

66 Birgit Brock-Utne, 'Language and Inequality: Global Challenges to Education' (2020) 42(5) *Compare: A Journal of Comparative and International Education* 773-793 DOI: https://doi.org/10.1080/03057925.2012.706453.

67 UNGEI, 'A Whole School Approach to Prevent School-Related Gender-Based Violence: Minimum Standards and Monitoring Framework' (UNGEI, 2018).

68 Carol Benson, 'Learners' Own Languages as Key to Achieving Sustainable Development Goal 4: Multilingual Education in Sub-Saharan Africa' (2019) *Language Issues in Comparative Education* 69.

69 Robert Yates, 'Universal Health Coverage: Progressive Taxes Are Key' (2015) 386 *The Lancet* 227-279 DOI: https://doi.org/10.1016/s0140-6736(15)60868-6.

In the healthcare sector, efforts to expand access to essential health services have focused on strengthening primary healthcare systems, implementing universal health coverage (UHC) policies, and increasing public spending on healthcare. Many countries in SSA have adopted UHC as a policy goal, aiming to ensure that all individuals have access to quality healthcare services without facing financial hardship.[70] Governments have implemented various financing mechanisms, such as national health insurance schemes, community-based health insurance, and performance-based financing, to improve the affordability and sustainability of healthcare services.[71]

Moreover, there has been a growing recognition of the importance of addressing the social determinants of health and promoting health equity in SSA. Policy interventions have increasingly focused on intersectoral collaboration and the integration of health considerations into broader development policies, such as education, agriculture, and social protection.[72] Community-based interventions, such as the training and deployment of community health workers, have been implemented to bridge the gap between formal healthcare services and marginalised communities, improving access to essential health services and health education.[73]

In the education sector, efforts to expand access to quality education have focused on abolishing school fees, increasing public spending on education, and improving the quality and relevance of education.[74] Many countries in SSA have introduced free primary education policies, aiming to remove financial barriers and ensure that all children have access to basic education.[75] Governments have also invested in school infrastructure, teacher training, and the provision of learning materials to improve the quality of education and create conducive learning environments.[76]

Furthermore, there has been a growing emphasis on promoting inclusive education and addressing the needs of marginalised and disadvantaged groups in SSA. Policy interventions have targeted gender disparities in education,

70 WHO, *Universal Health Coverage in Africa: A Framework for Action* (WHO, 2016).

71 Inke Mathauer et al., 'Extending Universal Health Coverage in Sub-Saharan Africa: An Assessment of Provider Payment Mechanisms' (2022) 22 Health Policy and Planning 817.

72 Kumanan Rasanathan et al., 'Primary Health Care and the Social Determinants of Health: Essential and Complementary Approaches for Reducing Inequities in Health' (2011) 65 Journal of Epidemiology & Community Health 656-660. DOI: https://doi.org/10.1136/jech.2009.093914.

73 Maryse C. Kok et al., 'How Does Context Influence Performance of Community Health Workers in Low- and Middle-Income Countries? Evidence from the Literature' (2015) 10 Health Research Policy and Systems 1 DOI: https://doi.org/10.1186/s12961-015-0001-3.

74 Birger Fredriksen, Sukhdeep Brar and Michael Trucano, *Getting Textbooks to Every Child in Sub-Saharan Africa: Strategies for Addressing the High Cost and Low Availability Problem* (World Bank, 2015).

75 UNESCO, Education for All 2000-2015: Achievements and Challenges (UNESCO, 2015).

76 World Bank, World Development Report 2018: Learning to Realize Education's Promise (World Bank, 2018).

aiming to increase girls' enrolment and retention in schools through measures such as scholarships, girls' empowerment programmes, and the provision of sanitary facilities.[77] Efforts have also been made to address the educational needs of children with disabilities, refugee and internally displaced children, and those from linguistic and ethnic minorities, through targeted interventions and inclusive education policies.[78]

Despite these policy interventions and institutional reforms, significant challenges persist in ensuring equitable access to healthcare and education in SSA. Limited resources, weak governance, and the complex interplay of socio-economic, cultural, and structural barriers continue to hinder progress in expanding access to these essential services.[79] Sustaining and scaling up successful interventions requires sustained political commitment, increased investments, and the strengthening of institutional capacities at all levels.[80] Collaborative efforts between governments, international partners, civil society organisations, and communities are crucial in driving systemic change and ensuring that no one is left behind in accessing quality healthcare and education in SSA.

Innovative Approaches and Best Practices

In addition to policy interventions and institutional reforms, innovative approaches and best practices have emerged in Sub-Saharan Africa (SSA) to address the challenges of access to healthcare and education. These innovations leverage technology, community engagement, and cross-sectoral collaboration to deliver services more effectively and reach marginalised populations.

In the healthcare sector, the use of digital health technologies has shown promise in improving access to healthcare services, particularly in remote and underserved areas. Mobile health (mHealth) interventions, such as SMS reminders for medication adherence, telemedicine consultations, and remote monitoring of chronic conditions, have been implemented to bridge the gap between patients and healthcare providers.[81] Additionally, the use of electronic health records (EHRs) and health information systems has facilitated the

77 Mercy Tembon and Lucia Fort (eds), *Girls Education in the 21st Century: Gender Equality, Empowerment, and Economic Growth* (World Bank, 2008).

78 UNESCO, Global Education Monitoring Report 2019: Migration, Displacement and Education - Building Bridges, not Walls (UNESCO, 2018).

79 Olusoji Adeyi et al., 'Health Status and Access to Healthcare in Sub-Saharan Africa' in Olusoji Adeyi (ed), Health and Development in Sub-Saharan Africa (World Bank, 2021).

80 Margaret E. Kruk et al., 'High-Quality Health Systems in the Sustainable Development Goals Era: Time for a Revolution' (2018) 6 The Lancet Global Health e1196.

81 Phat Luong et al, 'Test Message Medication Adherence Reminders Automated and Delivered at Scale Across Two Institutions: Testing the "Nudge" System: Pilot Study' (2021) 14(5) Circ Cardiovasc Qual Outcomes DOI: https://doi.org/10.1161%2FCIRCOUTCOMES.120.007015

collection and analysis of health data, enabling evidence-based decision-making and resource allocation.[82]

Community-based approaches have also proven effective in improving access to healthcare in SSA. The training and deployment of community health workers (CHWs) has been a successful strategy in extending healthcare services to rural and marginalised communities.[83] CHWs play a crucial role in health promotion, disease prevention, and the provision of basic healthcare services, serving as a link between communities and the formal healthcare system.[84] Moreover, community engagement and participatory approaches, such as community dialogues and participatory action research, have been employed to identify and address local health priorities, promote health-seeking behaviours, and foster community ownership of health interventions.[85]

In the education sector, the adoption of educational technologies has shown potential in expanding access to quality education, particularly in contexts of limited resources and infrastructure. The use of digital learning platforms, such as mobile learning apps and online courses, has enabled students to access educational content and resources beyond the traditional classroom setting.[86] Moreover, the integration of information and communication technologies (ICTs) into teacher training and professional development has enhanced the capacity of educators to deliver effective and engaging instruction.[87]

Innovative financing mechanisms have also been explored to improve access to education in SSA. Results-based financing approaches, such as performance-based contracts and impact bonds, have been implemented to incentivise the delivery of quality education and improve learning outcomes.[88] Additionally,

82 Peter Mechael et al., 'Barriers and Gaps Affecting mHealth in Low and Middle Income Countries: Policy White Paper' (WHO, 2010) available at < https://www.mobileactive.org/pdfs/mHealth_Barriers_White_Paper.pdf> accessed 29 May 2024.

83 Maryse C. Kok et al., 'Does Supportive Supervision Enhance Community Health Worker Motivation? A Mixed-Methods Study in Four African Countries' (2018) 9 Health Policy and Planning 988-998 DOI: https://doi.org/10.1093/heapol/czy082.

84 Henry B. Perry, Rose Zulliger, and Michael M. Rogers, 'Community Health Workers in Low-, Middle-, and High-Income Countries: An Overview of Their History, Recent Evolution, and Current Effectiveness' (2014) 35 *Annual Review of Public Health* 399-421 DOI: https://doi.org/10.1146/annurev-publhealth-032013-182354.

85 Zohra S Lassi et al, 'The Conceptual Framework and Assessment Methodology for the Systematic Reviews of Community-Based Interventions for the Prevention and Control of Infectious Diseases of Poverty' (2014) 3(22) *Infect Dis Poverty* DOI: https://doi.org/10.1186/2049-9957-3-22.

86 Mark West and Chew Han Ei, *Reading in the Mobile Era: A Study of Mobile Reading in Developing Countries* (UNESCO, 2014) available at < https://unesdoc.unesco.org/ark:/48223/pf0000227436> accessed 29 May 2024.

87 UNESCO, *Leveraging Information and Communication Technologies to Achieve the Post-2015 Education Goal* (UNESCO, 2015) available at < https://unesdoc.unesco.org/ark:/48223/pf0000243076> accessed 29 May 2024.

88 Emily Gustafsson-Wright and Sophie Gardiner, 'What Role Do Impact Bonds Have in the Achievement of the Global Goals?' (2016) available at < https://www.brookings.edu/arti-

Public-Private Partnerships (PPPs) have been leveraged to mobilise resources and expertise for school construction, curriculum development, and the provision of educational materials.[89]

Best practices in improving access to education in SSA have emphasised the importance of context-specific interventions, community involvement, and the empowerment of marginalised groups. Successful initiatives have adopted participatory approaches, engaging parents, teachers, and community leaders in the design and implementation of educational interventions.[90] Moreover, targeted interventions, such as scholarships, school feeding programmes, and gender-responsive pedagogy, have been effective in addressing the specific needs and barriers faced by disadvantaged groups, such as girls, children with disabilities, and those from low-income households.[91]

While these innovative approaches and best practices hold promise in improving access to healthcare and education in SSA, scaling up and sustaining these interventions remains a challenge. Limited resources, weak institutional capacities, and the need for long-term investments pose significant barriers to the widespread adoption and impact of these innovations.[92] Nonetheless, the lessons learned from these experiences provide valuable insights and guidance for policymakers, practitioners, and researchers working towards expanding access to healthcare and education in SSA.

Conclusion

Access to healthcare and education is a fundamental human right and a critical determinant of an individual's overall well-being and quality of life. However, in SSA, ensuring equitable access to these essential services remains a significant challenge, with far-reaching implications for the realisation of the right to an adequate standard of living.

---

cles/what-role-do-impact-bonds-have-in-the-achievement-of-the-global-goals/> accessed 29 May 2024.

89 UNICEF, *Public-Private Partnerships in Education: An Overview with Specific Reference to the Indian Context* (UNICEF, 2010) available at < https://www.unicef.org/uzbekistan/en/public-private-partnership-in-early-childhood-education> accessed 29 May 2024. See also Augustine Edobor Arimoro, 'Institutional Framework for Public-Private Partnerships in Nigeria: Is it a Case of Too Many Cooks for One Pot of Broth?' 40(2) *Business Law Review* 73-79 DOI: https://doi.org/10.54648/bula2019010.

90 Caroline Dyer, 'Evolving Approaches to Educating Children from Nomadic Communities' (2016) 46 *Prospects* 39-54 DOI: https://doi.org/10.1007/s11125-016-9381-6.

91 Vusi Gumede et al, 'Revisiting Poverty, Human Development and Inequality in Democratic South Africa' (2021) 15(2) *Indian Journal of Human Development* DOI: https://doi.org/10.1177/0973703021110329

92 Cynthia B. Lloyd and Paul C. Hewett, 'Primary Schooling in Sub-Saharan Africa: Recent Trends and Current Challenges' (2009) Population Council Working Paper 176 available at < https://knowledgecommons.popcouncil.org/cgi/viewcontent.cgi?article=1324&context=departments_sbsr-pgy> accessed 29 May 2024.

This chapter has provided a comprehensive examination of the multifaceted barriers to accessing healthcare and education in SSA, highlighting the complex interplay of socio-economic, political, and structural factors that perpetuate inequalities and hinder progress towards universal access. The analysis has shed light on the inadequate healthcare and educational infrastructure, financial barriers, socio-cultural impediments, and gender disparities that disproportionately affect marginalised and vulnerable populations in the region.

The chapter has also explored the wide-ranging implications of inadequate access to healthcare and education on various dimensions of human well-being, including health outcomes, educational attainment, and socio-economic development. The far-reaching consequences of these challenges, such as increased mortality rates, limited opportunities for social mobility, and the perpetuation of poverty and inequality, underscore the urgent need for concerted efforts to address these barriers and ensure equitable access to these essential services.

Moreover, the chapter has analysed the policy interventions, institutional reforms, and innovative approaches undertaken by governments, international organisations, and civil society actors to expand access to healthcare and education in SSA. While these efforts have yielded some progress and promising practices, significant challenges persist in ensuring the sustainability, scalability, and impact of these interventions.

Moving forward, addressing the challenges of access to healthcare and education in SSA requires a holistic and multisectoral approach that prioritises equity, inclusivity, and the empowerment of marginalised communities. This necessitates sustained investments in healthcare and educational infrastructure, the strengthening of health and education systems, and the implementation of targeted interventions to address the specific needs and barriers faced by disadvantaged groups.

Furthermore, fostering participatory and community-driven approaches, leveraging technology and innovation, and promoting intersectoral collaboration and partnerships are crucial in driving systemic change and ensuring that no one is left behind in accessing quality healthcare and education. By addressing these challenges and promoting equitable access to these essential services, SSA can make significant strides towards realising the right to an adequate standard of living for all its citizens and fostering inclusive and sustainable development in the region.

The insights and lessons gleaned from this chapter provide a foundation for subsequent chapters that will delve into strategies, best practices, and challenges in advancing socio-economic rights and promoting inclusive development in SSA. By shedding light on the complexities surrounding access to healthcare and education, this chapter contributes to a nuanced understanding of these vital issues and underscores the imperative of prioritising equitable access to these essential services in the pursuit of the right to an adequate standard of living in the region.

References

Adeyi O et al, 'Health Status and Access to Healthcare in Sub-Saharan Africa' in Olusoji Adeyi (ed), *Health and Development in Sub-Saharan Africa* (World Bank 2021).

Ainscow M, 'Promoting Inclusion and Equity in Education: Lessons from International Experiences' (2020) 6(1) *Nordic Journal of Studies in Education Policy* 7–16 https://doi.org/10.1080/20020317.2020.1729587.

Akyeampong K et al, *Access to Basic Education in Ghana: The Evidence and the Issues* (CREATE Country Analytic Report 2007).

Al-Tameemi RAN, 'Determinants of Poor Academic Performance among Undergraduate Students – A Systematic Review' (2023) 4 *International Journal of Educational Research Open* 100232 https://doi.org/10.1016/j.ijedro.2023.100232.

Antoninis M, 'Tackling the Largest Global Education Challenge? Secular and Religious Education in Northern Nigeria' (2014) 59 *World Development* 82–92 https://doi.org/10.1016/j.worlddev.2014.01.017.

Anyangwe EE, 'Promoting Gender Equity in Access to HIV Prevention, Care and Treatment in Sub-Saharan Africa' in F Nzwili (ed), *Where Are the Men?: Partnering with Men and Boys for Health and Gender Equity in Sub-Saharan Africa* (Hilton Publishing 2009).

Arimoro AE, 'The Corona Virus (COVID-19) Pandemic and the Challenge of Healthcare Infrastructure in Nigeria: What Role for Public-Private Partnerships?' (2020) 3 *Theoretical and Applied Law* 19–35 available at <https://www.taljournal.ru/jour/article/view/55?locale=en_US> accessed 28 May 2024.

Arimoro AE, 'Institutional Framework for Public-Private Partnerships in Nigeria: Is it a Case of Too Many Cooks for One Pot of Broth?' 40(2) *Business Law Review* 73–79 https://doi.org/10.54648/bula2019010.

Ataguba JE, 'Reassessing Catastrophic Health-Care Payments with a Nigerian Case Study' (2012) 10 *Health Economics, Policy and Law* 309–326 https://doi.org/10.1017/s1744133110000356.

Atun Ret et al, 'Health-System Reform and Universal Health Coverage in Latin America' (2015) 385 *The Lancet* 1230 https://doi.org/10.1016/s0140-6736(14)61646-9.

Bashir M et al, *Facing Forward: Schooling for Learning in Africa* (World Bank 2018).

Baten J et al, 'Educational Gender Inequality in Sub-Saharan Africa: A Long-Term Perspective' (2021) 47(3) *Population and Development Review* 813–849 https://doi.org/10.1111/padr.12430.

Beegle K and Christiaensen L (eds), *Accelerating Poverty Reduction in Africa* (World Bank 2019) available at <https://elibrary.worldbank.org/doi/abs/10.1596/978-1-4648-1232-3> accessed 28 May 2024.

Benson C, '"Learners" Own Languages as Key to Achieving Sustainable Development Goal 4: Multilingual Education in Sub-Saharan Africa' (2019) *Language Issues in Comparative Education* 69.

Brock-Utne B, 'Language and Inequality: Global Challenges to Education' (2020) 42(5) *Compare: A Journal of Comparative and International Education* 773–793 https://doi.org/10.1080/03057925.2012.706453.

Clark S and Brauner-Otto S, 'Divorce in Sub-Saharan Africa: Are Unions Becoming Less Stable?' (2015) 77 *Population and Development Review* 583 https://doi.org/10.1111/j.1728-4457.2015.00086.x.

de-Graft Aikins A et al, 'Explanatory Models of Diabetes in Urban Poor Communities in Accra, Ghana' (2015) 20(4) *Ethnicity & Health* 391–408 https://doi.org/10.1080/13557858.2014.921896.

Dhatt R et al, 'The Role of Women's Leadership and Gender Equity in Leadership and Health System Strengthening' (2017) 17(2) *Global Health, Epidemiology and Genomics* https://doi.org/10.1017/gheg.2016.22.

Dussault G and Franceschini MC, 'Not Enough There, Too Many Here: Understanding Geographical Imbalances in the Distribution of the Health Workforce' (2006) 5 *Human Resources for Health* 12 https://doi.org/10.1186%2F1478-4491-4-12.

Dyer C, 'Evolving Approaches to Educating Children from Nomadic Communities' (2016) 46 *Prospects* 39–54 https://doi.org/10.1007/s11125-016-9381-6.

Fredriksen B, *Education Resource Mobilization and Use in Developing Countries: Scope for Efficiency Gains through More Strategic Use of Education Aid* (Results for Development Institute 2011).

Fredriksen B, Brar S and Trucano M, *Getting Textbooks to Every Child in Sub-Saharan Africa: Strategies for Addressing the High Cost and Low Availability Problem* (World Bank 2015).

Ganle JK, 'Why Muslim Women in Northern Ghana Do Not Use Skilled Maternal Healthcare Services at Health Facilities: A Qualitative Study' (2015) 15(10) *BMC International Health and Human Rights* https://doi.org/10.1186/s12914-015-0048-9.

Gumede V et al, 'Revisiting Poverty, Human Development and Inequality in Democratic South Africa' (2021) 15(2) *Indian Journal of Human Development* 183–199 https://doi.org/10.1177/097370302110329.

Gustafsson-Wright E and Gardiner S, 'What Role Do Impact Bonds Have in the Achievement of the Global Goals?' (2016) available at <https://www.brookings.edu/articles/what-role-do-impact-bonds-have-in-the-achievement-of-the-global-goals/> accessed 29 May 2024.

Handa S et al, 'Can Unconditional Cash Transfers Raise Long-Term Living Standards? Evidence from Zambia' (2018) 133 *Journal of Development Economics* 42–65 https://doi.org/10.1016/j.jdeveco.2018.01.008.

Haque R et al, 'Women's Empowerment and Fertility Decision-Making in 53 Low and Middle Resource Countries: A Pooled Analysis of Demographic and Health Surveys' (2021) 11 *BMJ Open* https://dx.doi.org/10.1136/bmjopen-2020-045952.

Hubber P and Rollnick M, 'Tensions in the Teaching and Learning of Science in Developing Countries' in Mansoor Niaz and Bill Atweh (eds), *Science Education in Developing Countries* (Springer 2021).

Hutchinson J and Kettlewell K, 'Education to Employment: Complicated Transitions in a Changing World' (2015) 57(2) *Educational Research* 113–120 https://doi.org/10.1080/00131881.2015.1030848.

Ifeagwu SC et al, 'Health Financing for Universal Health Coverage in Sub-Saharan Africa: A Systematic Review' (2021) 6(8) *Global Health Research Policy* https://doi.org/10.1186%2Fs41256-021-00190-7.

Jones N et al, *Stemming Girls' Chronic Poverty: Catalysing Development Change by Building Just Social Institutions* (Chronic Poverty Research Centre 2010).

Joynes A and Jere C, 'Teenage Pregnancy and Motherhood in Sub-Saharan Africa: A Systematic Review of Enablers' (2022) 18 *PLoS One* e0264722.

Kalindi AM, 'Gender Inequities in Women's Access to Maternal Health Care Utilisation in Zambia: A Qualitative Analysis' (2023) *BMC Pregnancy and Childbirth* 755 https://doi.org/10.1186/s12884-023-06078-3.

Kaunda-Khangamwa BN et al, 'Adolescents Living with HIV, Complex Needs and Resilience in Blantyre, Malawi' (2020) 17(1) *AIDS Research and Therapy* https://doi.org/10.1186/s12981-020-00292-1.

Kinfu Y et al, 'The Health Worker Shortage in Africa: Are Enough Physicians and Nurses Being Trained?' (2009) 87 *Bulletin of the World Health Organization* 225.

Kodali PB, 'Achieving Universal Health Coverage in Low- and Middle-Income Countries: Challenges for Policy Post-Pandemic and Beyond' (2023) 16 *Risk Management Healthcare Policy* 607–621 https://doi.org/10.2147%2FRMHP.S366759.

Kok MC et al, 'Does Supportive Supervision Enhance Community Health Worker Motivation? A Mixed-Methods Study in Four African Countries' (2018) 9 *Health Policy and Planning* 988–998 https://doi.org/10.1093/heapol/czy082.

Kok MC et al, 'How Does Context Influence Performance of Community Health Workers in Low- and Middle-Income Countries? Evidence from the Literature' (2015) 10 *Health Research Policy and Systems* 1 https://doi.org/10.1186/s12961-015-0001-3.

Kombe G et al, 'The Human and Financial Resource Requirements for Scaling UP HIV/AIDS Services in Ethiopia' (2005) available at <https://pdf.usaid.gov/pdf_docs/Pnadc109.pdf> accessed 28 May 2024.

Kruk MK et al, 'High Quality Health Systems in the Sustainable Development Goals Era: Time for a Revolution' (2018) 6(11) *The Lancet Global Health* 1196–1252 https://doi.org/10.1016/S2214-109X(18)30386-3.

Lassi ZS et al, 'The Conceptual Framework and Assessment Methodology for the Systematic Reviews of Community-Based Interventions for the Prevention and Control of Infectious Diseases of Poverty' (2014) 3(22) *Infectious Diseases, the Environment and Poverty* https://doi.org/10.1186/2049-9957-3-22.

Lewin KM, *Strategies for Sustainable Financing of Secondary Education in Sub-Saharan Africa* (World Bank 2008).

Little AW, 'The Leap to Literacy: Transitions from Oral to Literate Societies' (2022) 84 *Prospects* 35.

Lloyd CB and Hewett PC, 'Primary Schooling in Sub-Saharan Africa: Recent Trends and Current Challenges' (2009) Population Council Working Paper 176 available at <https://knowledgecommons.popcouncil.org/cgi/viewcontent.cgi?article=1324&context=departments_sbsr-pgy> accessed 29 May 2024.

Luong P et al, 'Text Message Medication Adherence Reminders Automated and Delivered at Scale Across Two Institutions: Testing the "Nudge" System: Pilot Study' (2021) 14(5) *Circulation: Cardiovascular Quality and Outcomes* https://doi.org/10.1161%2FCIRCOUTCOMES.120.007015.

MacPherson EE et al, 'Gender Equity and Sexual Reproductive Health in Eastern and Southern Africa: A Critical Overview of the Literature' (2014) 7(1) *Global Health Action* https://doi.org/10.3402/gha.v7.23717.

Mathauer I et al, 'Extending Universal Health Coverage in Sub-Saharan Africa: An Assessment of Provider Payment Mechanisms' (2022) 22 *Health Policy and Planning* 817.

McIntyre D et al, 'What Are the Economic Consequences for Households of Illness and of Paying for Health Care in Low- and Middle-Income Country Contexts?' (2006) 62(4) *Social Science & Medicine* 858–865 https://doi.org/10.1016/j.socscimed.2005.07.001.

Mechael P et al, *Barriers and Gaps Affecting mHealth in Low and Middle Income Countries: Policy White Paper* (WHO 2010) available at <https://www.mobileactive.org/pdfs/mHealth_Barriers_White_Paper.pdf> accessed 29 May 2024.

Mingat A, Ledoux B, and Rakotomalala R, *Developing Post-Primary Education in Sub-Saharan Africa: Assessing the Financial Sustainability of Alternative Pathways* (World Bank 2010) available at <https://openknowledge.worldbank.org/bitstream/handle/10986/2429/538780PUB0post101Official0Use0Only1.pdf> accessed 28 May 2024.

Mkwananzi F and Walker M, 'Contextualizing the Role of Education in Female Employment in Sub-Saharan Africa: The Case of Kenya and South Africa' (2015) 128 *International Journal of Educational Development* 102511.

Mulumba M et al, 'Perceptions and Experiences of Access to Public Healthcare by People with Disabilities and Older People in Uganda' (2014) 13(76) *International Journal of Equity Health* https://doi.org/10.1186/s12939-014-0076-4.

Murray CJL and Frenk J, 'Ranking 37th — Measuring the Performance of the U.S. Health Care System' (2010) 362 *New England Journal of Medicine* 98–99 10.1056/NEJMp0910064.

Oketch M and Rolleston C, 'Policies on Free Primary and Secondary Education in East Africa: Retrospect and Prospect' (2007) 5 *Review of Research in Education* 131.

Onoka CA, 'Promoting Universal Financial Protection: Constraints and Enabling Factors in Scaling-Up Coverage with Social Health Insurance in Nigeria' (2013) 11 *Health Research and Systems* https://doi.org/10.1186/1478-4505-11-20.

Pauline Rose and Benjamin Alcott, *How Can Education Systems Become Equitable by 2030?* (DFID Think Pieces: Learning and Equity 2015).

Perry H, Zulliger R, and Rogers MM, 'Community Health Workers in Low-, Middle-, and High-Income Countries: An Overview of Their History, Recent Evolution, and Current Effectiveness' (2014) 35 *Annual Review of Public Health* 399–421 https://doi.org/10.1146/annurev-publhealth-032013-182354.

Pickering K, 'Indigenous Peoples and the COVID-19 Pandemic: A Systematic Scoping Review' (2023) 18(3) *Environmental Research Letters* 10.1088/1748-9326/acb804.

Raj A, 'When the Mother Is a Child: The Impact of Child Marriage on the Health and Human Rights of Girls' (2010) 95(110) *Archives of disease in childhood*931–935 https://doi.org/10.1136/adc.2009.178707.

Rasanathan K et al, 'Primary Health Care and the Social Determinants of Health: Essential and Complementary Approaches for Reducing Inequities in Health' (2011) 65 *Journal of Epidemiology & Community Health* 656–660 https://doi.org/10.1136/jech.2009.093914.

Rolleston C and James Z, *The Role of Schooling in Skill Development: Evidence from Young Lives in Ethiopia, India, Peru and Vietnam* (UNESCO Education For All Global Monitoring Report 2014).

Rout S, 'State Led Innovations for Achieving Universal Health Coverage in a Low Resource Setting Odisha, India: Opportunities and Challenges' (2021) 8(5)

International Journal of Community Medicine and Public Health 2338–2345 http://dx.doi.org/10.18203/2394-6040.ijcmph20211755.

Roy S, 'Unpaid Care Work: A Critical Analysis' (2022) available at <https://www.researchgate.net/publication/366642765_Unpaid_Care_Work_A_Critical_Analysis> accessed 28 May 2024.

Sen G and Ostlin P, 'Gender Inequality in Health: Why It Exists and How We Can Change It' (2008) 3(1) *Global Public Health* 1–12 https://doi.org/10.1080/17441690801900795.

Shannon G et al, 'Gender Equality in Science, Medicine, and Global Health: Where Are We At and Why Does it Matter?' (2019) 393(10171) *The Lancet* 560–569 https://doi.org/10.1016/S0140-6736(18)33135-0.

Singh R and Mukherjee P, *Comparison of the Effects of Government and Private Preschool Education on the Developmental Outcomes of Children: Evidence from Young Lives India* (Young Lives 2017) available at <https://www.younglives.org.uk/publications/comparison-effects-government-and-private-preschool-education-developmental-outcomes> accessed 28 May 2024.

Tembon M and Fort L (eds), *Girls Education in the 21st Century: Gender Equality, Empowerment, and Economic Growth* (World Bank 2008).

Tessema ZT et al, 'Determinants of Accessing Healthcare in Sub-Saharan Africa: A Mixed-Effect Analysis of Recent Demographic and Health Surveys from 36 Countries' (2022) 12(1) *BMJ Open* https://doi.org/10.1136%2Fbmjopen-2021-054397.

Trudell B, *The Impact of Language Policy and Practice on Children's Learning: Evidence from Eastern and Southern Africa* (UNICEF 2016) available at <https://www.unicef.org/esa/sites/unicef.org.esa/files/2018-09/UNICEF-2016-Language-and-Learning-FullReport.pdf> accessed 28 May 2024.

UNESCO, *Education for All 2000–2015: Achievements and Challenges* (UNESCO 2015).

UNESCO, *Global Education Monitoring Report 2019: Migration, Displacement and Education - Building Bridges, Not Walls* (UNESCO 2018).

UNESCO, *Global Education Monitoring Report 2020: Inclusion and Education: All Means All* (UNESCO 2020) available at <https://www.unesco.org/en/articles/global-education-monitoring-gem-report-2020> accessed 28 May 2024.

UNESCO, *Leveraging Information and Communication Technologies to Achieve the Post-2015 Education Goal* (UNESCO 2015) available at <https://unesdoc.unesco.org/ark:/48223/pf0000243076> accessed 29 May 2024.

UNESCO, *Pricing the Right to Education: The Cost of Reaching New Targets by 2030* (UNESCO 2015) Policy Paper 18 available at < https://unesdoc.unesco.org/ark:/48223/pf0000232197> accessed 28 May 2024.

UNESCO Institute for Statistics, *Education in Africa* (UNESCO 2019).

UNESCO Institute for Statistics, *SDG 4 Data Book: Global Education Indicators 2019* (UNESCO 2019).

UNGEI, *A Whole School Approach to Prevent School-Related Gender-Based Violence: Minimum Standards and Monitoring Framework* (UNGEI 2018).

UNICEF, *Public-Private Partnerships in Education: An Overview with Specific Reference to the Indian Context* (UNICEF 2010) available at <https://www.unicef.org/uzbekistan/en/public-private-partnership-in-early-childhood-education> accessed 29 May 2024.

United Nations General Assembly, 'International Covenant on Economic, Social and Cultural Rights' (1966) 993(11) *UN Treaty Series.*

Van de Poel E et al, 'Can Vouchers Deliver? An Evaluation of Subsidies for Maternal Health Care in Cambodia' (2014) 92 *Bulletin of the World Health Organization* 331.

Wagstaff A et al, 'Progress on Catastrophic Health Spending in 133 Countries: A Retrospective Observational Study' (2018) 6(2) *The Lancet Global Health* 169–179 https://doi.org/10.1016/s2214-109x(17)30429-1.

West M and Ei CH, *Reading in the Mobile Era: A Study of Mobile Reading in Developing Countries* (UNESCO 2014) available at <https://unesdoc.unesco.org/ark:/48223/pf0000227436> accessed 29 May 2024.

Whitaker KL et al, 'Addressing Language as a Barrier to Healthcare Access and Quality' (2022) 72 *British Journal of General Practice* 4–5 https://doi.org/10.3399/bjgp22X718013.

WHO, *Global Monitoring Report on Financial Protection in Health 2019* (WHO 2019) available at <https://www.who.int/publications/i/item/9789240003958> accessed 28 May 2024.

WHO, *Global Strategy on Human Resources for Health: Workforce 2030* (WHO 2016) available at <https://www.who.int/publications/i/item/9789241511131> accessed 28 May 2024.

WHO, *Public Spending on Health: A Closer Look at Global Trends* (WHO 2018) available at <https://www.who.int/publications/i/item/WHO-HIS-HGF-HFWorkingPaper-18.3> accessed 28 May 2024.

WHO, *Strategic Purchasing for Universal Health Coverage: Key Policy Issues and Questions: A Summary from Expert and Practitioners' Discussions* (WHO 2017) available at <https://iris.who.int/handle/10665/259423> accessed 28 May 2024.

WHO, *Universal Health Coverage in Africa: A Framework for Action* (WHO 2016).

World Bank, *World Development Report 2018: Learning to Realize Education's Promise* (World Bank 2018) available at <https://www.worldbank.org/en/publication/wdr2018> accessed 28 May 2024.

World Health Organization, *World Health Statistics 2022* (WHO 2022) available at <https://www.who.int/news/item/20-05-2022-world-health-statistics-2022> accessed 28 May 2024.

Yates R, 'Universal Health Coverage: Progressive Taxes Are Key' (2015) 386 *The Lancet* 227–279 https://doi.org/10.1016/s0140-6736(15)60868-6.

6 Access to Adequate Housing and Infrastructure

Introduction

Access to adequate housing and infrastructure is a fundamental human right and a crucial determinant of an individual's overall well-being and quality of life. The right to an adequate standard of living, as enshrined in various international human rights instruments, encompasses the right to adequate housing and access to essential infrastructure services.[1] However, in Sub-Saharan Africa (SSA), ensuring equitable access to these basic necessities remains a significant challenge, with far-reaching implications for the realisation of the right to an adequate standard of living.

Despite the recognition of housing as a basic human need and a critical factor in promoting social stability, economic development, and public health, SSA continues to face a severe housing crisis.[2] Rapid urbanisation, fuelled by population growth and rural-urban migration, has outpaced the capacity of governments and the private sector to provide adequate housing and infrastructure for the growing urban population.[3] As a result, a significant proportion of the urban population in SSA lives in informal settlements and slums, characterised by overcrowding, poor quality housing, and limited access to basic services.[4]

The challenges of housing and infrastructure development in SSA are multidimensional and deeply interconnected. Inadequate urban planning, weak institutional frameworks, and limited financial resources have contributed to the proliferation of unplanned settlements and the lack of essential

1 United Nations General Assembly, 'International Covenant on Economic, Social and Cultural Rights' (1966) UN Treaty Series, vol. 993, Article 11.

2 UN Habitat, *The Challenge of Slums: Global Report on Human Settlements 2003* (UN Habitat, 2003) available at < https://unhabitat.org/sites/default/files/download-manager-files/The%20Challenge%20of%20Slums%20-%20Global%20Report%20on%20Human%20Settlements%202003.pdf> accessed 27 June 2024.

3 Deborah Potts, 'The Slowing of Sun-Saharan Africa's Urbanization: Evidence and Implications for Urban Livelihoods' (2009) 21 *Environment and Urbanization* 253 DOI: 10.1177/0956247809103026.

4 Edgar Pieterse and Susan Parnell, *Africa's Urban Revolution* (Zed Books, 2014).

DOI: 10.4324/9781032628974-6

infrastructure services.[5] Moreover, the high cost of land, construction materials, and housing finance has made access to affordable housing a distant reality for many low-income households in the region.[6]

The implications of inadequate housing and infrastructure on the realisation of the right to an adequate standard of living in SSA are far-reaching and profound: poor housing conditions, characterised by overcrowding, lack of ventilation, and inadequate sanitation, pose significant health risks and contribute to the spread of communicable diseases.[7] Limited access to clean water and sanitation facilities further worsens the health burden and undermines efforts to promote public health and hygiene.[8] Moreover, inadequate transportation networks and the lack of reliable public transport systems limit access to economic opportunities, social services, and essential amenities, perpetuating patterns of social exclusion and inequality.[9]

Recognising the critical importance of addressing these challenges, governments, international organisations, and civil society actors in SSA have undertaken various efforts to improve housing and infrastructure development. These initiatives range from policy interventions and urban planning strategies to targeted programmes and community-based initiatives.[10] However, the effectiveness and sustainability of these efforts have been uneven, underscoring the need for a comprehensive and integrated approach to tackling the multidimensional barriers to adequate housing and infrastructure.

This chapter aims to provide a critical outlook of the challenges and complexities surrounding housing and infrastructure development in SSA, within the context of the right to an adequate standard of living. By analysing the multifaceted obstacles, exploring the implications of inadequate housing and infrastructure, and evaluating efforts to address these challenges, the chapter seeks to contribute to a nuanced understanding of these critical issues and inform strategies for advancing the realisation of the right to adequate housing and infrastructure in the region.

5 Carole Rakodi, 'Addressing Gendered Inequalities in Housing' in Caroline ON Moser (ed), Gender, Asset Accumulation and Just Cities: Pathways to Transformation (Routledge, 2015).

6 Lochner Marais et al., 'Informal Settlement Upgrading: Assessing the Literature and Experiences from Sub-Saharan Africa' (2014) Centre for Development Support Working Paper 3.

7 Oyebanji O. Oyebanji et al., 'A Systematic Review of Housing Quality and Health in Sub-Saharan Africa' (2022) 16 *International Journal of Environmental Research and Public Health* 2801.

8 UNICEF and WHO, Progress on Household Drinking Water, Sanitation and Hygiene 2000-2020: Five Years into the SDGs (UNICEF and WHO, 2021).

9 David Satterthwaite, 'The Sustainable Development Goals and Urban Inequality' (2022) 55 *Environment and Urbanization* 453 DOI: https://doi.org/10.1177/0956247816637501.

10 Adegun Olumuyiwa Bayo, 'Housing and Infrastructure Development in Informal Settlements: Debates and New Directions' (2021) 21 *Journal of Infrastructure Development* 31.

Challenges to Housing and Infrastructure in Sub-Saharan Africa

Rapid Urbanisation and Inadequate Urban Planning

SSA is experiencing rapid urbanisation, with urban population expected to double by 2050.[11] This unprecedented urban growth has put immense pressure on the region's already strained housing and infrastructure systems, leading to the proliferation of informal settlements and slums. Rapid urbanisation, fuelled by population growth, rural-urban migration, and the lack of adequate planning and management of urban development, has outpaced the capacity of governments and the private sector to provide adequate housing and infrastructure for the growing urban population.[12]

Inadequate urban planning is a major challenge to housing and infrastructure development in SSA. Many cities in the region have grown organically, without proper planning or zoning regulations, resulting in the haphazard development settlements and the lack of essential infrastructure services.[13] The absence of comprehensive urban development plans, weak institutional frameworks, and limited capacity of local authorities have contributed to the uncontrolled expansion of urban areas, often leading to the encroachment of settlements on environmentally sensitive areas such as wetlands and floodplains.[14]

Moreover, the lack of effective land-use planning and management has led to the inefficient use of urban land, with large tracts of land remaining undeveloped or underutilised, while low-income households are forced to settle in marginal and underserved areas.[15] The failure to anticipate and plan for urban growth has also resulted in the inadequate provision of basic services, such as water, sanitation, electricity, and transportation, further exacerbating the challenges faced by urban residents.[16]

The consequences of rapid urbanisation and inadequate urban planning are far-reaching, affecting the health, well-being, and quality of life of urban residents. Overcrowding, poor sanitation, and the lack of access to safe drinking

11 United Nations Department of Economic and Social Affairs, *World Urbanization Prospects: The 2018 Revision* (United Nations, 2019).

12 Sean Fox, 'Urbanization as a Global Historical Process: Theory and Evidence from Sub-Saharan Africa' (2012) 38 *Population and Development Review* 285 DOI: https://doi.org/10.1111/j.1728-4457.2012.00493.x

13 Vanessa Watson, 'African Urban Fantasies: Dreams or Nightmares?' (2014) 26 *Environment and Urbanization* 215-231 DOI: https://doi.org/10.1177/0956247813513705.

14 Shuaib Lwasa et al., 'Urban and Peri-Urban Agriculture and Forestry: Transcending Poverty Allevitaion to Climate Change Mitigation and Adaptation' (2013) 30 *Urban Climate* DOI: http://dx.doi.org/10.1016/j.uclim.2013.10.007

15 Sarah Charlton and Paula Meth, 'Lived Experiences of State Housing in Johannesburg and Durban' (2017) 93 *Transformation: Critical Perspectives on Southern Africa* 91.

16 David Satterthwaite, 'Missing the Millenium Development Goal Targets for Water and Sanitation in Urban Areas' (2016) 28(1) *Environment and Urbanization* 99 DOI: https://doi.org/10.1177/0956247816628435.

water in informal settlements contribute to the spread of communicable diseases and pose significant public health risks.[17] Moreover, the lack of proper drainage and stormwater management systems in unplanned settlements increases the vulnerability of residents to flooding and other natural hazards, further compounding their vulnerability and undermining their resilience.[18]

Addressing the challenges of rapid urbanisation and inadequate urban planning requires a comprehensive and integrated approach that involves multiple stakeholders, including governments, civil society organisations, and local communities. This includes the development and implementation of participatory urban development plans, the strengthening of institutional frameworks for urban governance, and the allocation of adequate resources for housing and infrastructure development.[19] Furthermore, there is a need for innovative approaches to land-use planning and management, such as the use of geographic information systems (GIS) and remote sensing technologies, to facilitate evidence-based decision-making and the efficient allocation of resources.[20]

Limited Access to Affordable Housing

Access to affordable housing is a critical challenge in SSA, particularly for low-income households in urban areas. The high cost of housing, coupled with limited access to housing finance and the lack of government support for affordable housing initiatives, has made homeownership an elusive dream for many urban residents in the region.[21] The affordability gap in housing is a major barrier to access, with the cost of the cheapest formal housing units often exceeding the incomes of the majority of urban households.[22] This affordability challenge is exacerbated by the high cost of land, construction materials, and infrastructure development, which drive up the prices of housing units

17 James IT Baines et al, 'Social Impact Assessment and Ethical Research Principles: Ethical Professional Practice in Impact Assessment Part II' (2013) 31(4) *Impact Assessment and Project Appraisal* 254-260 DOI: https://doi.org/10.1080/14615517.2013.850306

18 Hayley Leck and David Simon, 'Fostering Multiscalar Collaboration and Co-operation for Effective Governance of Climate Change Adaptation' (2013) 50(6) *Urban Studies* DOI: https://doi.org/10.1177/0042098012461675.

19 Vanessa Watson, 'Conflicting Rationalities: Implications for Planning Theory and Ethics' (2003) 4(4) *Planning Theory and Practice* 395-407 DOI: https://doi.org/10.1080/1464935032000146318.

20 Richard Sliuzas, 'Opportunities for Enhancing Communication, Learning and Decision Making Among Stakeholders in Urban Planning and Management using Geo-Information Technology' (ITC Dissertation 114, 2003).

21 Ibid.

22 Sock-Yong Phang and Matthias Helble, 'Housing Policies I Singapore' (2016) ADBI Working Paper 559 available at < https://r.search.yahoo.com/_ylt=AwrkPUdbRIRmskUVNwl-3Bwx.;_ylu=Y29sbwMEcG9zAzIEdnRpZAMEc2VjA3Ny/RV=2/RE=1719973084/RO=10/RU=https%3a%2f%2fwww.adb.org%2fsites%2fdefault%2ffiles%2fpublication%2f181599%2fadbi-wp559.pdf/RK=2/RS=w522RR2yrAbdvki9QCayj0NJQTE-> accessed 2 July 2024.

beyond the reach of low-income earners.[23] Moreover, the limited availability of serviced land for housing development, particularly in urban areas, further constrains the supply of affordable housing and contributes to the growth of informal settlements.[24]

Access to housing finance is another critical barrier to affordable housing in SSA. The underdeveloped mortgage markets, stringent lending requirements, and high interest rates in many countries in the region make it difficult for low-income households to access credit for housing.[25] The lack of credit history, collateral, and formal employment among low-income earners further limits their ability to secure housing loans from formal financial institutions.[26] Consequently, many urban residents are forced to rely on informal and often exploitative sources of housing finance, such as moneylenders and informal savings groups, which charge exorbitant interest rates and offer limited protection for borrowers.[27]

The limited government support for affordable housing initiatives in SSA has also contributed to the housing affordability crisis in the region. Many governments have prioritised the development of high-end housing projects and the provision of housing subsidies for middle- and high-income earners, at the expense of low-income households.[28] Moreover, the lack of clear policies and institutional frameworks for affordable housing development, coupled with the limited capacity of housing institutions and the absence of Public-Private Partnerships (PPPs), has hindered the development of sustainable and scalable affordable housing solutions.[29]

The consequences of limited access to affordable housing are far-reaching, affecting the health, well-being, and productivity of urban residents. Overcrowding, poor housing conditions, and the lack of basic services in informal settlements contribute to the spread of communicable diseases and pose

23 Franklin Obeng-Odoom, 'The State of African Cities 2014' (2014) 51(4) *Journal of Asian and African Studies* DOI: https://doi.org/10.1177/0021909614547604.

24 Femke Van Noorloos et al, 'Incremental Housing as a Node for Intersecting Flows of City-Making: Rethinking the Housing Shortage in the Global South'(2019) 32(1) *Environment & Urbanization* DOI: https://doi.org/10.1177/0956247819887679.

25 El-haj M Bah et al, *Housing Market Dynamics in Africa* (Palgrave Macmillan 2018) available at <https://link.springer.com/book/10.1057/978-1-137-59792-2> accessed 2 July 2024.

26 Andrew Jones and Lisa Stead, 'Can People on Low Incomes Access Affordable Housing Loans in Urban Africa and Asia? Examples of Innovative Housing Finance Models from Reall's Global Network' (2020) 32(1) *Environment & Urbanization* DOI: https://doi.org/10.1177/0956247819899557.

27 Maggie Mwoka et al, 'Housing as a Social Determinant of Health: Evidence from Singapore, the UK, and Kenya: The 3-D Commission' (2021) 98 *Journal of Urban Health* 15-30 DOI: https://doi.org/10.1007%2Fs11524-021-00557-8.

28 Nancy Kwak, *A World of Homeowners: American Power and the Politics of Housing Aid* (University of Chicago Press, 2015) DOI: https://doi.org/10.7208/chicago/9780226282497.001.0001.

29 Timothy Gbanga Nubi et al, *Housing and SDGs in Urban Africa* (Springer Nature 2021).

significant health risks, particularly for vulnerable groups such as children, the elderly, and people with disabilities.[30] Similarly, the high cost of housing forces many low-income households to allocate a significant portion of their incomes to rent or mortgage payments, leaving little for other essential needs such as food, healthcare, and education.[31]

Addressing the challenge of affordable housing in SSA requires a multifaceted strategy that involves the collaboration of governments, the private sector, and civil society. This includes the development of comprehensive housing policies and strategies that prioritise the needs of low-income households, and the promotion of innovative financing mechanisms for affordable housing.[32] Again, there is the need for the development of alternative housing solutions, such as incremental housing, community-led housing initiatives, and the use of local building materials and technologies, to reduce the costs of housing and improve affordability for low-income households.[33]

Poor Quality Housing and Insufficient Basic Services

Poor quality housing and insufficient basic services are pervasive challenges in SSA, particularly in informal settlements and low-income urban areas. The lack of access to adequate housing, coupled with the absence of essential services such as water, sanitation, and electricity, poses significant risks to the health, safety, and well-being of millions of people residing in the region.[34]

The quality of housing in many informal settlements in SSA is characterised by poor structural conditions, inadequate ventilation, and the use of substandard building materials.[35] Houses are often constructed using temporary or makeshift materials such as corrugated iron sheets, plastic sheets, and mud bricks, which provide little protection against the elements and are prone to rapid deterioration.[36] The high population densities and overcrowding in informal settlements contribute to the spread of communicable diseases such

30 Ibid.

31 Sumila Gulyani and Ellen M. Bassett, 'The Living Conditions Diamond: An Analytical and Theoretical Framework for Understanding Slums' (2010) 21 *Environment and Planning A: Economy and Space* DOI: https://doi.org/10.1068/a42520.

32 Annelies Zoomers et al, 'The Rush for Land in an Urbanizing World: From Land Grabbing Toward Developing Safe, Resilient, and Sustainable Cities and Landscapes' (2017) 92 *World Development* 242-252 DOI: https://doi.org/10.1016/j.worlddev.2016.11.016.

33 Watson, op cit (n19) above.

34 Ibid.

35 Zafu Assefa Teferi and Peter Newman, 'Slum Regeneration and Sustainability: Applying Extended Metabolism Model and the SDGs' (2017) 9(12) *Sustainability* 2273 DOI: http://dx.doi.org/10.3390/su9122273.

36 Richard Florida, 'Slums, Favelas and Shantytowns: What's in a Name?' (2017) Bloomberg CityLab.

as tuberculosis and respiratory infections and increase the risk of fire outbreaks and other hazards.[37]

The lack of access to basic services, such as clean water, sanitation, and electricity further worsens the challenges posed by poor quality housing in SSA. Many informal settlements lack access to safe drinking water, with residents often relying on contaminated sources or traveling long distances to collect water from communal standpipes.[38] The absence of adequate sanitation facilities, such as toilets and sewerage systems, leads to the widespread practice of open defecation and the improper disposal of waste, which poses significant health risks and contributes to environmental degradation.[39]

Furthermore, the lack of access to electricity in many informal settlements limits the ability of residents to engage in productive activities, such as studying or running small businesses, and exposes them to the risks associated with the use of kerosene lamps and other hazardous lighting sources.[40] The absence of street lighting and the lack of public spaces also contribute to increased insecurity and the risk of gender-based violence in informal settlements.[41]

The poor quality of housing and the lack of basic services in informal settlements have far-reaching implications for the health, well-being, and productivity of urban residents. Exposure to hazardous living conditions and the lack of access to essential services contributes to high rates of morbidity and mortality, particularly among children and other vulnerable groups.[42] The time and energy spent on collecting water and managing household waste divert resources away from productive activities and limit the ability of residents to engage in income generating opportunities.[43]

Addressing the challenges of poor quality housing and insufficient basic services in SSA requires a multisectoral approach that involves the collaboration of governments, civil society organisations, and local communities. This includes the development and implementation of slum upgrading programmes that prioritise the provision of basic services and the improvement of housing conditions, the strengthening of institutional frameworks for urban

37 Ibid.

38 Christa Brelsford et al., Heterogeneity and Scale of Sustainable Development in Cities' (2017)34 *PNAS* 8963-8968 DOI: https://doi.org/10.1073/pnas.1606033114.

39 Jamie Bartram et al., 'Global Monitoring of Water Supply and Sanitation: History, Methods and Future Challenges' (2014) 11 *International Journal of Environmental Research and Public Health* 8137 DOI: https://doi.org/10.3390/ijerph110808137.

40 Andrew Scott et al., Accelerating Access to Electricity in Africa with Off-Grid Solar: The Impact of Solar Household Solutions (Overseas Development Institute, 2016).

41 Ibid.

42 Samson Kinyanjui et al., 'Water, Sanitation, Hygiene, and Waste Management for the Prevention and Control of COVID-19 in Informal Settlements and Slums' (2022) 17 *Global Health: Science and Practice* 63.

43 Innocent K. Tumwebaze et al., 'Access to Adequate Water, Sanitation and Hygiene in Slum Households: Experiences from Kampala, Uganda' (2014) 16 Water and Environment Journal 269.

governance, and the promotion of community-led initiatives for housing and service delivery.[44]

Innovative service delivery in informal settlements can be significantly improved by implementing decentralised water and sanitation systems, deploying renewable energy technologies, and establishing community-managed waste collection and recycling schemes.[45] This solution leverages local resources and community engagement to create sustainable infrastructure, while reducing dependency on centralised systems that often struggle to serve these areas effectively. By empowering residents to manage their own services through these decentralised approaches, communities can achieve better access to essential utilities while building local capacity and environmental sustainability

Inadequate Transportation Networks and Connectivity

Inadequate transportation networks and limited connectivity are significant challenges to housing and infrastructure development in SSA. The lack of efficient and affordable transportation systems in many cities in the region hinders access to employment opportunities, social services, and essential amenities, perpetuating patterns of spatial inequality and social exclusion.[46]

The transportation infrastructure in many SSA cities is characterised by poorly maintained roads, limited public transport options, and the absence of pedestrian and cycling facilities.[47] The rapid growth of urban populations and the increasing motorisation rates have put immense pressure on the existing transportation networks, leading to chronic congestion, high levels of air pollution, and increased road safety risks.[48] The lack of integrated land-use and transportation planning has resulted in the spatial mismatch between housing and employment centres, forcing many urban residents to undertake long and costly commutes to access economic opportunities.[49]

Public transportation systems in many SSA cities are often inadequate, unreliable, and unaffordable for low-income households. The limited coverage and

44 Vanessa Watson, 'Seeing from the South: Refocusing Urban Planning on the Globe's Central Urban Issues' (2009) 46 *Urban Studies* 2259.

45 Jonathan Silver, 'Incremental Infrastructures: Material Improvisation and Social Collaboration Across Post-Colonial Accra' (2014) 51 Urban Geography 1011.

46 Patrick M. Wamala et al., 'Sustainable Urban Mobility in Sub-Saharan Africa: Assessing the Sustainability of the Matatu System in Kampala City' (2022) 12 *Sustainability* 9750.

47 Chioma C. Amadi et al., 'The Impact of Roadside Pollution in an Emerging African Megacity: The Lagos Metropolis Experience' (2022) 169 *Science of the Total Environment* 155157.

48 Daniel Oviedo et al., 'The Elusive Quest for Integration in the Planning and Delivery of Urban Transport in Sub-Saharan Africa: The Case of Maputo, Mozambique' (2021) 33 *Planning Theory & Practice* 46

49 Liza Rose Cirolia, 'Fractured Fiscal Authority and Fragmented Infrastructures: Financing Sustainable Urban Development in Sub-Saharan Africa' (2020) 30 *Habitat International* 102233.

frequency of bus and rail services, coupled with the high cost of fares, make it difficult for many urban residents to access essential services and participate in social and economic activities.[50] Moreover, the informal transport sector, which includes minibuses, motorcycles, and three-wheelers, while providing a critical service in many cities, is often unregulated and operates under precarious conditions, posing significant safety risks for passengers and operators.[51]

The lack of connectivity between different modes of transportation and the absence of integrated fare systems further exacerbates the challenges faced by urban commuters in SSA. The fragmentation of transportation services and the lack of coordination between different operators make it difficult for passengers to plan and execute seamless journeys, leading to increased travel times and costs.[52] Moreover, the absence of reliable travel information and the lack of digital payment systems limit the ability of commuters to make informed decisions and access transportation services efficiently.[53]

The consequences of inadequate transportation networks and limited connectivity are far-reaching, affecting the economic productivity, social inclusion, and quality of life of urban residents in SSA. The time and cost burden of commuting disproportionately affects low-income households, limiting their access to employment opportunities and essential services.[54] Moreover, the lack of safe and affordable transportation options disproportionately impacts women, children, and people with disabilities who often face additional barriers to mobility and are at higher risk of violence and harassment in public spaces.[55]

Addressing the challenges of inadequate transportation networks and limited connectivity in SSA requires a comprehensive and integrated approach that involves the collaboration of governments, the private sector, and civil society organisations. This includes the development and implementation of sustainable urban mobility plans that prioritise the needs of pedestrians, cyclists, and public transport users, the investment in high-quality transportation infrastructure, and the promotion of transit-oriented development.[56]

50 Christo Venter et al., 'The Equity Impacts of Bus Rapid Transit: A Review of the Evidence and Implications for Sustainable Transport' (2018) 74 *International Journal of Sustainable Transportation* 140.

51 Ibid.

52 Anvita Arora and Geetam Tiwari, 'A Framework for Assessing Level of Service of Informal Public Transport Services' (2016) 3 *Transportation Research Procedia* 1.

53 Jacqueline M. Klopp et al., 'Harmonized Indicators for Informal Public Transport Data Collection in Sub-Saharan African Cities' (2021) 7 *Journal of Transport Geography* 103156.

54 Roger Behrens et al., 'Low-Income Household Travel Expenditure in Sub-Saharan African Cities: Unpacking the Implications of Affordability and Accessibility' (2022) 36 Transport Policy 158

55 Yonatan Kelder et al., '#MeToo? The Role of Gender, Socio-Economic Status and Transport in Commuter Vulnerability to Crime in Johannesburg' (2022) 22 *Urban Studies* 3.

56 Ibid.

Moreover, there is a need for innovative approaches to transportation service delivery, such as the use of demand-responsive transport systems, shared mobility platforms, and integrated fare payment systems.[57] The integration of transportation planning with broader urban development and poverty reduction strategies is also critical for promoting the long-term sustainability and inclusivity of urban transportation systems in SSA.[58]

Implications of Inadequate Housing and Infrastructure on the Right to an Adequate Standard of Living

Health Risks and Vulnerability

Inadequate housing and infrastructure in SSA have significant implications for the health and well-being of urban residents, particularly those living in informal settlements and low-income areas. The lack of access to safe and adequate housing, coupled with the absence of essential services such as clean water, sanitation, and waste management, exposes millions of people to a range of health risks and increases their vulnerability to disease and injury.[59]

Poor housing conditions, characterised by overcrowding, inadequate ventilation, and the use of substandard building materials, contribute to the spread of communicable diseases such as tuberculosis, respiratory infections, and diarrheal diseases.[60] The high population densities in informal settlements facilitate the transmission of airborne diseases, while the lack of proper sanitation and hygiene facilities increases the risk of waterborne illnesses.[61] Moreover, exposure to indoor air pollution from the use of solid fuels for cooking and heating, a common practice in many low-income households, is a major risk factor for respiratory diseases and contributes to high rates of morbidity and mortality, particularly among women and children.[62]

The absence of safe drinking water and adequate sanitation facilities in many informal settlements further exacerbates the health risks faced by residents. The reliance on contaminated water sources and the practice of open defecation contribute to the spread of diarrheal diseases, which are a leading cause

57 Joachim Ezeadichie et al., 'Crowdsourced Mapping of Paratransit in Kigali, Rwanda' (2022) 7 *Journal of Transport Geography* 103418.

58 Jackie Walters, 'Overview of Public Transport Policy Developments in South Africa' (2013) 39 *Research in Transportation Economics* 34.

59 Ibid.

60 Ibid.

61 Blessing U. Mberu et al., 'Health and Health-Related Indicators in Slum, Rural, and Urban Communities: A Comparative Analysis' (2016) 9 *Global Health Action* 33163 DOI: https://doi.org/10.3402/gha.v9.33163.

62 Donee Alexander et al., 'Burden of Disease from Household Air Pollution for 2016' (2018) 78 *International Journal of Public Health* 573.

of child mortality in SSA.[63] Moreover, the lack of proper waste management systems and the accumulation of solid waste in public spaces create breeding grounds for disease vectors such as mosquitoes and rodents, increasing the risk of vector-borne diseases such as malaria and dengue fever.[64]

Inadequate housing and infrastructure also increase the vulnerability of urban residents to injury and violence. The use of substandard building materials and the lack of proper construction techniques make many houses in informal settlements prone to collapse, particularly during extreme weather events such as heavy rains and floods.[65] Moreover, the absence of safe public spaces and the lack of street lighting contribute to increased insecurity and the risk of gender-based violence, particularly for women and girls.[66]

The health risks and vulnerabilities associated with inadequate housing and infrastructure have far-reaching consequences for the well-being and productivity of urban residents in SSA. The high burden of disease and injury not only affects the quality of life of individuals and families but also imposes significant economic costs on households and health systems.[67] Moreover, the disproportionate impact of poor housing and infrastructure on low-income and marginalised communities perpetuates patterns of health inequality and social exclusion, undermining efforts to achieve universal health coverage and the right to an adequate standard of living.[68]

Addressing the health risks and vulnerabilities associated with inadequate housing and infrastructure in SSA requires a multisectoral approach that prioritises the provision of safe and adequate housing, the improvement of basic services, and the strengthening of primary healthcare systems. This includes the development and implementation of slum upgrading programmes that focus on the provision of essential services such as water, sanitation, and waste management, the promotion of healthy housing design and construction

63 Samson Kinyanjui et al., 'Water, Sanitation, Hygiene, and Waste Management for the Prevention and Control of COVID-19 in Informal Settlements and Slums' (2022) 17 *Global Health: Science and Practice* 63.

64 Gideon Abagna Azunre et al, 'Urban Informalities in Sub-Saharan Africa (SSA): A Solution for or Barrier against Sustainable City Development' (2022) 152 *World Development* DOI: https://doi.org/10.1016/j.worlddev.2021.105782.

65 Abimbola Windapo and Olaitan Olugboyega, 'Housing Quality Assessment System for Developing Countries: The Delphi Method Approach' (2021) 3 *Journal of African Real Estate Research* 97.

66 Ayobami Popoola et al., 'Bridging the Security Gap in Poor Urban Neighbourhoods Through Neighbourhood Planning' (2021) 19 *Urban Design International* 167.

67 Yanfeng Ouyang et al., 'Health Impacts of Ambient Air Pollution in Sub-Saharan Africa: Evidence from the Demographic and Health Surveys' (2021) 202 *Environmental Research* 111701.

68 Babatunde A. Ahonsi, 'Inclusive Health Delivery in an Urban African Context: Reflections and Options for Action' (2020) 12 *Social Sciences* 133.

practices, and the integration of health considerations into urban planning and development policies.[69]

Moreover, there is a need for targeted interventions that address the specific health needs and vulnerabilities of different population groups, such as women, children, the elderly, and people with disabilities. This includes the provision of maternal and child health services, the promotion of health education and behaviour change communication, and the strengthening of community-based health systems.[70] The engagement and empowerment of local communities in the design and implementation of health interventions are also critical for promoting the long-term sustainability and effectiveness of these efforts.[71]

Limited Economic Opportunities and Social Exclusion

Inadequate housing and infrastructure in Sub-Saharan Africa (SSA) have significant implications for the economic opportunities and social inclusion of urban residents, particularly those living in informal settlements and low-income areas. The lack of access to adequate housing, coupled with the absence of essential services and infrastructure, creates barriers to employment, education, and social participation, perpetuating cycles of poverty and marginalisation.[72]

Poor housing conditions and the lack of basic services in informal settlements limit the ability of residents to engage in productive economic activities and access employment opportunities. The time and energy spent on collecting water, managing waste, and navigating inadequate transportation networks divert resources away from income-generating activities and limit the ability of individuals to seek and maintain stable employment.[73] Moreover, the lack of access to electricity and reliable energy sources constrains the growth of home-based enterprises and small businesses, which are critical sources of livelihood for many low-income households in SSA.[74]

69 Melanie Lombard, 'Informality as Structure or Agency? Exploring Shed Housing in the UK as Informal Practice' (2019) 56 *International Journal of Urban and Regional Research* 569.

70 Esther Awuor Owino et al., 'Community-Based Solid Waste Management Approaches for Sustainable Development: A Case Study of Waste Management Groups in Kisumu, Kenya' (2021) 10 *Frontiers in Sustainable Cities* 678495.

71 Blessing Mberu et al., 'Bringing Sexual and Reproductive Health in the Urban Contexts to the Forefront of the Development Agenda: The Case for Prioritizing the Urban Poor' (2014) 9 *Maternal and Child Health Journal* 1572.

72 Liza Rose Cirolia and Warren Smit, 'Fractured Approaches to Urban Transformation: Analyzing Parallel Perspectives in South Africa' (2017) 42 *Transformation: Critical Perspectives on Southern Africa* 86.

73 Innocent Chirisa and Elmond Bandauko, 'African Cities and the Water-Food-Climate-Energy Nexus: An Agenda for Sustainability and Resilience at a Local Level' (2015) 50 *Urban Forum* 391.

74 Jon Phillips et al., *Energy Access and Forced Migration* (Chatham House, 2019).

Inadequate housing and infrastructure also have significant implications for educational attainment and human capital development in SSA. The lack of safe and adequate housing, coupled with the absence of basic services such as electricity and sanitation, creates an unconducive environment for learning and studying, particularly for children and youth.[75] The time and energy spent on household chores and the management of basic needs, such as water collection and waste disposal, reduce the time available for schooling and homework, leading to lower educational outcomes and limited future economic opportunities.[76]

Moreover, the spatial segregation and marginalisation of informal settlements in many SSA cities contribute to the social exclusion and stigmatisation of their residents. The lack of access to essential services and infrastructure, coupled with the poor quality of housing, reinforces patterns of inequality and discrimination, limiting the ability of individuals and communities to participate fully in social, economic, and political life.[77] The absence of safe public spaces and the lack of community facilities, such as parks, libraries, and community centres, further exacerbate the social isolation and marginalisation of low-income communities, undermining efforts to promote social cohesion and inclusive urban development.[78]

The limited economic opportunities and social exclusion associated with inadequate housing and infrastructure have far-reaching consequences for the well-being and prosperity of urban residents in SSA. The persistent marginalisation and deprivation of low-income communities not only affect the quality of life of individuals and families but also undermine the overall economic and social development of cities and regions.[79] Moreover, the exclusion and stigmatisation of informal settlements and their residents perpetuate patterns of inequality and social injustice, undermining efforts to achieve inclusive and sustainable urban development.[80]

Addressing the challenges of limited economic opportunities and social exclusion associated with inadequate housing and infrastructure in SSA requires a multifaceted approach that prioritises the provision of affordable and adequate housing, the improvement of basic services and infrastructure, and the promotion of inclusive urban development. This includes the development and implementation of slum upgrading programmes that focus on the

75 Sarah Sabates-Wheeler and Ian MacAuslan, 'Migration and Social Protection: Exposing Problems of Access' (2007) 35 *Development* 26.

76 Stephen Devereux and Rachel Sabates-Wheeler, 'Transformative Social Protection' (2004) IDS Working Paper 232.

77 Edgar Pieterse et al., *New Urban Worlds: Inhabiting Dissonant Times* (Polity Press, 2017).

78 David Satterthwaite, 'Reducing Urban Poverty: Some Lessons from Experience' (2002) 13 *Environment and Urbanization* 167.

79 Ibid.

80 Marie Huchzermeyer, 'Troubling Continuities: Use and Utility of the Term 'Slum'' in Gordon MacLeod and Colin McFarlane (eds), *Thinking Through Urban Research* (Sage, 2021).

provision of essential services, the creation of economic opportunities, and the enhancement of community participation and empowerment.[81]

Moreover, there is a need for targeted interventions that address the specific needs and vulnerabilities of different population groups, such as women, youth, and people with disabilities. This includes the provision of skills training and entrepreneurship support, the promotion of inclusive education and vocational training, and the strengthening of social protection systems.[82] The engagement and empowerment of local communities in the design and implementation of economic and social development initiatives are also critical for promoting the long-term sustainability and effectiveness of these efforts.[83]

Reduced Access to Essential Services and Amenities

Inadequate housing and infrastructure in Sub-Saharan Africa (SSA) have significant implications for the access of urban residents to essential services and amenities, such as healthcare, education, and public spaces. The lack of access to these services and amenities, particularly in informal settlements and low-income areas, undermines the quality of life and well-being of individuals and communities, perpetuating patterns of deprivation and inequality.[84]

The absence of adequate healthcare facilities and services in many informal settlements in SSA limits the ability of residents to access timely and quality healthcare, leading to poor health outcomes and increased morbidity and mortality rates.[85] The lack of primary healthcare centres, coupled with the limited availability of healthcare professionals and essential medicines, forces many residents to travel long distances or rely on informal and often unregulated healthcare providers, increasing the risks of complications and delayed treatment.[86] Moreover, the lack of access to safe drinking water and sanitation facilities in many informal settlements exacerbates the burden of communicable diseases, particularly among children and other vulnerable groups.[87]

Inadequate housing and infrastructure also have significant implications for access to education and learning opportunities in SSA. The lack of safe and adequate housing, coupled with the absence of basic services such as electricity

81 David Satterthwaite et al., 'Building Resilience to Climate Change in Informal Settlements' (2020) 31 *One Earth* 143.

82 Ibid.

83 Olumuyiwa B. Adegun, 'Infrastructure Development and the Prospect of Inclusive Growth in Nigerian Informal Settlements' (2022) 32 *Urban Forum* 147.

84 Michele Acuto et al., 'Infrastructural Deficits and Potential in African Cities' (2022) 1 *Urban Studies* 10.

85 Ibid.

86 Jude Mukundane and Wim Naudé, 'Healthcare Access and Quality in Sub-Saharan Africa: Evidence from a Stochastic Frontier Analysis' (2022) 21 *International* Health 157

87 Samson Kinyanjui et al., 'Water, Sanitation, Hygiene, and Waste Management for the Prevention and Control of COVID-19 in Informal Settlements and Slums' (2022) 17 *Global Health: Science and Practice* 63.

and sanitation, creates an unconducive environment for learning and studying, particularly for children and youth.[88] The distance and time required to travel to schools, often located outside of informal settlements, can discourage attendance and increase dropout rates, particularly for girls and children from low-income households.[89] Moreover, the lack of access to learning materials, such as textbooks and computers, and the limited availability of trained teachers in many informal settlements further undermine the quality of education and learning outcomes.[90]

The absence of safe and accessible public spaces and amenities, such as parks, libraries, and community centres, in many informal settlements in SSA further exacerbates the social isolation and marginalisation of their residents. The lack of these spaces and amenities limits opportunities for social interaction, recreation, and community engagement, undermining efforts to promote social cohesion and inclusive urban development.[91] Moreover, the absence of safe public spaces disproportionately affects women, children, and people with disabilities, who often face additional barriers to mobility and participation in public life.[92]

The reduced access to essential services and amenities associated with inadequate housing and infrastructure has far-reaching consequences for the well-being and development of urban residents in SSA. The persistent deprivation and marginalisation of low-income communities not only affect the quality of life of individuals and families but also undermine the overall social and economic development of cities and regions.[93] Moreover, the lack of access to essential services and amenities perpetuates patterns of inequality and social injustice, undermining efforts to achieve inclusive and sustainable urban development.[94]

Addressing the challenges of reduced access to essential services and amenities associated with inadequate housing and infrastructure in SSA requires a multisectoral approach that prioritises the provision of affordable and adequate

88 Sinem Sefa Akay, 'Informal Settlements, Shelter Deprivations and Development Challenges in Sub-Saharan Africa' (2021) 79 *Local Economy* 1007.

89 Kofi Awuviry-Newton et al., 'Disability and Education: Gaps and Barriers in Disability Inclusion and Support Systems in Low-and Middle-Income Sub-Saharan African Countries' (2021) 16 *Frontiers in Education* 754140.

90 Uduak Okon, 'The Effects of Household Crowding on School Attendance in Urban Informal Neighbourhoods of the Lagos Metropolis, Nigeria' (2022) 68 *Genus* 7

91 Diana Mitlin, 'Catalysing Local Government Engagement with Urban Poverty Reduction' (2022) 49 *Journal of International Development* 792.

92 Deborah Potts, 'Gendered Space and Economic Opportunity in African Cities' (2022) 44 *Journal of Southern African Studies* 111.

93 Ambe J. Njoh and Elizabeth N.M. Ayuk-Etang, 'Deterrents to Informal Urbanism in Sub-Saharan Africa: The Case for Prioritising Financial Interventions Over Repressive Measures' (2021) 31 *Urban Forum* 291.

94 Rafael Pereira, 'Gendered Mobilities and Transport Access in Sub-Saharan Africa' (2022) 1 *Frontiers in Future Transportation* 871874.

housing, the improvement of basic services and infrastructure, and the promotion of inclusive urban development. This includes the development and implementation of slum upgrading programmes that focus on the provision of healthcare, education, and community facilities, the creation of safe and accessible public spaces, and the enhancement of community participation and empowerment.[95]

Moreover, there is a need for targeted interventions that address the specific needs and vulnerabilities of different population groups, such as women, children, and people with disabilities. This includes the provision of gender-responsive healthcare and education services, the creation of safe and inclusive public spaces, and the strengthening of social protection systems.[96] The engagement and empowerment of local communities in the design and implementation of urban development initiatives are also critical for promoting the long-term sustainability and effectiveness of these efforts.[97]

Efforts to Improve Housing and Infrastructure in SSA

Policy Interventions and Institutional Reforms

Recognising the critical importance of improving housing and infrastructure in Sub-Saharan Africa (SSA), governments, international organisations, and civil society actors have undertaken various policy interventions and institutional reforms aimed at addressing the multifaceted challenges faced by the region.

In the housing sector, efforts to expand access to affordable and adequate housing have focused on the development and implementation of national housing policies, the strengthening of housing finance systems, and the promotion of inclusive and participatory approaches to housing delivery.[98] Many countries in SSA have adopted national housing policies that prioritise the needs of low-income households and aim to create an enabling environment for the provision of affordable and adequate housing.[99] These policies have included measures such as the provision of serviced land for housing development, the establishment of housing subsidy programmes, and the promotion of Public-Private Partnerships in housing delivery.[100]

95 Megan Chapman et al., 'Urban Africa: Risk Knowledge - A Research Agenda' (2022) 54 *Urban Studies* 2735.

96 Joseph Macarthy et al., *Confronting the Urban Housing Crisis in the Global South: Adequate, Secure, and Affordable Housing* (World Resources Institute, 2020).

97 Jane Weru et al., 'A Pathway to Urban Inclusion in Nairobi' (2022) 54 *Environment and Urbanization* 70.

98 Lochner Marais et al., 'The Housing Policy Paradox in South Africa: Challenges and Prospects' (2022) 32 Housing Policy Debate 1.

99 Kecia Rust, Housing Finance in Africa: A Review of Some of Africa's Housing Finance Markets (Centre for Affordable Housing Finance in Africa, 2022).

100 Olumuyiwa Ogunmakinde and Manya Mooya, 'The Role of Housing Microfinance in Informal Settlements Upgrading in South Africa' (2022) 12 *Sustainability* 1715.

Moreover, there has been a growing recognition of the importance of strengthening housing finance systems in SSA to improve access to affordable housing. Governments and international organisations have implemented various initiatives to develop and deepen housing finance markets, such as the establishment of housing finance institutions, the introduction of innovative financing mechanisms, and the promotion of microfinance for housing.[101] These efforts have aimed to increase the availability and affordability of housing finance, particularly for low-income households and those in the informal sector.[102]

In the infrastructure sector, policy interventions and institutional reforms have focused on improving the planning, financing, and delivery of essential infrastructure services, such as water, sanitation, electricity, and transportation. Many countries in SSA have adopted national infrastructure development plans that prioritise investments in critical infrastructure sectors and aim to create an enabling environment for private sector participation in infrastructure development.[103] These plans have included measures such as the establishment of infrastructure investment funds, the promotion of Public-Private Partnerships in infrastructure delivery, and the strengthening of regulatory frameworks for infrastructure services.[104]

Moreover, there has been a growing emphasis on promoting inclusive and sustainable approaches to infrastructure development in SSA. Governments and international organisations have increasingly recognised the importance of integrating social, economic, and environmental considerations into infrastructure planning and delivery and have implemented various initiatives to promote community participation, gender equality, and environmental sustainability in infrastructure projects.[105] These efforts have aimed to ensure that infrastructure investments not only improve access to essential services but also contribute to broader development objectives, such as poverty reduction, social inclusion, and climate resilience.[106]

Despite these policy interventions and institutional reforms, significant challenges persist in improving housing and infrastructure in SSA. Limited financial resources, weak institutional capacities, and the complex interplay of socio-economic, cultural, and political factors continue to hinder progress in

101 Issa Faye and Thouraya Triki, *Housing Finance in Africa* (African Development Bank, 2013).

102 Judith Ojo-Aromokudu and Pauline Adebayo, 'Strategies for Addressing Housing Affordability in the Global South: A Literature Review' (2022) 86 *Town Planning Review* 245.

103 African Development Bank, Financing Africa's Infrastructure: New Strategies, Mechanisms, and Instruments (2021).

104 Ben Arimah and Raf Tuts, Rethinking Urban Infrastructure in Africa: Don't Build Your Way Out of the Problem (LSE Cities, 2022).

105 Sylvia Croese and Edgar Pieterse, Reframing the New Urban Agenda in the Context of COVID-19: Implications for Urban Equality, Sustainability and Partnerships (IIED, 2021).

106 Daniel Hoornweg and Kevin Pope, 'Socioeconomic Pathways and Regional Distribution of the World's 101 Largest Cities' (2014) 4 Global Cities Institute Working Paper 4.

expanding access to affordable and adequate housing and infrastructure services.[107] Moreover, the effectiveness and sustainability of these interventions have been uneven, with some initiatives yielding positive results while others have faced challenges in implementation and impact.[108]

Addressing the challenges of housing and infrastructure development in SSA requires sustained political commitment, increased investments, and the strengthening of institutional capacities at all levels. This includes the development and implementation of comprehensive and integrated housing and infrastructure policies that prioritise the needs of low-income and marginalised communities, the mobilisation of domestic and international resources for housing and infrastructure development, and the promotion of inclusive and participatory approaches to urban planning and governance.[109] Moreover, there is a need for continued innovation and experimentation in housing and infrastructure delivery models, leveraging the potential of new technologies, financing mechanisms, and partnerships to accelerate progress towards the realisation of the right to adequate housing and infrastructure in SSA.[110]

Innovative Approaches and Best Practices

In addition to policy interventions and institutional reforms, innovative approaches and best practices have emerged in Sub-Saharan Africa (SSA) to address the challenges of housing and infrastructure development. These innovations leverage technology, community engagement, and cross-sectoral collaboration to deliver housing and infrastructure services more effectively and reach marginalised populations.

In the housing sector, the adoption of incremental housing approaches has shown promise in improving access to affordable and adequate housing for low-income households in SSA. Incremental housing involves the provision of basic housing units or serviced plots that can be progressively upgraded and expanded over time, based on the needs and resources of the household.[111] This approach has been successfully implemented in various countries in SSA, such as South Africa, Kenya, and Ethiopia, and has demonstrated the potential to deliver affordable and flexible housing solutions at scale.[112]

107 Ambe J Njoh, 'Models of Urban Land Use in Sub-Saharan Africa: Explaining the Failure of the State' (2022) 19 *Afrika Focus* 143.

108 Sarah Charlton, 'Spanning the Spectrum: Infrastructural Experiences in South Africa's State Housing Programme' (2018) *40 International Development Planning Review* 97.

109 Ibid.

110 Nic Cheeseman (ed), *The African City* (Cambridge University Press, 2022).

111 Abubakar Danladi Isah and Chichebe Muslim, 'Incremental Housing Development in Abuja, Nigeria: Challenges and Prospects' (2021) 11 Civil Engineering and Architecture 1259.

112 Liza Rose Cirolia, 'Fractured Fiscal Authority and Fragmented Infrastructures: Financing Sustainable Urban Development in Sub-Saharan Africa' (2020) 30 Habitat International 102233.

Moreover, the use of alternative building materials and technologies has emerged as an innovative approach to reducing the cost and environmental impact of housing construction in SSA. The use of local materials, such as compressed earth blocks, bamboo, and recycled materials, has been promoted as a sustainable and cost-effective alternative to conventional building materials such as cement and steel.[113] Additionally, the adoption of prefabrication and modular construction techniques has shown potential in reducing construction time and costs, while improving the quality and durability of housing units.[114]

In the infrastructure sector, the use of decentralised and community-based approaches has proven effective in improving access to essential services, particularly in informal settlements and low-income areas. Decentralised infrastructure systems, such as small-scale water and sanitation facilities, renewable energy systems, and community-managed waste collection services, have been implemented in various countries in SSA, demonstrating the potential to deliver affordable and sustainable infrastructure solutions at the local level.[115]

Moreover, the adoption of participatory and inclusive approaches to infrastructure planning and delivery has emerged as a best practice in SSA. The engagement of local communities in the design, implementation, and management of infrastructure projects has been shown to improve the relevance, ownership, and sustainability of these interventions.[116] Participatory approaches, such as community-led urban upgrading and co-production of infrastructure services, have been successfully implemented in various countries in SSA, such as Kenya, Tanzania, and Uganda, and have demonstrated the potential to deliver more equitable and resilient infrastructure solutions.[117]

The use of digital technologies and data-driven approaches has also emerged as an innovative approach to improving the planning, delivery, and management of housing and infrastructure services in SSA. The adoption of geographic information systems (GIS), remote sensing, and mobile technologies has enabled the collection and analysis of spatial data on housing and infrastructure conditions, facilitating evidence-based decision-making and resource

113 Holger Wallbaum et al., 'Sustainable Construction in Sub-Saharan Africa: Reflection and Way Forward' (2021) 8 *Frontiers in Built Environment* 863350.

114 Matthew French and Daniel Ting, 'Sustainable Social Housing: An Inconvenient Truth - The Exclusion of Social Agency and Environmental Impact in Sustainability Assessments' (2022) 173 *Energy and Buildings* 112090.

115 Silver Mugisha et al., 'Pro-Poor Water Services and Infrastructure in Urban Africa: Challenges and Opportunities' (2021) 9 *Water Security* 100086.

116 Pasif Rashidi et al., 'Towards Participatory Infrastructuring: The Case of Makerspaces in Nairobi's Informal Settlements' (2022) 1 Proceedings of the Association for Computing Machinery on Human-Computer Interaction 40.

117 Debdulal Thakur et al., 'Community-Managed Sanitation: A Systematic Review of Evidence from Low-and Middle-Income Countries' (2022) 15 *Frontiers in Environmental Science* 790754.

allocation.[118] Moreover, the use of digital platforms and mobile applications has improved the accessibility and transparency of housing and infrastructure services, enabling citizens to report issues, access information, and provide feedback on service delivery.[119]

While these innovative approaches and best practices hold promise in improving housing and infrastructure development in SSA, scaling up and sustaining these interventions remains a challenge. Limited financial resources, weak institutional capacities, and the need for long-term investments pose significant barriers to the widespread adoption and impact of these innovations.[120] Nonetheless, the lessons learned from these experiences provide valuable insights and guidance for policymakers, practitioners, and researchers working towards expanding access to affordable and adequate housing and infrastructure services in SSA.

Conclusion

Adequate housing and infrastructure are fundamental components of the right to an adequate standard of living, playing a crucial role in promoting the health, well-being, and socio-economic development of individuals and communities. However, in Sub-Saharan Africa (SSA), ensuring equitable access to these basic necessities remains a significant challenge, with far-reaching implications for the realisation of this fundamental human right.

This chapter has provided a comprehensive examination of the multifaceted challenges to housing and infrastructure development in SSA, highlighting the complex interplay of socio-economic, political, and structural factors that perpetuate inequalities and hinder progress towards adequate housing and infrastructure for all. The analysis has shed light on the challenges posed by rapid urbanisation, inadequate urban planning, limited access to affordable housing, poor quality housing, insufficient basic services, inadequate transportation networks, and limited access to clean water and sanitation facilities, which disproportionately affect low-income and marginalised communities in the region.

The chapter has also explored the wide-ranging implications of inadequate housing and infrastructure on various dimensions of human well-being, including health risks and vulnerability, limited economic opportunities and social exclusion, and reduced access to essential services and amenities. The far-reaching consequences of these challenges, such as increased morbidity and mortality rates, perpetuation of poverty and inequality, and undermining

118 Michal Apollo et al., 'Geospatial Information, Citizen Science and Spatial Data Infrastructures for Sustainable Development Goals in Africa' (2022) 12 *ISPRS International Journal of Geo-Information* 190.

119 Ibid.

120 Sylvia Croese and Edgar Pieterse, *Reframing the New Urban Agenda in the Context of COVID-19: Implications for Urban Equality, Sustainability and Partnerships* (IIED, 2021).

of social cohesion and inclusive development, underscore the urgent need for concerted efforts to address these barriers and ensure equitable access to adequate housing and infrastructure.

Moreover, the chapter has critically evaluated the policy interventions, institutional reforms, and innovative approaches undertaken by governments, international organisations, and civil society actors to improve housing and infrastructure development in SSA. While these efforts have yielded some progress and promising practices, significant challenges persist in ensuring the sustainability, scalability, and impact of these interventions.

Moving forward, addressing the challenges of housing and infrastructure development in SSA requires a holistic and multisectoral approach that prioritises equity, inclusivity, and the empowerment of marginalised communities. This necessitates sustained investments in affordable and adequate housing, the strengthening of urban planning and governance frameworks, and the implementation of targeted interventions to address the specific needs and vulnerabilities of different population groups.

Furthermore, fostering participatory and community-driven approaches, leveraging technology and innovation, and promoting cross-sectoral collaboration and partnerships are crucial in driving systemic change and ensuring that no one is left behind in accessing adequate housing and infrastructure. By addressing these challenges and promoting equitable access to these basic necessities, SSA can make significant strides towards realising the right to an adequate standard of living for all its citizens and fostering inclusive and sustainable urban development in the region.

The insights and lessons gleaned from this chapter provide a foundation for subsequent chapters that will delve into strategies, best practices, and challenges in advancing housing and infrastructure development and promoting inclusive urbanisation in SSA. By shedding light on the complexities surrounding housing and infrastructure, this chapter contributes to a nuanced understanding of these critical issues and underscores the imperative of prioritising equitable access to adequate housing and infrastructure in the pursuit of the right to an adequate standard of living in the region.

References

Acuto M et al, 'Infrastructural Deficits and Potential in African Cities' (2022) 1 *Urban Studies* 10.

Adegun OB, 'Infrastructure Development and the Prospect of Inclusive Growth in Nigerian Informal Settlements' (2022) 32 *Urban Forum* 147.

African Development Bank, *Financing Africa's Infrastructure: New Strategies, Mechanisms, and Instruments* (African Development Bank 2021).

Ahonsi BA, 'Inclusive Health Delivery in an Urban African Context: Reflections and Options for Action' (2020) 12 *Social Sciences* 133.

Akay SS, 'Informal Settlements, Shelter Deprivations and Development Challenges in Sub-Saharan Africa' (2021) 79 *Local Economy* 1007.

Alexander D et al, 'Burden of Disease from Household Air Pollution for 2016' (2018) 78 *International Journal of Public Health* 573.

Amadi CC et al, 'The Impact of Roadside Pollution in an Emerging African Megacity: The Lagos Metropolis Experience' (2022) 169 *Science of the Total Environment* 155157.

Apollo M et al, 'Geospatial Information, Citizen Science and Spatial Data Infrastructures for Sustainable Development Goals in Africa' (2022) 12 *ISPRS International Journal of Geo-Information* 190.

Arimah B and Tuts R, *Rethinking Urban Infrastructure in Africa: Don't Build Your Way Out of the Problem* (LSE Cities 2022).

Aromokudu JO and Adebayo P, 'Strategies for Addressing Housing Affordability in the Global South: A Literature Review' (2022) 86 *Town Planning Review* 245.

Arora A and Tiwari G, 'A Framework for Assessing Level of Service of Informal Public Transport Services' (2016) 3 *Transportation Research Procedia* 1.

Azunre GA et al, 'Urban Informalities in Sub-Saharan Africa (SSA): A Solution for or Barrier against Sustainable City Development' (2022) 152 *World Development* https://doi.org/10.1016/j.worlddev.2021.105782.

Bah EM et al, *Housing Market Dynamics in Africa* (Palgrave Macmillan 2018) available at <https://link.springer.com/book/10.1057/978-1-137-59792-2> accessed 2 July 2024.

Baines JITet al, 'Social Impact Assessment and Ethical Research Principles: Ethical Professional Practice in Impact Assessment Part II' (2013) 31(4) *Impact Assessment and Project Appraisal* 254–260 https://doi.org/10.1080/14615517.2013.850306.

Bartram Jet al, 'Global Monitoring of Water Supply and Sanitation: History, Methods and Future Challenges' (2014) 11 *International Journal of Environmental Research and Public Health* 8137 https://doi.org/10.3390/ijerph110808137.

Bayo AO, 'Housing and Infrastructure Development in Informal Settlements: Debates and New Directions' (2021) 21 *Journal of Infrastructure Development* 31.

Behrens R et al, 'Low-Income Household Travel Expenditure in Sub-Saharan African Cities: Unpacking the Implications of Affordability and Accessibility' (2022) 36 *Transport Policy* 158.

Chapman M et al, 'Urban Africa: Risk Knowledge - A Research Agenda' (2022) 54 *Urban Studies* 2735.

Charlton S, 'Spanning the Spectrum: Infrastructural Experiences in South Africa's State Housing Programme' (2018) 40 *International Development Planning Review* 97.

Charlton S and Meth P, 'Lived Experiences of State Housing in Johannesburg and Durban' (2017) 93 *Transformation: Critical Perspectives on Southern Africa* 91.

Cheeseman N (ed), *The African City* (Cambridge University Press 2022).

Chirisa I and Bandauko E, 'African Cities and the Water-Food-Climate-Energy Nexus: An Agenda for Sustainability and Resilience at a Local Level' (2015) 50 *Urban Forum* 391.

Christa Brelsford et al, 'Heterogeneity and Scale of Sustainable Development in Cities' (2017) 34 *PNAS* 8963–8968 https://doi.org/10.1073/pnas.1606033114.

Cirolia LR, 'Fractured Fiscal Authority and Fragmented Infrastructures: Financing Sustainable Urban Development in Sub-Saharan Africa' (2020) 30 *Habitat International* 102233.

Cirolia LR and Smit W, 'Fractured Approaches to Urban Transformation: Analyzing Parallel Perspectives in South Africa' (2017) 42 *Transformation: Critical Perspectives on Southern Africa* 86.
Croese S and Pieterse E, *Reframing the New Urban Agenda in the Context of COVID-19: Implications for Urban Equality, Sustainability and Partnerships* (IIED 2021).
Devereux S and Sabates-Wheeler R, 'Transformative Social Protection' (2004) IDS Working Paper 232.
Ezeadichie J et al, 'Crowdsourced Mapping of Paratransit in Kigali, Rwanda' (2022) 7 *Journal of Transport Geography* 103418.
Faye I and Triki T, *Housing Finance in Africa* (African Development Bank 2013).
Florida R, *Slums, Favelas and Shantytowns: What's in a Name?* (Bloomberg CityLab 2017).
Fox S, 'Urbanization as a Global Historical Process: Theory and Evidence from Sub-Saharan Africa' (2012) 38 *Population and Development Review* 285–310 https://doi.org/10.1111/j.1728-4457.2012.00493.x
French M and Ting D, 'Sustainable Social Housing: An Inconvenient Truth - The Exclusion of Social Agency and Environmental Impact in Sustainability Assessments' (2022) 173 *Energy and Buildings* 112090.
Gulyani S and Bassett EM, 'The Living Conditions Diamond: An Analytical and Theoretical Framework for Understanding Slums' (2010) 21 *Environment and Planning A: Economy and Space* https://doi.org/10.1068/a42520.
Hofmann P and Manian K, 'Aggregated Inconvenience: Redefining the Boundaries of Housing and Home in Resettlement Housing' (2021) 41 *Urban Planning and Transport Research* 81.
Hoornweg D and Pope K, 'Socioeconomic Pathways and Regional Distribution of the World's 101 Largest Cities' (2014) 4 *Global Cities Institute Working Paper* 4.
Isah AD and Muslim C, 'Incremental Housing Development in Abuja, Nigeria: Challenges and Prospects' (2021) 11 *Civil Engineering and Architecture* 1259.
Jones A and Stead L, 'Can People on Low Incomes Access Affordable Housing Loans in Urban Africa and Asia? Examples of Innovative Housing Finance Models from Reall's Global Network' (2020) 32(1) *Environment & Urbanization* 155-174 https://doi.org/10.1177/0956247819899557.
Kelder Y et al, '#MeToo? The Role of Gender, Socio-Economic Status and Transport in Commuter Vulnerability to Crime in Johannesburg' (2022) 22 *Urban Studies* 3.
Kinyanjui S et al, 'Water, Sanitation, Hygiene, and Waste Management for the Prevention and Control of COVID-19 in Informal Settlements and Slums' (2022) 17 *Global Health: Science and Practice* 63.
Klopp JM et al, 'Harmonized Indicators for Informal Public Transport Data Collection in Sub-Saharan African Cities' (2021) 7 *Journal of Transport Geography* 103156.
Kwak N, *A World of Homeowners: American Power and the Politics of Housing Aid* (University of Chicago Press 2015) https://doi.org/10.7208/chicago/9780226282497.001.0001.
Leck H and Simon D, 'Fostering Multiscalar Collaboration and Co-operation for Effective Governance of Climate Change Adaptation' (2013) 50(6) *Urban Studies* 1221–1238 https://doi.org/10.1177/0042098012461675.
Lombard M, 'Informality as Structure or Agency? Exploring Shed Housing in the UK as Informal Practice' (2019) 56 *International Journal of Urban and Regional Research* 569.

Lwasa S et al, 'Urban and Peri-Urban Agriculture and Forestry: Transcending Poverty Allevitaion to Climate Change Mitigation and Adaptation' (2013) 30 *Urban Climate* http://dx.doi.org/10.1016/j.uclim.2013.10.007 .

Macarthy J et al. *Confronting the Urban Housing Crisis in the Global South: Adequate, Secure, and Affordable Housing* (World Resources Institute 2020).

Maggie Mwoka et al, 'Housing as a Social Determinant of Health: Evidence from Singapore, the UK, and Kenya: The 3-D Commission' (2021) 98 *Journal of Urban Health* 15–30 https://doi.org/10.1007%2Fs11524-021-00557-8.

Marais L et al, 'The Housing Policy Paradox in South Africa: Challenges and Prospects' (2022) 32 *Housing Policy Debate* 1.

Marais L et al, 'Informal Settlement Upgrading: Assessing the Literature and Experiences from Sub-Saharan Africa' (2014) *Centre for Development Support Working Paper* 3.

Mberu BU et al, 'Bringing Sexual and Reproductive Health in the Urban Contexts to the Forefront of the Development Agenda: The Case for Prioritizing the Urban Poor' (2014) 9 *Maternal and Child Health Journal* 1572.

Mberu BU et al, 'Health and Health-Related Indicators in Slum, Rural, and Urban Communities: A Comparative Analysis' (2016) 9 *Global Health Action* 33163 https://doi.org/10.3402/gha.v9.33163.

Mitlin D, 'Catalysing Local Government Engagement with Urban Poverty Reduction' (2022) 49 *Journal of International Development* 792.

Mugisha S et al, 'Pro-Poor Water Services and Infrastructure in Urban Africa: Challenges and Opportunities' (2021) 9 *Water Security* 100086.

Mukundane J and Naudé W, 'Healthcare Access and Quality in Sub-Saharan Africa: Evidence from a Stochastic Frontier Analysis' (2022) 21 *International* Health 157.

Njoh AJ, 'Models of Urban Land Use in Sub-Saharan Africa: Explaining the Failure of the State' (2022) 19 *Afrika Focus* 143.

Njoh AJ and Ayuk-Etang ENM, 'Deterrents to Informal Urbanism in Sub-Saharan Africa: The Case for Prioritising Financial Interventions Over Repressive Measures' (2021) 31 *Urban Forum* 291.

Noorloos FV et al, 'Incremental Housing as a Node for Intersecting Flows of City-Making: Rethinking the Housing Shortage in the Global South' (2019) 32(1) *Environment & Urbanization* 37–54 https://doi.org/10.1177/0956247819887679.

Nubi TG et al, *Housing and SDGs in Urban Africa* (Springer Nature 2021).

Obeng-Odoom F, 'The State of African Cities 2014' (2014) 51(4) *Journal of Asian and African Studies* 389–397 https://doi.org/10.1177/0021909614547604.

Ogunmakinde O and Mooya M, 'The Role of Housing Microfinance in Informal Settlements Upgrading in South Africa' (2022) 12 *Sustainability* 1715.

Okon U, 'The Effects of Household Crowding on School Attendance in Urban Informal Neighbourhoods of the Lagos Metropolis, Nigeria' (2022) 68 *Genus* 7.

Ouyang Y et al, 'Health Impacts of Ambient Air Pollution in Sub-Saharan Africa: Evidence from the Demographic and Health Surveys' (2021) 202 *Environmental Research* 111701.

Oviedo D et al, 'The Elusive Quest for Integration in the Planning and Delivery of Urban Transport in Sub-Saharan Africa: The Case of Maputo, Mozambique' (2021) 33 *Planning Theory & Practice* 46.

Owino EA et al, 'Community-Based Solid Waste Management Approaches for Sustainable Development: A Case Study of Waste Management Groups in Kisumu, Kenya' (2021) 10 *Frontiers in Sustainable Cities* 678495.

Oyebanji OO et al, 'A Systematic Review of Housing Quality and Health in Sub-Saharan Africa' (2022) 16 *International Journal of Environmental Research and Public Health* 2801.

Pereira R, 'Gendered Mobilities and Transport Access in Sub-Saharan Africa' (2022) 1 *Frontiers in Future Transportation* 871874.

Phang S and Helble M, 'Housing Policies I Singapore' (2016) ADBI Working Paper 559 available at <https://r.search.yahoo.com/_ylt=AwrkPUdbRIRmskUVNwl3Bwx.;_ylu=Y29sbwMEcG9zAzIEdnRpZAMEc2VjA3Ny/RV=2/RE=1719973084/RO=10/RU=https%3a%2f%2fwww.adb.org%2fsites%2fdefault%2ffiles%2fpublication%2f181599%2fadbi-wp559.pdf/RK=2/RS=w522RR2yrAbdvki9QCayj0NJQTE-> accessed 2 July 2024.

Phillips J et al, *Energy Access and Forced Migration* (Chatham House 2019).

Pieterse E et al, *New Urban Worlds: Inhabiting Dissonant Times* (Polity Press 2017).

Pieterse E and Parnell S, *Africa's Urban Revolution* (Zed Books 2014).

Popoola A et al, 'Bridging the Security Gap in Poor Urban Neighbourhoods Through Neighbourhood Planning' (2021) 19 *Urban Design International* 167.

Potts D, 'Gendered Space and Economic Opportunity in African Cities' (2022) 44 *Journal of Southern African Studies* 111.

Potts D, 'The Slowing of Sun-Saharan Africa's Urbanization: Evidence and Implications for Urban Livelihoods' (2009) 21 *Environment and Urbanization* 253 https://doi.org/10.1177/0956247809103026.

Rakodi C, 'Addressing Gendered Inequalities in Housing' in Caroline ON Moser (ed), *Gender, Asset Accumulation and Just Cities: Pathways to Transformation* (Routledge 2015).

Rashidi P et al, 'Towards Participatory Infrastructuring: The Case of Makerspaces in Nairobi's Informal Settlements' (2022) 1 *Proceedings of the Association for Computing Machinery on Human-Computer Interaction* 40.

Rust K, *Housing Finance in Africa: A Review of Some of Africa's Housing Finance Markets* (Centre for Affordable Housing Finance in Africa 2022).

Sabates-Wheeler S and MacAuslan I, 'Migration and Social Protection: Exposing Problems of Access' (2007) 35 *Development* 26.

Satterthwaite D, 'Missing the Millenium Development Goal Targets for Water and Sanitation in Urban Areas' (2016) 28(1) *Environment and Urbanization* 99 https://doi.org/10.1177/0956247816628435.

Satterthwaite D, 'Reducing Urban Poverty: Some Lessons from Experience' (2002) 13 *Environment and Urbanization* 167.

Satterthwaite D, 'The Sustainable Development Goals and Urban Inequality' (2022) 55 *Environment and Urbanization* 453 https://doi.org/10.1177/0956247816637501.

Scott A et al, *Accelerating Access to Electricity in Africa with Off-Grid Solar: The Impact of Solar Household Solutions* (Overseas Development Institute 2016).

Silver J, 'Incremental Infrastructures: Material Improvisation and Social Collaboration Across Post-Colonial Accra' (2014) 51 *Urban Geography* 1011.

Sliuzas R, *Opportunities for Enhancing Communication, Learning and Decision Making Among Stakeholders in Urban Planning and Management using Geo-Information Technology* (ITC Dissertation 2003) 114.

Teferi ZA and Newman P, 'Slum Regeneration and Sustainability: Applying Extended Metabolism Model and the SDGs' (2017) 9(12) *Sustainability* 2273 http://dx.doi.org/10.3390/su9122273.

Thakur D et al, 'Community-Managed Sanitation: A Systematic Review of Evidence from Low-and Middle-Income Countries' (2022) 15 *Frontiers in Environmental Science* 790754.

UN Habitat, *The Challenge of Slums: Global Report on Human Settlements 2003* (UN Habitat 2003) available at <https://unhabitat.org/sites/default/files/download-manager-files/The%20Challenge%20of%20Slums%20-%20Global%20Report%20on%20Human%20Settlements%202003.pdf> accessed 27 June 2024.

UNICEF and WHO, *Progress on Household Drinking Water, Sanitation and Hygiene 2000–2020: Five Years into the SDGs* (UNICEF and WHO 2021).

United Nations Department of Economic and Social Affairs, *World Urbanization Prospects: The 2018 Revision* (United Nations 2019).

United Nations General Assembly, 'International Covenant on Economic, Social and Cultural Rights' (1966) 993(11) *UN Treaty Series.*

Venter C et al, 'The Equity Impacts of Bus Rapid Transit: A Review of the Evidence and Implications for Sustainable Transport' (2018) 74 *International Journal of Sustainable Transportation* 140.

Wallbaum H et al, 'Sustainable Construction in Sub-Saharan Africa: Reflection and Way Forward' (2021) 8 *Frontiers in Built Environment* 863350.

Walters J, 'Overview of Public Transport Policy Developments in South Africa' (2013) 39 *Research in Transportation Economics* 34.

Wamala PM et al, 'Sustainable Urban Mobility in Sub-Saharan Africa: Assessing the Sustainability of the Matatu System in Kampala City' (2022) 12 *Sustainability* 9750.

Watson V, 'African Urban Fantasies: Dreams or Nightmares?' (2014) 26 *Environment and Urbanization* 215–231 https://doi.org/10.1177/0956247813513705.

Watson V, 'Conflicting Rationalities: Implications for Planning Theory and Ethics' (2003) 4(4) *Planning Theory and Practice* 395–407 https://doi.org/10.1080/1464935032000146318.

Watson V, 'Seeing from the South: Refocusing Urban Planning on the Globe's Central Urban Issues' (2009) 46 *Urban Studies* 2259.

Weru J et al, 'A Pathway to Urban Inclusion in Nairobi' (2022) 54 *Environment and Urbanization* 70.

Windapo A and Olugboyega O, 'Housing Quality Assessment System for Developing Countries: The Delphi Method Approach' (2021) 3 *Journal of African Real Estate Research* 97.

Zoomers A et al, 'The Rush for Land in an Urbanizing World: From Land Grabbing Toward Developing Safe, Resilient, and Sustainable Cities and Landscapes' (2017) 92 *World Development* 242–252 https://doi.org/10.1016/j.worlddev.2016.11.016.

7 Environmental Degradation and Climate Change

Introduction

Environmental degradation and climate change have emerged as critical challenges of our time, with far-reaching implications for sustainable development, human well-being, and the realisation of fundamental human rights. In Sub-Saharan Africa (SSA), these challenges are particularly acute, as the region grapples with a complex interplay of socio-economic, political, and environmental factors that exacerbate vulnerability and undermine the enjoyment of the right to an adequate standard of living.[1]

The impacts of environmental degradation and climate change in SSA are multifaceted and profound, affecting various dimensions of human development and well-being. Deforestation, desertification, loss of biodiversity, land degradation, and water scarcity are among the pressing environmental challenges faced by the region, with far-reaching consequences for food security, livelihoods, and public health.[2] Moreover, the increased frequency and intensity of extreme weather events, such as droughts, floods, and heatwaves, further compound the vulnerability of communities and ecosystems, undermining resilience and adaptive capacity.[3]

The adverse effects of environmental degradation and climate change in SSA are not evenly distributed, with vulnerable and marginalised populations bearing a disproportionate burden of the impacts. Rural communities, smallholder farmers, women, and indigenous peoples are among the groups most at risk, as they often rely heavily on natural resources for their livelihoods and have limited access to resources and support systems to cope with environmental

1 United Nations General Assembly, 'Transforming our world: the 2030 Agenda for Sustainable Development' (2015) A/RES/70/1.

2 IPCC, Climate Change 2022: Impacts, Adaptation and Vulnerability. Contribution of Working Group II to the Sixth Assessment Report of the Intergovernmental Panel on Climate Change (Cambridge University Press, 2022).

3 World Bank, Accelerating Climate-Resilient and Low-Carbon Development: Africa Climate Business Plan - Third Implementation Progress Report and Forward Look (World Bank, 2021).

DOI: 10.4324/9781032628974-7

shocks and stresses.[4] Moreover, the impacts of environmental degradation and climate change can exacerbate existing inequalities and social vulnerabilities, perpetuating poverty, food insecurity, and displacement.[5]

The realisation of the right to an adequate standard of living in SSA is closely intertwined with the state of the environment and the impacts of climate change. Access to clean water, sufficient and nutritious food, adequate housing, and sustainable livelihoods are all fundamental components of this right and are directly affected by environmental degradation and climate variability.[6] As such, addressing these challenges is not only an environmental imperative but also a human rights obligation, requiring concerted efforts to protect and fulfil the rights of individuals and communities in the face of growing environmental risks.[7]

Recognising the urgency of the situation, governments, international organisations, and civil society actors in SSA have undertaken various efforts to address environmental degradation and climate change. These efforts range from policy initiatives and adaptation strategies to mitigation measures and international collaborations aimed at building resilience, reducing vulnerability, and promoting sustainable development.[8] However, the effectiveness and scale of these efforts have been uneven, underscoring the need for more comprehensive, integrated, and rights-based approaches to tackling these complex challenges.

This chapter aims to provide a critical examination of the impacts of environmental degradation and climate change on the realisation of the right to an adequate standard of living in SSA. By exploring the multifaceted consequences of these challenges, analysing the disproportionate impacts on vulnerable populations, and evaluating the efforts undertaken to address them, the chapter seeks to contribute to a more nuanced understanding of the intricate relationship between environmental sustainability, socio-economic development, and human rights in the region. In doing so, it underscores the urgency for robust environmental policies, sustainable development practices, and international cooperation to safeguard the right to an adequate standard of living in the face of growing environmental risks.

4 UNEP, Adaptation Gap Report 2021: The Gathering Storm - Adapting to Climate Change in a Post-Pandemic World (UNEP, 2021).
5 Ahmadou Aly Mbaye and Landry Signé, Change and Development in Africa (Brookings Institution Press, 2022).
6 Olivier De Schutter, 'Climate Change and the Human Right to Adequate Food' in Ottavio Quirico and Mouloud Boumghar (eds), Climate Change and Human Rights: An International and Comparative Law Perspective (Routledge, 2016).
7 Sumudu Atapattu, 'Climate Change and Human Rights in Africa' in Ademola Oluborode Jegede (ed), *Human Rights and the Environment under African Union Law* (Palgrave Macmillan, 2020).
8 African Union, *African Strategy on Climate Change* (African Union, 2022).

Consequences of Environmental Degradation and Climate Change in SSA

Deforestation and Loss of Biodiversity

Deforestation and the loss of biodiversity are among the most pressing environmental challenges faced by Sub-Saharan Africa (SSA), with far-reaching consequences for the region's ecosystems, livelihoods, and the realisation of the right to an adequate standard of living. The rapid loss of forest cover and the degradation of natural habitats have led to the erosion of vital ecosystem services, the decline of species diversity, and the increased vulnerability of communities to environmental shocks and stresses.

SSA is home to some of the world's most diverse and critical forest ecosystems, including the Congo Basin rainforest, the second-largest tropical rainforest after the Amazon.[9] These forests play a crucial role in regulating the global climate, maintaining water cycles, and providing habitats for a wide range of plant and animal species. However, the region has experienced significant deforestation in recent decades, driven by a complex interplay of factors, including agricultural expansion, logging, urbanisation, and the demand for fuelwood and charcoal.[10]

The loss of forest cover has profound implications for biodiversity, as forests are home to a significant proportion of the region's plant and animal species. Deforestation fragments habitats, disrupts ecological processes, and increases the risk of species extinction, with cascading effects on ecosystem functioning and resilience.[11] Moreover, the loss of forest biodiversity undermines the livelihoods and well-being of local communities, who often rely on forest resources for food, medicine, and income generation.[12]

The consequences of deforestation and biodiversity loss extend beyond the immediate environmental impacts, affecting various dimensions of human development and the enjoyment of the right to an adequate standard of living. The degradation of forest ecosystems can exacerbate soil erosion, reduce soil fertility, and contribute to the siltation of rivers and streams, affecting agricultural productivity and water quality.[13] Moreover, the loss of forest cover can alter local and regional climate patterns, increasing the frequency and intensity

9 FAO, 'The State of the World's Forests 2022: Forest Pathways for Green Recovery and Building Inclusive, Resilient and Sustainable Economies' (FAO, 2022).

10 Olufunso A. Somorin et al., 'The Congo Basin Forests in a Changing Climate: Policy Discourses on Adaptation and Mitigation (REDD+)' (2012) 22 *Global Environmental Change* 288.

11 Yadvinder Malhi and Luiz E.O.C. Aragão, 'The African Rainforests in the Anthropocene' in Kathryn Reyerson (ed), *The Medieval Globe, Volume 4: A Global History of Early Modern Deforestation* (Arc Humanities Press, 2023).

12 Luke Preece et al., 'Quantifying the Contribution of Non-Timber Forest Products to the Livelihoods of Communities in the Miombo Woodlands: A Systematic Review' (2021) 6 *Trees, Forests and People* 100136.

13 Meine van Noordwijk, 'Integrated Natural Resource Management as Pathway to Poverty Reduction: Innovating Practices, Institutions and Policies' (2019) 172 *Agricultural Systems* 60.

of extreme weather events such as droughts and floods, which disproportionately affect vulnerable communities.[14]

Addressing the challenges of deforestation and biodiversity loss in SSA requires a multifaceted approach that recognises the complex drivers and impacts of these issues. This includes the development and implementation of sustainable forest management practices, the promotion of agroforestry and other land-use practices that integrate conservation and livelihood objectives, and the strengthening of governance frameworks and institutions for forest and biodiversity management.[15]

There is a need for greater recognition of the rights and roles of local communities and indigenous peoples in forest conservation and management. The traditional knowledge and practices of these communities can provide valuable insights for sustainable forest management, and their active participation in decision-making processes can help ensure that conservation efforts are socially just and equitable.[16]

Addressing deforestation and biodiversity loss also requires tackling the underlying drivers of these challenges, such as poverty, inequality, and unsustainable consumption patterns. This necessitates a broader transformation towards more sustainable and inclusive development pathways, which prioritise the conservation and sustainable use of natural resources, while also addressing the social and economic needs of communities.[17]

Land Degradation and Desertification

Land degradation and desertification are significant environmental challenges in Sub-Saharan Africa (SSA), with far-reaching implications for food security, livelihoods, and the realisation of the right to an adequate standard of living. These challenges are driven by a complex interplay of factors, including unsustainable land-use practices, overgrazing, deforestation, and climate change, which lead to the loss of soil fertility, the reduction of vegetation cover, and the expansion of drylands and desert-like conditions.[18]

14 Cheikh Mbow et al., 'What Drives the Vulnerability of Pastoralists to Global Environmental Change? A Qualitative Meta-Analysis' (2019) 54 *Global Environmental Change* 56.

15 Lalisa A. Duguma et al., 'Community Forestry Frameworks in Sub-Saharan Africa and the Impact on Sustainable Development' (2018) 21 *Ecology and Society* 21.

16 Phil Franks et al., 'Who has been left behind? Why sustainable development goals fail the Arab world' (2018) 10 *World Development* 540.

17 Frank Sperling et al., 'Resilient Sustainable Development - Emerging Concepts for Africa's Transformation towards Sustainability and Resilience' (2020) 25 *Current Opinion in Environmental Sustainability* 73.

18 Alisher Mirzabaev et al., 'Desertification' in Priyadarshi R. Shukla et al. (eds), 'Climate Change and Land: An IPCC Special Report on Climate Change, Desertification, Land Degradation, Sustainable Land Management, Food Security, and Greenhouse Gas Fluxes in Terrestrial Ecosystems' (IPCC, 2019).

SSA is particularly vulnerable to land degradation and desertification due to its heavy reliance on agriculture and natural resources, coupled with high rates of population growth and poverty. The region is home to vast areas of drylands, including the Sahel and the Horn of Africa, which are characterised by low and erratic rainfall, high temperatures, and fragile ecosystems.[19] These areas are particularly susceptible to land degradation, as the combination of climatic factors and human activities, such as overgrazing and unsustainable farming practices, can lead to the rapid loss of vegetation cover and soil erosion.[20]

The consequences of land degradation and desertification for food security and livelihoods in SSA are significant. The loss of soil fertility and the reduction of vegetation cover can lead to declines in agricultural productivity, increased crop failures, and reduced availability of forage for livestock.[21] This can have devastating impacts on rural communities who often rely on agriculture and livestock rearing for their livelihoods and food security. Moreover, the expansion of drylands and desert-like conditions can lead to the displacement of communities, as agricultural lands become unproductive and water resources become scarce.[22]

Land degradation and desertification also have significant implications for the enjoyment of the right to an adequate standard of living in SSA. The loss of agricultural productivity and the displacement of communities can lead to increased poverty, food insecurity, and malnutrition, undermining the ability of individuals and households to meet their basic needs.[23] Moreover, the degradation of land and water resources can exacerbate existing inequalities and vulnerabilities, particularly for women and marginalised communities who often have limited access to resources and support systems to cope with environmental shocks and stresses.[24]

Addressing the challenges of land degradation and desertification in SSA requires a comprehensive and integrated approach that recognises the complex drivers and impacts of these issues. This includes the promotion of sustainable

19 Barron Joseph Orr et al., 'Scientific Conceptual Framework for Land Degradation Neutrality: A Report of the Science-Policy Interface' (United Nations Convention to Combat Desertification, 2017).

20 Lindsay C. Stringer et al., 'Improving the Relevance of Drylands Ecological Restoration Research: Steps Towards Implementing the UNCCD Ecological Restoration Plan of Work' (2022) 101 *Restoration Ecology* e13732.

21 Ermias Aynekulu et al., 'The Economics of Land Degradation in Africa' (2020) 3 *Land Degradation Neutrality: A Business Perspective*.

22 Sophie Pascale et al., 'Desertification Risk in the Sahel: Why Land Use and Land Cover Are Important' (2022) 28 *Regional Environmental Change* 63.

23 Ephraim Nkonya et al., 'The Unholy Cross: Profitability and Adoption of Climate-Smart Agriculture Practices in Africa South of the Sahara' (2018) 10 *International Journal of Agricultural Sustainability* 586.

24 Helen Young, *Nutrition in Africa's Drylands: A Conceptual Framework for Addressing Acute Malnutrition* (Feinstein International Center, Tufts University, 2020).

land management practices, such as agroforestry, conservation agriculture, and integrated soil fertility management, which can help restore degraded lands, improve soil health, and enhance agricultural productivity.[25]

Moreover, there is a need for greater investment in research and development to identify and promote drought-resistant crops and livestock breeds as well as to develop and disseminate technologies and practices that can help communities adapt to changing environmental conditions.[26] This should be coupled with efforts to strengthen the capacity of local institutions and communities to manage and protect their land and water resources and to build resilience to environmental shocks and stresses.[27]

Addressing land degradation and desertification also requires tackling the underlying drivers of these challenges, such as poverty, inequality, and unsustainable consumption patterns. This necessitates a broader transformation towards more sustainable and inclusive development pathways, which prioritise the conservation and sustainable use of natural resources, while also addressing the social and economic needs of communities.[28]

Water Scarcity and Drought

Water scarcity and drought are critical environmental challenges in Sub-Saharan Africa (SSA), with far-reaching implications for human well-being, socio-economic development, and the realisation of the right to an adequate standard of living. The region is characterised by a high degree of spatial and temporal variability in water availability, with many areas experiencing chronic water stress and recurrent droughts.[29] These challenges are exacerbated by a range of factors, including population growth, urbanisation, climate change, and unsustainable water management practices.

Water scarcity in SSA is a multifaceted issue, encompassing both physical and economic dimensions. Physical water scarcity refers to the insufficient availability of water resources to meet the demands of the population, while economic water scarcity refers to the lack of infrastructure and institutional capacity to access and distribute available water resources.[30] Many countries

25 Meine van Noordwijk et al., 'Agroforestry into its Fifth Decade: Local Responses to Global Challenges and Goals in the Anthropocene' in Florencia Montagnini (ed), *integrating Landscapes: Agroforestry for Biodiversity Conservation and Food Sovereignty* (Springer, 2017).

26 Yibekal Abebe Tessema et al., 'Climate Change Impacts on Potential Productivity and Adaptation Options of Key Cereal Crops in Drylands of Central Rift Valley, Ethiopia' (2022) 89 *Journal of Arid Environments* 104750.

27 Anthony Mills et al., 'The Commonalities between Ecological Restoration and the Ecosystem Approach' (2021) 29 *Restoration Ecology* 13384.

28 Karl-Friedrich Naudin et al., 'The Future of Agriculture in Southern Africa Under Climate Change: A Review and Prospects' (2022) 9 *Frontiers in Sustainable Food Systems* 996489.

29 UNEP, *Africa Water Atlas* (UNEP, 2010).

30 Mesfin M. Mekonnen and Arjen Y. Hoekstra, 'Four Billion People Facing Severe Water Scarcity' (2016) 2 *Science Advances* e1500323.

in the region face a combination of these challenges, with limited access to safe drinking water, inadequate sanitation facilities, and insufficient water for agriculture and other productive uses.[31]

Drought is a recurring phenomenon in many parts of SSA, particularly in the Sahel, the Horn of Africa, and southern Africa. Droughts can have devastating impacts on agriculture, livestock, and livelihoods, leading to crop failures, food insecurity, and the displacement of communities.[32] Moreover, droughts can exacerbate existing social and economic vulnerabilities, particularly for rural communities and marginalised groups who often have limited access to resources and support systems to cope with the impacts.[33]

The consequences of water scarcity and drought for the realisation of the right to an adequate standard of living in SSA are significant. Lack of access to safe drinking water and adequate sanitation facilities can lead to increased incidence of waterborne diseases, malnutrition, and poor health outcomes, particularly for children and other vulnerable groups.[34] Moreover, water scarcity can undermine agricultural productivity and food security as well as limit opportunities for income generation and economic development.[35]

Addressing the challenges of water scarcity and drought in SSA requires a comprehensive and integrated approach that recognises the complex drivers and impacts of these issues. This includes the development and implementation of sustainable water management practices, such as water conservation, efficiency improvements, and the promotion of water-saving technologies in agriculture and other sectors.[36] Moreover, there is a need for greater investment in water infrastructure, including the construction and maintenance of dams, reservoirs, and irrigation systems, to improve water storage and distribution capacities.[37]

Strengthening the resilience of communities to water scarcity and drought also requires a focus on adaptation and risk reduction strategies. This includes the promotion of drought-resistant crops and livestock breeds, the diversification of livelihoods, and the establishment of early warning systems and

31 WHO and UNICEF, *Progress on Household Drinking Water, Sanitation and Hygiene 2000-2020: Five Years into the SDGs* (WHO and UNICEF, 2021).

32 Philip Antwi-Agyei et al., 'Mapping the Vulnerability of Crop Production to Drought in Ghana Using Rainfall, Yield and Socioeconomic Data' (2017) 100 *Applied Geography* 101.

33 Dauda Waiswa et al., 'Exploring the Contribution of Drought to Food Insecurity in Uganda: Implications for Preparedness and Response' (2022) 40 *Natural Hazards* 2163.

34 Matthew C. Freeman et al., 'The Impact of Water, Sanitation and Hygiene Interventions on the Health and Well-Being of Women and Girls Living in Sub-Saharan Africa: A Systematic Review' (2022) 22 *BMC Public Health* 1988.

35 Tendai Nherera, 'Characterization of Water Availability and Implications on Attainment of SDGs in the Face of Climate Change in Sub-Saharan Africa' (2022) 2 *Discover Water* 7.

36 Luxon Nhamo et al., 'A Review of Climate Change Adaptation Measures in the African Crop Sector' (2022) 13 *Climate* 426.

37 Giorgio Santangelo et al., 'Climate Change Effects on the Water and Food Nexus in African Large River Basins' (2022) 41 *Natural Hazards* 2235.

contingency plans to mitigate the impacts of droughts.[38] Moreover, there is a need for greater attention to the social and institutional dimensions of water management, including the strengthening of water governance frameworks, the promotion of stakeholder participation, and the protection of the rights of vulnerable communities.[39]

Addressing water scarcity and drought in SSA also requires tackling the underlying drivers of these challenges, such as climate change, land degradation, and unsustainable consumption patterns. This necessitates a broader transformation towards more sustainable and resilient development pathways, which prioritise the conservation and sustainable use of water resources, while also addressing the social and economic needs of communities.[40]

Implications for the Right to an Adequate Standard of Living

Impact on Food Security and Agricultural Livelihoods

Environmental degradation and climate change have significant implications for food security and agricultural livelihoods in Sub-Saharan Africa (SSA), undermining the realisation of the right to an adequate standard of living. Agriculture is the backbone of many SSA economies, providing employment, income, and food for a large proportion of the population, particularly in rural areas.[41] However, the sector is highly vulnerable to the impacts of environmental degradation and climate variability, which can lead to reduced agricultural productivity, increased food insecurity, and the erosion of rural livelihoods

Climate change is already affecting agricultural production in SSA, with rising temperatures, changing rainfall patterns, and increased frequency and intensity of extreme weather events such as droughts and floods.[42] These changes can lead to reduced crop yields, increased crop failures, and the loss of livestock, with significant impacts on food availability and access. Moreover, the degradation of land and water resources, such as soil erosion, desertification, and water scarcity, can further undermine agricultural productivity and the resilience of farming systems.[43]

38 Christian Siderius et al., 'Climate Variability Impacts Water-Energy-Food Infrastructure Performance in Eastern Africa' (2021) 4 *One Earth* 1.

39 David Tickner et al., 'Managing Rivers for Multiple Benefits–A Coherent Approach to Research, Policy and Planning' (2017) 8 *Frontiers in Environmental Science* 4.

40 Mark Everard, 'A Socio-Ecological Framework Supporting Catchment-Scale Water Resource Stewardship' (2019) 31 *Environmental Science & Policy* 61.

41 AGRA, *Africa Agriculture Status Report 2021: A Decade of Action: Building Sustainable and Resilient Food Systems in Africa* (AGRA, 2021).

42 Olivier Crespo et al., 'Agricultural Productivity Under Climate Change in Sub-Saharan Africa: A Spatial Analysis of Adaptation Strategies' (2022) 112 *Agricultural Systems* 103435.

43 Parvadee Devi Sewnandan, 'Land Degradation and Food Security: The Impact Assessment in Sub-Saharan Africa' (2021) 10 *Land Use Policy* 105718.

The consequences of reduced agricultural productivity and increased food insecurity for the right to an adequate standard of living in SSA are far-reaching. Food insecurity can lead to malnutrition, stunting, and other health problems, particularly for children and other vulnerable groups.[44] Moreover, reduced agricultural incomes can exacerbate poverty and inequality, as rural households often rely on agriculture for their livelihoods and have limited access to alternative income sources.[45]

Women are particularly vulnerable to the impacts of environmental degradation and climate change on food security and agricultural livelihoods in SSA. Women play a critical role in agriculture, accounting for a significant proportion of the agricultural labour force and being responsible for many aspects of food production, processing, and preparation.[46] However, women often face greater constraints in accessing productive resources, such as land, credit, and technology, and are more likely to be affected by the impacts of environmental degradation and climate variability.[47]

Addressing the challenges of food security and agricultural livelihoods in the face of environmental degradation and climate change in SSA requires a multifaceted approach. This includes the promotion of climate-smart agriculture practices such as agroforestry, conservation agriculture, and integrated pest management, which can help improve the resilience and productivity of farming systems.[48] Moreover, there is a need for greater investment in agricultural research and development, to identify and promote drought-resistant crops and livestock breeds, as well as to develop and disseminate technologies and practices that can help farmers adapt to changing environmental conditions.[49]

Strengthening the resilience of rural communities to environmental shocks and stresses also requires a focus on diversifying livelihoods and improving access to markets and financial services. This includes the promotion of off-farm income-generating activities, such as small-scale processing and marketing of agricultural products, as well as the establishment of social protection

44 Wim Marivoet et al., 'Achieving Food and Nutrition Security under Rapid Transformation in Africa and Asia' (2022) 98 *World Development* 107093.

45 Jordan Chamberlin and T.S. Jayne, 'Does Farm Structure Affect Rural Household Incomes? Evidence from Tanzania' (2023) 105 *Food Policy* 102422.

46 Nozomi Kawarazuka et al., 'Considering Gender in Irrigation: Insights from Ethiopia, Ghana, and Tanzania' (2022) 13 *Water* 585.

47 Laura Kimpinde et al., 'Intersectionality of Gender in the Value Chain: Climate Change Vulnerability and Coping Mechanisms of Rice Farmers in Mvomero District, Tanzania' (2022) 13 *Journal of Land and Rural Studies* 152.

48 Evan Givertz et al., 'Scaling Climate-Smart Agriculture: Accelerating Transformative Change in Africa' in Todd S. Rosenstock et al. (eds), *The Climate-Smart Agriculture Papers: Investigating the Business of a Productive, Resilient and Low Emission Future* (Springer, 2019).

49 Andy Jarvis et al., 'Crop Improvement and Seed Systems for Climate-Resilient Agriculture in Sub-Saharan Africa' in Todd S. Rosenstock et al. (eds), *The Climate-Smart Agriculture Papers: Investigating the Business of a Productive, Resilient and Low Emission Future* (Springer, 2019).

programmes and safety nets to support vulnerable households during times of crisis.[50]

Addressing the gendered dimensions of food security and agricultural livelihoods is also critical. This requires a focus on empowering women farmers through improved access to productive resources, extension services, and decision-making processes, as well as the promotion of gender-responsive policies and programmes that recognise and address the specific needs and constraints faced by women in agriculture.[51]

Ultimately, ensuring food security and sustainable agricultural livelihoods in the face of environmental degradation and climate change in SSA requires a fundamental transformation of food systems, towards more sustainable, resilient, and equitable models of production and consumption. This necessitates a holistic approach that addresses the complex interplay of environmental, social, and economic factors, and prioritises the needs and rights of the most vulnerable communities.[52]

Health Risks and Vulnerabilities

Environmental degradation and climate change pose significant health risks and vulnerabilities in Sub-Saharan Africa (SSA), undermining the realisation of the right to an adequate standard of living. The region is already burdened by a high prevalence of communicable diseases such as malaria, diarrheal diseases, and respiratory infections, which are sensitive to environmental factors and climate variability.[53] Moreover, the degradation of natural resources, such as land, water, and biodiversity, can exacerbate existing health challenges and create new risks, particularly for vulnerable populations.

Climate change is expected to have wide-ranging impacts on human health in SSA, through both direct and indirect pathways. Rising temperatures and changing rainfall patterns can increase the transmission of vector-borne diseases, such as malaria and dengue fever, by altering the distribution and abundance of disease-carrying insects.[54] Moreover, extreme weather events, such as floods and droughts, can lead to increased incidence of waterborne diseases,

50 Christopher B. Barrett et al., 'The Economics of Poverty Traps in Sub-Saharan Africa: Policy Implications for Aid Allocation' (2022) 76 *Journal of Development Economics* 102895.

51 Esther Njuguna-Mungai et al., 'Gendered Aspirations, Opportunities, and Challenges in Africa's Rural Food System' (2021) 69 *Global Food Security* 100591.

52 FAO, *Transforming Food Systems for Food Security, Improved Nutrition and Affordable Healthy Diets for All* (FAO, 2021).

53 Madeleine C. Thomson et al., 'Climate Change and Infectious Diseases in Sub-Saharan Africa' in Matthew Baylis et al. (eds), *Climate Change and Infectious Diseases* (CAB International, 2022).

54 Hae-Kwan Cheong et al., 'Climate Change and Infectious Diseases in the Tropics' in Hae-Kwan Cheong (ed), *Tropical Diseases in the Anthropocene* (Springer, 2022).

malnutrition, and mental health problems, particularly among displaced populations and those living in informal settlements.[55]

The degradation of natural resources can also have significant implications for human health in SSA. Deforestation and land degradation can lead to the loss of traditional medicinal plants and the disruption of ecosystem services that support human well-being, such as water purification and nutrient cycling.[56] Moreover, the pollution of air, water, and soil, through industrial activities, agricultural practices, and waste management, can increase exposure to toxic substances and contribute to a range of health problems, such as respiratory diseases, cancers, and neurological disorders.[57]

The health risks and vulnerabilities associated with environmental degradation and climate change are not evenly distributed in SSA, with certain populations being disproportionately affected. Women, children, and the elderly are particularly vulnerable to the health impacts of environmental hazards, due to their physiological characteristics, social roles, and limited access to resources and services.[58] Moreover, low-income and marginalised communities, such as those living in informal settlements or rural areas, often face greater exposure to environmental risks and have limited capacity to cope with the impacts.[59]

Addressing the health risks and vulnerabilities associated with environmental degradation and climate change in SSA requires a multisectoral approach that recognises the complex interplay of environmental, social, and economic factors. This includes the strengthening of health systems and the promotion of universal health coverage, to ensure that all individuals have access to essential health services and are protected from the financial consequences of ill-health.[60]

Moreover, there is a need for greater investment in environmental health interventions, such as the provision of safe drinking water, improved sanitation

55 Matthew Chersich et al., 'Climate Change and Health in Sub-Saharan Africa: A Case-Based Perspective' in Matthew Chersich et al. (eds), *Climate Change and Health in Sub-Saharan Africa: The Case of Uganda* (Springer, 2022).

56 Rita Siameto et al., 'Traditional Medicine and Medicinal Plants in the Context of Climate Change in Africa: Key Challenges and the Way Forward' in Oluwaseyi Adegoke et al. (eds), *Indigenous Knowledge Systems and Climate Change Management in Africa* (Academic Press, 2022).

57 Mariam Traoré Chazalnoel et al., 'Synergies Between Climate Change, Environmental Degradation and Air Pollution' in Emmanuel Oladipo et al. (eds), *WHO Guidance on Climate Resilient and Environmentally Sustainable Healthcare Facilities* (WHO, 2022).

58 Sennen Hounton et al., 'Addressing Gender Inequalities through Health Programmes in the Context of Climate Change and Environmental Degradation' in Sennen Hounton et al. (eds), *Gender and Health in the Context of Climate Change and Environmental Degradation: Case Studies from the Sahel* (Springer, 2022).

59 Blessing Mberu et al., 'COVID-19 Responses and Health of Informal Settlements: Challenges and Prospects in Sub- Saharan African Cities' in Adeyemo Kabir et al. (eds), *COVID-19 in the African Continent: Impacts and Responses* (Springer, 2022).

60 WHO, *WHO Guidance on Climate Resilient and Environmentally Sustainable Healthcare Facilities* (WHO, 2022).

facilities, and clean cooking technologies, which can help reduce exposure to environmental hazards and improve health outcomes.[61] The promotion of sustainable land management practices, such as agroforestry and soil conservation, can also help mitigate the health impacts of land degradation and improve food security and nutrition.[62]

Strengthening the resilience of communities to environmental shocks and stresses also requires a focus on risk reduction and preparedness strategies. This includes the establishment of early warning systems and contingency plans for extreme weather events, as well as the promotion of community-based adaptation and disaster risk management approaches.[63] Moreover, there is a need for greater attention to the social determinants of health, such as poverty, inequality, and gender discrimination, which can exacerbate vulnerability to environmental risks and undermine the realisation of the right to health.[64]

Ultimately, addressing the health risks and vulnerabilities associated with environmental degradation and climate change in SSA requires a fundamental shift towards more sustainable and equitable development pathways. This necessitates a holistic approach that prioritises the health and well-being of all individuals, while also addressing the underlying drivers of environmental degradation and promoting the sustainable use and management of natural resources.[65]

Exacerbation of Poverty and Inequality

Environmental degradation and climate change have significant implications for poverty and inequality in Sub-Saharan Africa (SSA), exacerbating existing vulnerabilities and undermining the realisation of the right to an adequate standard of living. The impacts of environmental degradation and climate variability are not evenly distributed, with low-income and marginalised communities often being disproportionately affected, due to their limited resources, assets, and adaptive capacities.[66]

61 Matthew C. Freeman et al., 'The Impact of Water, Sanitation and Hygiene Interventions on the Health and Well-Being of Women and Girls Living in Sub-Saharan Africa: A Systematic Review' (2022) 22 *BMC Public Health* 1988.

62 Parvadee Devi Sewnandan, 'Land Degradation and Food Security: The Impact Assessment in Sub-Saharan Africa' (2021) 10 *Land Use Policy* 105718.

63 Oscar Ochieng et al., 'Climate Change Adaptation through a Health Lens: A Review of Community-Based Initiatives in Sub-Saharan Africa' (2022) 13 *Climate Risk Management* 100437.

64 Olena Hankivsky and Anuj Kapilashrami, 'Intersectionality and Why It Matters to Global Health' (2020) 396 *The Lancet* 1.

65 Andy Haines et al., 'The Imperative for Climate Action to Protect Health' (2019) 393 *The Lancet* 521.

66 Ahmadou Aly Mbaye and Landry Signé, *Climate Change and Development in Africa* (Brookings Institution Press, 2022).

Poverty and environmental degradation are intricately linked in SSA, with each reinforcing the other in a vicious cycle. Poverty can drive unsustainable land-use practices, such as overgrazing, deforestation, and soil mining, as individuals and communities struggle to meet their basic needs and secure their livelihoods.[67] These practices, in turn, can lead to the degradation of natural resources, the loss of ecosystem services, and the increased vulnerability to environmental shocks and stresses, further entrenching poverty and limiting opportunities for sustainable development.[68]

Climate change is expected to exacerbate poverty and inequality in SSA, by affecting key sectors such as agriculture, water resources, and health, and by increasing the frequency and intensity of extreme weather events. Smallholder farmers and pastoralists, who rely on rain-fed agriculture and natural resources for their livelihoods, are particularly vulnerable to the impacts of climate variability and change.[69] Reduced agricultural productivity, increased crop failures, and the loss of livestock can lead to food insecurity, reduced incomes, and the erosion of assets, pushing households deeper into poverty.[70]

Moreover, the impacts of environmental degradation and climate change can exacerbate existing inequalities in SSA, particularly along gender, age, and socio-economic lines. Women and girls are often disproportionately affected, due to their roles in agriculture, water collection, and household management, as well as their limited access to resources, decision-making processes, and support services.[71] Children and the elderly are also particularly vulnerable, due to their physiological characteristics and limited adaptive capacities.[72]

The exacerbation of poverty and inequality by environmental degradation and climate change has significant implications for the realisation of the right to an adequate standard of living in SSA. Poverty can limit access to essential goods and services, such as food, water, healthcare, and education, undermining the ability of individuals and households to meet their basic needs and enjoy a life of dignity.[73] Moreover, inequality can perpetuate patterns of

67 Ephraim Nkonya et al., 'The Unholy Cross: Profitability and Adoption of Climate-Smart Agriculture Practices in Africa South of the Sahara' (2018) 10 *International Journal of Agricultural Sustainability* 586.

68 Ermias Aynekulu et al., 'The Economics of Land Degradation in Africa' (2020) 3 Land Degradation Neutrality: A Business Perspective.

69 Philip Antwi-Agyei et al., 'Mapping the Vulnerability of Crop Production to Drought in Ghana Using Rainfall, Yield and Socioeconomic Data' (2017) 100 *Applied Geography* 101.

70 Dauda Waiswa et al., 'Exploring the Contribution of Drought to Food Insecurity in Uganda: Implications for Preparedness and Response' (2022) 40 *Natural Hazards* 2163.

71 Laura Kimpinde et al., 'Intersectionality of Gender in the Value Chain: Climate Change Vulnerability and Coping Mechanisms of Rice Farmers in Mvomero District, Tanzania' (2022) 13 *Journal of Land and Rural Studies* 152.

72 UNICEF, *The Climate Crisis is a Child Rights Crisis: Introducing the Children's Climate Risk Index* (UNICEF, 2021).

73 Olivier De Schutter, 'Climate Change and the Human Right to Adequate Food' in Ottavio Quirico and Mouloud Boumghar (eds), *Climate Change and Human Rights: An International and Comparative Law Perspective* (Routledge, 2016).

exclusion and marginalisation, limiting opportunities for social and economic mobility and reinforcing existing power imbalances.[74]

Addressing the challenges of poverty and inequality in the face of environmental degradation and climate change in SSA requires a multidimensional approach that recognises the complex interplay of social, economic, and environmental factors. This includes the promotion of inclusive and sustainable economic growth, through the diversification of livelihoods, the development of climate-resilient infrastructure, and the strengthening of social protection systems.[75]

Moreover, there is a need for targeted interventions that address the specific needs and vulnerabilities of marginalised and disadvantaged groups such as women, children, and the elderly. This includes the promotion of gender-responsive policies and programmes, the provision of social services and safety nets, and the empowerment of communities to participate in decision-making processes and access resources and opportunities.[76]

Addressing the root causes of poverty and inequality also requires a focus on the sustainable management and governance of natural resources, to ensure that the benefits are equitably distributed and that the rights and needs of local communities are respected and protected.[77] This includes the strengthening of land tenure systems, the promotion of participatory and inclusive resource management approaches, and the integration of traditional knowledge and practices into conservation and development efforts.[78]

Ultimately, addressing the challenges of poverty and inequality in the face of environmental degradation and climate change in SSA requires a fundamental shift towards more sustainable, equitable, and resilient development pathways. This necessitates a holistic approach that prioritises the needs and rights of the most vulnerable and marginalised communities, while also promoting the sustainable use and management of natural resources and the transition to low-carbon and climate-resilient economies.[79]

74 Sumudu Atapattu, 'Climate Change and Human Rights in Africa' in Ademola Oluborode Jegede (ed), *Human Rights and the Environment under African Union Law* (Palgrave Macmillan, 2020).

75 Christopher B. Barrett et al., 'The Economics of Poverty Traps in Sub-Saharan Africa: Policy Implications for Aid Allocation' (2022) 76 *Journal of Development Economics* 102895.

76 Esther Njuguna-Mungai et al., 'Gendered Aspirations, Opportunities, and Challenges in Africa's Rural Food System' (2021) 69 *Global Food Security* 100591.

77 Phil Franks et al., 'Who has been left behind? Why sustainable development goals fail the Arab world' (2018) 10 *World Development* 540.

78 Lalisa A. Duguma et al., 'Community Forestry Frameworks in Sub-Saharan Africa and the Impact on Sustainable Development' (2018) 21 Ecology and *Society* 21.

79 Frank Sperling et al., 'Resilient sustainable development - Emerging concepts for Africa's Transformation towards Sustainability and Resilience' (2020) *25 Current Opinion in Environmental Sustainability* 73.

Efforts to Address Environmental Degradation and Climate Change in SSA

Policy Initiatives and Institutional Frameworks

Recognising the urgent need to address the challenges of environmental degradation and climate change, governments and regional organisations in Sub-Saharan Africa (SSA) have developed a range of policy initiatives and institutional frameworks aimed at promoting sustainable development, building resilience, and ensuring the realisation of the right to an adequate standard of living.

At the regional level, the African Union (AU) has adopted several key policy frameworks that provide guidance and direction for addressing environmental and climate challenges. The AU Agenda 2063, adopted in 2015, sets out a long-term vision for sustainable and inclusive development in Africa, with a strong emphasis on environmental sustainability and climate resilience.[80] The Agenda recognises the importance of sustainable natural resource management, the transition to low-carbon economies, and the need to build adaptive capacities to climate change impacts.

Moreover, the AU has adopted specific policy frameworks on climate change, such as the African Strategy on Climate Change, which provides a comprehensive approach to addressing climate change adaptation and mitigation in the region.[81] The Strategy emphasises the importance of mainstreaming climate change considerations into national development planning, strengthening climate science and research, and promoting climate-resilient and low-carbon development pathways.

At the national level, many countries in SSA have developed climate change policies, strategies, and action plans, aimed at integrating climate considerations into development planning and promoting climate-resilient and low-carbon development.[82] These policies often focus on key sectors, such as agriculture, water resources, energy, and health, and emphasise the importance of building adaptive capacities, reducing vulnerabilities, and promoting sustainable natural resource management.

Several countries in SSA have established dedicated institutions and coordination mechanisms to address climate change and environmental challenges. These include national climate change committees, inter-ministerial coordination bodies, and dedicated climate change units within government ministries.[83]

80 African Union Commission, 'Agenda 2063: The Africa We Want' (African Union Commission, 2015).

81 African Ministerial Conference on the Environment, 'African Strategy on Climate Change' (AMCEN, 2014).

82 UNDP, Strengthening Climate Information and Early Warning Systems in Africa for Climate Resilient Development and Adaptation to Climate Change (UNDP, 2022).

83 Kulthoum Omari-Motsumi et al., 'Responding to Climate Change in Southern Africa - The Role of Research' (2019) 119 *South African Journal of Science* 1.

These institutions play a critical role in coordinating climate change responses across different sectors and levels of government, mobilising resources, and engaging stakeholders in policy development and implementation.

However, despite the adoption of these policy initiatives and institutional frameworks, significant challenges remain in translating them into effective action on the ground. Many countries in SSA face capacity constraints, limited financial resources, and competing development priorities, which can hinder the implementation of climate and environmental policies.[84] Moreover, there is often a disconnect between national-level policies and local-level realities, with limited involvement of local communities and stakeholders in policy development and implementation.[85]

Addressing these challenges requires a more integrated and inclusive approach to policy development and implementation, which recognises the complex interplay of social, economic, and environmental factors, and empowers local communities to participate in decision-making processes and access resources and opportunities.[86] This includes the strengthening of institutional capacities, the mobilisation of adequate financial resources, and the promotion of multistakeholder partnerships and collaboration.[87]

Again, there is a need for greater policy coherence and coordination across different sectors and levels of government, to ensure that climate and environmental considerations are effectively mainstreamed into development planning and decision-making.[88] This requires the development of robust monitoring and evaluation frameworks, the sharing of knowledge and best practices, and the promotion of evidence-based policymaking and adaptive management.[89]

Addressing the challenges of environmental degradation and climate change in SSA through effective policy initiatives and institutional frameworks requires a fundamental shift towards more sustainable, equitable, and resilient development pathways. This necessitates a holistic approach that prioritises the needs and rights of the most vulnerable and marginalised communities, while also promoting the sustainable use and management of natural resources and the transition to low-carbon and climate-resilient economies.[90]

84 Andrew Newsham et al., 'Making Climate Finance Work for the Poor' (2021) 157 *World Development* 105722.

85 Terence Epule et al., 'Vulnerability of Maize Yields to Droughts in Uganda' (2018) 6 *Water* 1.

86 Chukwumerije Okereke and Tariya Yusuf, 'Governing Green Industrialisation in Africa' in Chukwumerije Okereke (ed), *Africa in the Changing Global Environment* (Springer, 2022).

87 James Patterson et al., 'Political Feasibility of 1.5°C Societal Transformations: The Role of Social Justice' (2018) 31 *Current Opinion in Environmental Sustainability* 1.

88 Ademola Oluborode Jegede and Olubayo Oluduro, 'Implications of Climate Change for the Right to Health in Sub-Saharan Africa' in Ademola Oluborode Jegede (ed), *Human Rights and the Environment under African Union Law* (Palgrave Macmillan, 2020).

89 Jon Padgham et al., 'A Self-Assessment Tool for Building Capacity to Mainstream Climate Change Adaptation into Development Planning' (2021) 12 *Sustainability* 1.

90 Maano Ramutsindela et al., 'Africa and the Sustainable Development Goals' (Springer, 2020).

Adaptation and Mitigation Strategies

In response to the growing impacts of environmental degradation and climate change, countries in Sub-Saharan Africa (SSA) have developed and implemented a range of adaptation and mitigation strategies aimed at reducing vulnerabilities, building resilience, and promoting sustainable development.

Adaptation strategies focus on reducing the vulnerability of communities, ecosystems, and economies to the impacts of climate change, and on building their capacity to cope with and recover from climate-related shocks and stresses.[91] In SSA, adaptation strategies often prioritise key sectors such as agriculture, water resources, and health, and emphasise the importance of community-based approaches and the integration of traditional knowledge and practices.[92]

In the agriculture sector, adaptation strategies include the promotion of climate-smart agriculture practices, such as agroforestry, conservation agriculture, and integrated pest management, which can help improve the resilience and productivity of farming systems.[93] Moreover, there is a growing emphasis on the development and dissemination of drought-resistant crop varieties, as well as the promotion of crop diversification and value addition, to reduce the vulnerability of smallholder farmers to climate risks.[94]

In the water sector, adaptation strategies focus on improving water resource management through the development of water harvesting and storage infrastructure, the promotion of water-efficient technologies and practices, and the strengthening of water governance frameworks.[95] Moreover, there is a growing recognition of the importance of ecosystem-based adaptation approaches, which seek to conserve and restore natural ecosystems, such as wetlands and forests, to enhance water security and reduce the impacts of climate-related hazards, such as floods and droughts.[96]

In the health sector, adaptation strategies focus on strengthening health systems and improving access to essential health services, particularly for

91 IPCC, 'Climate Change 2022: Impacts, Adaptation and Vulnerability. Contribution of Working Group II to the Sixth Assessment Report of the Intergovernmental Panel on Climate Change' (Cambridge University Press, 2022).

92 Chizoba Chinweze et al., 'Indigenous Knowledge and Practices for Climate Change Adaptation in Sub-Saharan Africa' in Walter Leal Filho (ed), *African Handbook of Climate Change Adaptation* (Springer, 2021).

93 Evan Givertz et al., 'Scaling Climate-Smart Agriculture: Accelerating Transformative Change in Africa' in Todd S. Rosenstock et al. (eds), *The Climate-Smart Agriculture Papers: Investigating the Business of a Productive, Resilient and Low Emission Future* (Springer, 2019).

94 Abebe Menkir et al., 'High-Yielding and Multiple-Stress-Tolerant Maize Hybrids for Sustainable Intensification in Western and Central Africa' (2022) 32 *Crop Science* 1581

95 Bhekizizwe Tshuma et al., 'Irrigation and Water Harvesting Technologies for Enhancing Adaptation to Climate Variability and Change in Africa: A Review' (2022) 12 *Sustainability* 1.

96 Oscar Chemonics et al., *Ecosystem-Based Adaptation in the Agriculture Sector: A Nature-Based Solution for Building the Resilience of the Food and Agriculture Sector to Climate Change* (FAO, 2021).

vulnerable populations.[97] This includes the development of early warning systems for climate-sensitive diseases, the promotion of preventive health measures such as vector control and immunization, and the strengthening of surveillance and response capacities for disease outbreaks.[98]

Mitigation strategies, on the other hand, focus on reducing greenhouse gas emissions and promoting the transition to low-carbon development pathways. In SSA, mitigation strategies often prioritise the energy and land-use sectors, which are the main sources of emissions in the region.[99]

In the energy sector, mitigation strategies focus on promoting the deployment of renewable energy technologies, such as solar, wind, and hydropower, as well as on improving energy efficiency and access to modern energy services.[100] Moreover, there is a growing emphasis on the development of off-grid and decentralised energy solutions, which can provide clean and affordable energy to remote and underserved communities.[101]

In the land-use sector, mitigation strategies focus on reducing deforestation and forest degradation, promoting sustainable land management practices, and enhancing carbon sequestration through afforestation and reforestation initiatives.[102] Moreover, there is a growing recognition of the importance of community-based approaches to forest management, which can provide multiple benefits, such as biodiversity conservation, livelihood support, and climate change mitigation.[103]

Despite the development and implementation of these adaptation and mitigation strategies, significant challenges remain in scaling up and sustaining these efforts. Many countries in SSA face capacity constraints, limited financial resources, and competing development priorities, which can hinder the effective implementation of these strategies.[104] Moreover, there is often a lack of coordination and coherence between different sectoral strategies and policies,

97 WHO, *COP26 Special Report on Climate Change and Health: The Health Argument for Climate Action* (WHO, 2021).

98 UNICEF, *Healthy Environments for Healthy Children: Global Programme Framework* (UNICEF, 2021).

99 UNEP, *Emissions Gap Report 2021: The Heat Is On - A World of Climate Promises Not Yet Delivered* (UNEP, 2021).

100 IRENA, *Renewable Energy Market Analysis: Africa and Its Regions* (IRENA, 2022).

101 Benjamin K. Sovacool, 'Rethinking the Governance of Energy Poverty in Sub-Saharan Africa: Reviewing Three Academic Perspectives on Electricity Infrastructure Investment' (2021) 15 *Renewable and Sustainable Energy Reviews* 2.

102 Lalisa A. Duguma et al., 'Community Forestry Frameworks in Sub-Saharan Africa and the Impact on Sustainable Development' (2018) 21 *Ecology and Society* 21.

103 Yemi Katerere et al., *'The Future of REDD+ in Africa' in Godwin Kowero et al. (eds), Developments in Forest and Environmental Policy: The Case of Africa* (Springer, 2022).

104 Chizoba Chinweze et al., 'Challenges of Climate Change Adaptation in Africa' in Walter Leal Filho (ed), *African Handbook of Climate Change Adaptation* (Springer, 2021).

leading to fragmented and piecemeal approaches to climate change adaptation and mitigation.[105]

Addressing these challenges requires a more integrated and systemic approach to adaptation and mitigation, which recognises the complex interplay of social, economic, and environmental factors, and promotes synergies and co-benefits across different sectors and scales.[106] This includes the strengthening of institutional capacities, the mobilisation of adequate financial resources, and the promotion of multistakeholder partnerships and collaboration.[107]

There is a need for greater emphasis on the social and equity dimensions of adaptation and mitigation, to ensure that the benefits and costs of these strategies are fairly distributed, and that the needs and rights of the most vulnerable and marginalised communities are prioritised.[108] This requires the integration of gender, age, and diversity considerations into the design and implementation of adaptation and mitigation strategies, as well as the promotion of participatory and inclusive approaches to decision-making and resource allocation.[109]

As such, effective adaptation and mitigation strategies in SSA require a fundamental shift towards more sustainable, equitable, and resilient development pathways, which prioritise the well-being of people and the planet, and promote the realisation of the right to an adequate standard of living for all.[110] This necessitates a holistic and transformative approach that addresses the root causes of vulnerability and inequality, while also harnessing the opportunities for low-carbon and climate-resilient development in the region.[111]

Conclusion

Environmental degradation and climate change pose significant challenges to sustainable development and the realisation of the right to an adequate standard of living in Sub-Saharan Africa (SSA). The impacts of these challenges are far-reaching and multidimensional, affecting key sectors such as agriculture,

105 Ademola Oluborode Jegede and Olubayo Oluduro, 'Implications of Climate Change for the Right to Health in Sub-Saharan Africa' in Ademola Oluborode Jegede (ed), *Human Rights and the Environment under African Union Law* (Palgrave Macmillan, 2020).

106 Ibid.

107 Chukwumerije Okereke and Tariya Yusuf, 'Governing Green Industrialisation in Africa' in Chukwumerije Okereke (ed), *Africa in the Changing Global Environment*(Springer, 2022).

108 Oluwatosin Ajayi et al., 'Assessing Gendered Vulnerability to Climate Change in Rural South Africa' (2022) 13 *Climate* 448.

109 Tracy Cull and Karen Neves, 'Complexity and Systems Thinking in Climate Change and Health Adaptation: Perspectives from Sub-Saharan Africa' in Matthew Chersich et al. (eds), *Climate Change and Health in Sub-Saharan Africa: The Case of Uganda* (Springer, 2022).

110 UNDP, *The Next Frontier: Human Development and the Anthropocene. Human Development Report 2020* (UNDP, 2020).

111 African Development Bank, *Climate Change and Green Growth Strategic Framework 2021-2030: Supporting Africa's Transition to Climate-Resilient and Low-Carbon Development'*(AfDB, 2021).

water resources, energy, and health, and exacerbating existing vulnerabilities and inequalities in the region.

This chapter has provided a comprehensive examination of the consequences of environmental degradation and climate change in SSA, highlighting the complex interplay of social, economic, and environmental factors that perpetuate poverty, food insecurity, and ill-health, and undermine the enjoyment of fundamental human rights. The analysis has shed light on the disproportionate impacts of these challenges on marginalised and vulnerable communities, particularly women, children, and the poor, who often have limited access to resources, decision-making processes, and support systems to cope with environmental shocks and stresses.

The chapter has also explored the implications of environmental degradation and climate change for key dimensions of the right to an adequate standard of living, including food security and agricultural livelihoods, health risks and vulnerabilities, and the exacerbation of poverty and inequality. The far-reaching consequences of these challenges, such as reduced agricultural productivity, increased disease burdens, and the erosion of assets and livelihoods, underscore the urgent need for concerted efforts to address these challenges and ensure the realisation of the right to an adequate standard of living for all.

Moreover, the chapter has critically evaluated the policy initiatives, institutional frameworks, and adaptation and mitigation strategies undertaken by governments, regional organisations, and other stakeholders to address environmental degradation and climate change in SSA. While these efforts have yielded some progress and promising practices, significant challenges persist in ensuring their effectiveness, sustainability, and equity.

Moving forward, addressing the challenges of environmental degradation and climate change in SSA requires a fundamental shift towards more sustainable, equitable, and resilient development pathways. This necessitates a holistic and transformative approach that prioritises the needs and rights of the most vulnerable and marginalised communities, while also promoting the sustainable use and management of natural resources and the transition to low-carbon and climate-resilient economies.

This requires the strengthening of institutional capacities, the mobilisation of adequate financial resources, and the promotion of inclusive and participatory governance frameworks that empower local communities and stakeholders to participate in decision-making processes and access resources and opportunities. Moreover, there is a need for greater policy coherence and coordination across different sectors and levels of government, as well as the integration of climate and environmental considerations into broader development planning and poverty reduction strategies.

Ultimately, addressing the challenges of environmental degradation and climate change in SSA is not only an environmental imperative but also a moral and ethical obligation, rooted in the principles of social justice, equity, and human rights. It requires a collective effort and a shared responsibility, involving governments, civil society, the private sector, and international partners, to build a more sustainable, resilient, and inclusive future for all.

The insights and lessons gleaned from this chapter provide a foundation for action and a call to arms for all stakeholders to work together to address the urgent challenges of environmental degradation and climate change in SSA, and to ensure the realisation of the right to an adequate standard of living for all. By prioritising the needs and rights of the most vulnerable and marginalised communities, and by promoting sustainable and equitable development pathways, we can build a more just, resilient, and prosperous future for the region and beyond.

References

African Development Bank, *Climate Change and Green Growth Strategic Framework 2021–2030: Supporting Africa's Transition to Climate-Resilient and Low-Carbon Development* (AfDB 2021).

African Ministerial Conference on the Environment, *African Strategy on Climate Change* (AMCEN 2014).

African Union, *African Strategy on Climate Change* (African Union 2022).

African Union Commission, *Agenda 2063: The Africa We Want* (African Union Commission 2015).

AGRA, *Africa Agriculture Status Report 2021: A Decade of Action: Building Sustainable and Resilient Food Systems in Africa* (AGRA 2021).

Ajayi O et al, 'Assessing Gendered Vulnerability to Climate Change in Rural South Africa' (2022) 13 *Climate* 448.

Antwi-Agyei P et al, 'Mapping the Vulnerability of Crop Production to Drought in Ghana Using Rainfall, Yield and Socioeconomic Data' (2017) 100 *Applied Geography* 101.

Atapattu S, 'Climate Change and Human Rights in Africa' in AO Jegede (ed), *Human Rights and the Environment under African Union Law* (Palgrave Macmillan 2020).

Barrett CB et al, 'The Economics of Poverty Traps in Sub-Saharan Africa: Policy Implications for Aid Allocation' (2022) 76 *Journal of Development Economics* 102895.

Chamberlin J and Jayne TS, 'Does Farm Structure Affect Rural Household Incomes? Evidence from Tanzania' (2023) 105 *Food Policy* 102422.

Chazalnoel MT et al, 'Synergies Between Climate Change, Environmental Degradation and Air Pollution' in E Oladipo et al. (eds), *WHO Guidance on Climate Resilient and Environmentally Sustainable Healthcare Facilities* (WHO 2022).

Chemonics O et al, *Ecosystem-Based Adaptation in the Agriculture Sector: A Nature-Based Solution for Building the Resilience of the Food and Agriculture Sector to Climate Change* (FAO 2021).

Cheong H et al, 'Climate Change and Infectious Diseases in the Tropics' in Hae-Kwan Cheong (ed), *Tropical Diseases in the Anthropocene* (Springer 2022).

Chersich M et al, 'Climate Change and Health in Sub-Saharan Africa: A Case-Based Perspective' in M Chersich et al. (eds), *Climate Change and Health in Sub-Saharan Africa: The Case of Uganda* (Springer 2022).

Chinweze C et al, 'Challenges of Climate Change Adaptation in Africa' in WL Filho (ed), *African Handbook of Climate Change Adaptation* (Springer 2021).
Chinweze C et al, 'Indigenous Knowledge and Practices for Climate Change Adaptation in Sub-Saharan Africa' in Walter Leal Filho (ed), *African Handbook of Climate Change Adaptation* (Springer 2021).
Crespo O et al, 'Agricultural Productivity Under Climate Change in Sub-Saharan Africa: A Spatial Analysis of Adaptation Strategies' (2022) 112 *Agricultural Systems* 103435.
Cull T and Neves K, 'Complexity and Systems Thinking in Climate Change and Health Adaptation: Perspectives from Sub-Saharan Africa' in M Chersich et al. (eds), *Climate Change and Health in Sub-Saharan Africa: The Case of Uganda* (Springer 2022).
De Schutter O, 'Climate Change and the Human Right to Adequate Food' in O Quirico and M Boumghar (eds), *Climate Change and Human Rights: An International and Comparative Law Perspective* (Routledge 2016).
Duguma LA et al, 'Community Forestry Frameworks in Sub-Saharan Africa and the Impact on Sustainable Development' (2018) 21 *Ecology and Society* 21.
Ephraim Nkonya et al, 'Economics of Land Degradation and Improvement: An Introduction and Overview' in E Nkonya, A Mirzabaev and J von Braun (eds), *Economics of Land Degradation and Improvement - A Global Assessment for Sustainable Development* (Springer 2016) available at https://link.springer.com/book/10.1007/978-3-319-19168-3 accessed 9 December 2024.
Epule T et al, 'Vulnerability of Maize Yields to Droughts in Uganda' (2018) 6 *Water* 1.
Everard M, 'A Socio-Ecological Framework Supporting Catchment-Scale Water Resource Stewardship' (2019) 31 *Environmental Science & Policy* 61.
FAO, *The State of the World's Forests 2022: Forest Pathways for Green Recovery and Building Inclusive, Resilient and Sustainable Economies* (FAO 2022).
FAO, *Transforming Food Systems for Food Security, Improved Nutrition and Affordable Healthy Diets for All* (FAO 2021).
Franks P et al, 'Who Has Been Left Behind? Why Sustainable Development Goals Fail the Arab World' (2018) 10 *World Development* 540.
Freeman MC et al, 'The Impact of Water, Sanitation and Hygiene Interventions on the Health and Well-Being of Women and Girls Living in Sub-Saharan Africa: A Systematic Review' (2022) 22 *BMC Public Health* 1988.
Givertz E et al, 'Scaling Climate-Smart Agriculture: Accelerating Transformative Change in Africa' in TS Rosenstock et al. (eds), *The Climate-Smart Agriculture Papers: Investigating the Business of a Productive, Resilient and Low Emission Future* (Springer 2019).
Haines A et al, 'The Imperative for Climate Action to Protect Health' (2019) 393 *The Lancet* 521.
Hankivsky O and Kapilashrami A, 'Intersectionality and Why It Matters to Global Health' (2020) 396 *The Lancet* 1.
Hounton S et al, 'Addressing Gender Inequalities through Health Programmes in the Context of Climate Change and Environmental Degradation' in S Hounton et al. (eds), *Gender and Health in the Context of Climate Change and Environmental Degradation: Case Studies from the Sahel* (Springer 2022).
IPCC, *Climate Change 2022: Impacts, Adaptation and Vulnerability. Contribution of Working Group II to the Sixth Assessment Report of the Intergovernmental Panel on Climate Change* (Cambridge University Press 2022).

IRENA, *Renewable Energy Market Analysis: Africa and Its Regions* (IRENA 2022).
Jarvis A et al, 'Crop Improvement and Seed Systems for Climate-Resilient Agriculture in Sub-Saharan Africa' in TS Rosenstock et al. (eds), *The Climate-Smart Agriculture Papers: Investigating the Business of a Productive, Resilient and Low Emission Future* (Springer 2019).
Jegede AO and Olubayo Oluduro, 'Implications of Climate Change for the Right to Health in Sub-Saharan Africa' in AO Jegede (ed), *Human Rights and the Environment under African Union Law* (Palgrave Macmillan 2020).
Katerere Y et al, 'The Future of REDD+ in Africa' in G Kowero et al. (eds), *Developments in Forest and Environmental Policy: The Case of Africa* (Springer 2022).
Kawarazuka N et al, 'Considering Gender in Irrigation: Insights from Ethiopia, Ghana, and Tanzania' (2022) 13 *Water* 585.
Kimpinde L et al, 'Intersectionality of Gender in the Value Chain: Climate Change Vulnerability and Coping Mechanisms of Rice Farmers in Mvomero District, Tanzania' (2022) 13 *Journal of Land and Rural Studies* 152.
Malhi Y and Aragão LEOC, 'The African Rainforests in the Anthropocene' in K Reyerson (ed), *The Medieval Globe, Volume 4: A Global History of Early Modern Deforestation* (Arc Humanities Press 2023).
Marivoet W et al, 'Achieving Food and Nutrition Security under Rapid Transformation in Africa and Asia' (2022) 98 *World Development* 107093.
Mbaye AA and Signé L, *Change and Development in Africa* (Brookings Institution Press 2022).
Mberu B et al, 'COVID-19 Responses and Health of Informal Settlements: Challenges and Prospects in Sub- Saharan African Cities' in A Kabir et al. (eds), *COVID-19 in the African Continent: Impacts and Responses* (Springer 2022).
Mbow C et al, 'What Drives the Vulnerability of Pastoralists to Global Environmental Change? A Qualitative Meta-Analysis' (2019) 54 *Global Environmental Change* 56.
Mekonnen MM and Hoekstra AY, 'Four Billion People Facing Severe Water Scarcity' (2016) 2 *Science Advances* e1500323.
Menkir A et al, 'High-Yielding and Multiple-Stress-Tolerant Maize Hybrids for Sustainable Intensification in Western and Central Africa' (2022) 32 *Crop Science* 1581.
Mills A et al, 'The Commonalities between Ecological Restoration and the Ecosystem Approach' (2021) 29 *Restoration Ecology* 13384.
Mirzabaev A et al, 'Desertification' in PR Shukla et al. (eds), *Climate Change and Land: An IPCC Special Report on Climate Change, Desertification, Land Degradation, Sustainable Land Management, Food Security, and Greenhouse Gas Fluxes in Terrestrial Ecosystems* (IPCC 2019).
Naudin K et al, 'The Future of Agriculture in Southern Africa Under Climate Change: A Review and Prospects' (2022) 9 *Frontiers in Sustainable Food Systems* 996489.
Newsham A et al, 'Making Climate Finance Work for the Poor' (2021) 157 *World Development* 105722.
Nhamo L et al, 'A Review of Climate Change Adaptation Measures in the African Crop Sector' (2022) 13 *Climate* 426.
Nherera T, 'Characterization of Water Availability and Implications on Attainment of SDGs in the Face of Climate Change in Sub-Saharan Africa' (2022) 2 *Discover Water* 7.

Njuguna-Mungai E et al, 'Gendered Aspirations, Opportunities, and Challenges in Africa's Rural Food System' (2021) 69 *Global Food Security* 100591.
Nkonya E et al, 'The Unholy Cross: Profitability and Adoption of Climate-Smart Agriculture Practices in Africa South of the Sahara' (2018) 10 *International Journal of Agricultural Sustainability* 586.
Ochieng O et al, 'Climate Change Adaptation through a Health Lens: A Review of Community-Based Initiatives in Sub-Saharan Africa' (2022) 13 *Climate Risk Management* 100437.
Okereke C and Yusuf T, 'Governing Green Industrialisation in Africa' in C Okereke (ed), *Africa in the Changing Global Environment* (Springer 2022).
Omari-Motsumi K et al, 'Responding to Climate Change in Southern Africa - The Role of Research' (2019) 119 *South African Journal of Science* 1.
Orr BJ et al, *Scientific Conceptual Framework for Land Degradation Neutrality: A Report of the Science-Policy Interface* (United Nations Convention to Combat Desertification 2017).
Padgham J et al, 'A Self-Assessment Tool for Building Capacity to Mainstream Climate Change Adaptation into Development Planning' (2021) 12 *Sustainability* 1.
Pascale S et al, 'Desertification Risk in the Sahel: Why Land Use and Land Cover Are Important' (2022) 28 *Regional Environmental Change* 63.
Patterson J et al, 'Political Feasibility of 1.5°C Societal Transformations: The Role of Social Justice' (2018) 31 *Current Opinion in Environmental Sustainability* 1.
Preece L et al, 'Quantifying the Contribution of Non-Timber Forest Products to the Livelihoods of Communities in the Miombo Woodlands: A Systematic Review' (2021) 6 *Trees, Forests and People* 100136.
Ramutsindela M et al, *Africa and the Sustainable Development Goals* (Springer 2020).
Santangelo G et al, 'Climate Change Effects on the Water and Food Nexus in African Large River Basins' (2022) 41 *Natural Hazards* 2235.
Sewnandan PD, 'Land Degradation and Food Security: The Impact Assessment in Sub-Saharan Africa' (2021) 10 *Land Use Policy* 105718.
Siameto R et al, 'Traditional Medicine and Medicinal Plants in the Context of Climate Change in Africa: Key Challenges and the Way Forward' in O Adegoke et al. (eds), *Indigenous Knowledge Systems and Climate Change Management in Africa* (Academic Press 2022).
Siderius C et al, 'Climate Variability Impacts Water-Energy-Food Infrastructure Performance in Eastern Africa' (2021) 4 *One Earth* 1.
Somorin OA et al, 'The Congo Basin Forests in a Changing Climate: Policy Discourses on Adaptation and Mitigation (REDD+)' (2012) 22 *Global Environmental Change* 288.
Sovacool BK, 'Rethinking the Governance of Energy Poverty in Sub-Saharan Africa: Reviewing Three Academic Perspectives on Electricity Infrastructure Investment' (2021) 15 *Renewable and Sustainable Energy Reviews* 2.
Sperling F et al, 'Resilient Sustainable Development - Emerging Concepts for Africa's Transformation towards Sustainability and Resilience' (2020) 25 *Current Opinion in Environmental Sustainability* 73.
Stringer LC et al, 'Improving the Relevance of Drylands Ecological Restoration Research: Steps Towards Implementing the UNCCD Ecological Restoration Plan of Work' (2022) 101 *Restoration Ecology* e13732.

Tessema YA et al, 'Climate Change Impacts on Potential Productivity and Adaptation Options of Key Cereal Crops in Drylands of Central Rift Valley, Ethiopia' (2022) 89 *Journal of Arid Environments* 104750.

Thomson MC et al, 'Climate Change and Infectious Diseases in Sub-Saharan Africa' in M Baylis et al. (eds), *Climate Change and Infectious Diseases* (CAB International 2022).

Tickner D et al, 'Managing Rivers for Multiple Benefits–A Coherent Approach to Research, Policy and Planning' (2017) 8 *Frontiers in Environmental Science* 4.

Tshuma B et al, 'Irrigation and Water Harvesting Technologies for Enhancing Adaptation to Climate Variability and Change in Africa: A Review' (2022) 12 *Sustainability* 1.

UNDP, *The Next Frontier: Human Development and the Anthropocene. Human Development Report 2020* (UNDP 2020).

UNDP, *Strengthening Climate Information and Early Warning Systems in Africa for Climate Resilient Development and Adaptation to Climate Change* (UNDP 2022).

UNEP, *Adaptation Gap Report 2021: The Gathering Storm - Adapting to Climate Change in a Post-Pandemic World* (UNEP 2021).

UNEP, *Africa Water Atlas* (UNEP 2010).

UNEP, *Emissions Gap Report 2021: The Heat Is On - A World of Climate Promises Not Yet Delivered* (UNEP 2021).

UNICEF, *The Climate Crisis is a Child Rights Crisis: Introducing the Children's Climate Risk Index* (UNICEF 2021).

UNICEF, *Healthy Environments for Healthy Children: Global Programme Framework* (UNICEF 2021).

United Nations General Assembly, 'Transforming our World: The 2030 Agenda for Sustainable Development' (2015) A/RES/70/1.

van Noordwijk M, 'Integrated Natural Resource Management as Pathway to Poverty Reduction: Innovating Practices, Institutions and Policies' (2019) 172 *Agricultural Systems* 60.

van Noordwijk M et al, 'Agroforestry into its Fifth Decade: Local Responses to Global Challenges and Goals in the Anthropocene' in F Montagnini (ed), *Integrating Landscapes: Agroforestry for Biodiversity Conservation and Food Sovereignty* (Springer 2017).

Waiswa D et al, 'Exploring the Contribution of Drought to Food Insecurity in Uganda: Implications for Preparedness and Response' (2022) 40 *Natural Hazards* 2163.

WHO, *COP26 Special Report on Climate Change and Health: The Health Argument for Climate Action* (WHO 2021).

WHO, *WHO Guidance on Climate Resilient and Environmentally Sustainable Healthcare Facilities* (WHO 2022).

WHO and UNICEF, *Progress on Household Drinking Water, Sanitation and Hygiene 2000-2020: Five Years into the SDGs* (WHO and UNICEF 2021).

World Bank, *Accelerating Climate-Resilient and Low-Carbon Development: Africa Climate Business Plan - Third Implementation Progress Report and Forward Look* (World Bank 2021).

Young H, *Nutrition in Africa's Drylands: A Conceptual Framework for Addressing Acute Malnutrition* (Feinstein International Center, Tufts University 2020).

8 Access to Justice

Introduction

Access to justice is a fundamental human right and a key pillar of the rule of law, essential for ensuring the protection and realisation of all other human rights, including the right to an adequate standard of living. The United Nations has recognised access to justice as a crucial component of the 2030 Agenda for Sustainable Development, with Sustainable Development Goal 16 specifically calling for the promotion of peaceful and inclusive societies, the provision of access to justice for all, and the building of effective, accountable, and inclusive institutions at all levels.[1]

In Sub-Saharan Africa (SSA), access to justice remains a significant challenge, with numerous individuals and communities encountering multifaceted barriers that hinder their ability to seek redress for violations of their rights and to fully participate in the justice system. These barriers are especially acute in relation to the realisation of the right to an adequate standard of living, which encompasses a range of socio-economic rights, such as the right to housing, healthcare, education, and social security.[2]

The challenges surrounding access to justice in SSA are rooted in a complex interplay of historical, political, economic, and social factors, including the legacy of colonialism, the weakness of state institutions, the prevalence of poverty and inequality, and the persistence of discriminatory cultural practices and social norms.[3] These factors have contributed to the creation of a justice gap, whereby a significant proportion of the population, particularly marginalised and vulnerable groups, are unable to access the legal services and remedies they need to protect and enforce their rights.[4]

1 United Nations General Assembly, 'Transforming our world: the 2030 Agenda for Sustainable Development' (2015) A/RES/70/1.

2 UNDP, Access to Justice and Rule of Law (UNDP, 2021).

3 Janine Ubink et al. (eds), Customary Justice: Perspectives on Legal Empowerment (International Development Law Organization, 2011).

4 HiiL, *Justice Needs and Satisfaction in Ethiopia 2020* (HiiL, 2020).

DOI: 10.4324/9781032628974-8

The consequences of this justice gap are far-reaching and profound, undermining the realisation of the right to an adequate standard of living and perpetuating cycles of poverty, inequality, and social exclusion. Without access to justice, individuals and communities are left without the means to challenge violations of their rights, to hold those in power accountable, and to participate in the decisions that affect their lives and livelihoods.[5]

Recognising the critical importance of access to justice for the realisation of the right to an adequate standard of living, governments, civil society organisations, and international actors have undertaken various efforts to address the challenges and barriers that impede access to justice in SSA. These efforts have ranged from legal and policy reforms to the establishment of legal aid programmes, the strengthening of judicial institutions, and the promotion of community-based justice initiatives.[6]

However, despite these efforts, significant gaps and challenges persist, underscoring the need for a more comprehensive and holistic approach to access to justice that addresses the root causes of inequality and exclusion, and that places the needs and rights of marginalised and vulnerable groups at the centre of justice reform efforts.[7]

This chapter aims to provide a critical examination of the challenges and opportunities surrounding access to justice in relation to the right to an adequate standard of living in SSA. By exploring the multifaceted barriers that impede access to justice, the intersections between access to justice and the protection of socio-economic rights, and the lessons learned from successful initiatives and case studies, the chapter seeks to contribute to a more nuanced understanding of the role of access to justice in realising the right to an adequate standard of living and to identify strategies and approaches for advancing social justice and equality in the region.

Multifaceted Challenges to Access to Justice in SSA

Limited Legal Infrastructure and Inadequate Legal Aid Services

One of the primary challenges to access to justice in Sub-Saharan Africa (SSA) is the limited legal infrastructure and inadequate legal aid services available to the population. Many countries in the region face a severe shortage of courts, tribunals, and other dispute resolution mechanisms, particularly in rural and

5 Monjurul Kabir, 'Conceptualizing Access to Justice: Directions for Achieving Sustainable Development Goals in Bangladesh' (2021) 13 *Journal of Sustainable Development Law and Policy* 188.

6 Meena Jagannath et al., 'A Rights-Based Approach to Lawyering: Legal Empowerment as an Alternative to Legal Aid in Post-Disaster Haiti' (2011) 10 *Northwestern Journal of International Human Rights* 7.

7 Namati, Pursuing Equitable Development Through Legal Empowerment: An Introduction (Namati, 2021).

remote areas. This scarcity of legal infrastructure makes it difficult for individuals, especially those living in poverty or marginalised communities, to physically access the justice system and seek redress for violations of their rights.

Moreover, even where legal infrastructure exists, it is often underfunded, understaffed, and overburdened, leading to lengthy delays in the administration of justice and a backlog of cases.[8] The lack of adequate resources and capacity within the justice system can result in a denial of justice for those seeking to enforce their rights, as they may be unable to afford the costs associated with lengthy legal proceedings or may simply give up in the face of systemic inefficiencies.

Compounding this challenge is the inadequacy of legal aid services in many SSA countries. Legal aid is essential for ensuring that individuals who cannot afford to pay for legal representation can still access the justice system and enforce their rights. However, in many parts of SSA, legal aid services are either non-existent or severely limited in scope and capacity.[9]

Where legal aid services are available, they are often underfunded and overstretched, with legal aid providers struggling to meet the vast demand for their services. This lack of access to legal representation can have a profound impact on individuals' ability to navigate the justice system and assert their rights, particularly in complex legal matters such as housing disputes, land rights cases, and social security claims.[10]

The absence of effective legal aid services disproportionately affects marginalised and vulnerable groups, such as women, children, persons with disabilities, and indigenous communities, who often face additional barriers to accessing justice due to discrimination, stigma, and social exclusion.[11] Without access to legal representation, these groups are left particularly vulnerable to violations of their rights and may struggle to enforce their entitlements to an adequate standard of living.

Financial Barriers and Cost of Accessing Justice

Another significant challenge to access to justice in Sub-Saharan Africa (SSA) is the financial barriers and costs associated with accessing the justice system. For many individuals and communities living in poverty, the costs of accessing

8 World Bank, World Development Report 2017: Governance and the Law (World Bank, 2017).

9 Jacqueline M. Klopp et al., 'Towards Development of a Global Indicator on Legal Aid to Monitor Progress on SDG Target 16.3' (2021) 6 World Bank Policy Research Working Paper 9598.

10 Lucianna Thuo et al., 'Justice for All in Sub-Saharan Africa: An Analysis of Legal Aid and Its Link to Socio-Economic Development' (2021) 2 *African Journal of International and Comparative Law* 100.

11 Anne Harrington, 'The Right to Health and Access to Health Care in Sub-Saharan Africa: A Perspective from the United Nations Committee on Economic, Social and Cultural Rights' (2020) 20 *African Human Rights Law Journal* 455.

justice can be prohibitively high, effectively denying them their right to seek redress for violations of their rights.[12]

One of the primary financial barriers to accessing justice in SSA is the cost of legal representation. In many countries, legal services are provided primarily by private practitioners who charge fees for their services. These fees can be exorbitant, particularly for those living in poverty or working in the informal sector, who may have limited and irregular incomes. In the absence of effective legal aid services, the cost of legal representation can put access to justice out of reach for a significant proportion of the population.

In addition to legal fees, individuals seeking to access justice in SSA may also face a range of other costs, including court fees, transportation costs, and the costs of obtaining necessary documentation or evidence. These costs can accumulate quickly, making it difficult for individuals to sustain legal action, particularly in cases that involve lengthy proceedings or multiple court appearances.[13]

The financial barriers to accessing justice have a disproportionate impact on women and girls, who often have less access to and control over financial resources than men. This can make it particularly difficult for women to access the justice system in cases involving family law, inheritance disputes, and gender-based violence, where the costs of legal representation and the risks of retaliation may be high.[14]

The costs of accessing justice can also serve as a deterrent for individuals seeking to enforce their rights to an adequate standard of living. For example, individuals may be reluctant to challenge evictions or assert their rights to housing or land due to the costs associated with legal proceedings, even where they have a strong case. Similarly, individuals may be deterred from seeking redress for violations of their rights to health, education, or social security, particularly where the costs of accessing justice are perceived to outweigh the potential benefits.[15]

Cultural and Social Benefits to Accessing Justice

In addition to financial and institutional barriers, cultural and social factors can also serve as significant impediments to accessing justice in Sub-Saharan Africa (SSA). These barriers can take many forms, including discriminatory attitudes and practices, social stigma, and cultural norms that discourage individuals from seeking redress for violations of their rights.

12 Meena Jagannath et al. (n 6).

13 Olabisi D. Akinkugbe, 'Towards a More Efficient Legal Aid System in Nigeria' (2022) 10 *Obiter* 25.

14 Anne Daugherty-Lindsay et al., 'Women's Access to Justice in Sub-Saharan Africa: Challenges, Opportunities and the Role of Legal Aid' (2022) 60 *Commonwealth Law Bulletin* 301.

15 Taiwo Ajala, 'Human Rights and Access to Justice in Sub-Saharan Africa' (2021) 21 *African Human Rights Law Journal* 1.

One of the most pervasive cultural barriers to accessing justice in SSA is the persistence of discriminatory attitudes and practices based on gender, ethnicity, religion, and other identities. Women and girls, in particular, face significant obstacles in accessing justice due to deeply entrenched gender inequalities and discriminatory social norms.[16] In many SSA countries, women's rights are not fully recognised or protected under the law, and women may face discrimination and bias in the justice system itself, including from police, prosecutors, and judges.[17]

Cultural attitudes that prioritise the preservation of family and community harmony over individual rights can also serve as a barrier to accessing justice in SSA. In some communities, there may be strong social pressures to resolve disputes informally through traditional or customary mechanisms, rather than through the formal justice system.[18] While these informal mechanisms can play an important role in promoting social cohesion and resolving conflicts, they may also perpetuate power imbalances and discriminatory practices, particularly against women and marginalised groups.[19]

Social stigma and the fear of reprisals can also deter individuals from seeking justice, particularly in cases involving sensitive or taboo issues such as sexual and gender-based violence, HIV/AIDS, and mental health. Victims of these violations may face significant social and cultural barriers to reporting crimes or seeking redress, including shame, blame, and the risk of further violence or discrimination.[20]

Cultural and social barriers can also intersect with other forms of marginalisation, such as poverty and disability, to create further obstacles to accessing justice. For example, individuals living in poverty may face discrimination and stigma based on their socio-economic status, while persons with disabilities may encounter attitudinal and physical barriers in the justice system that limit their ability to participate fully and assert their rights.[21]

Overcoming cultural and social barriers to accessing justice requires a multifaceted approach that addresses the underlying drivers of discrimination and

16 Catherine A. MacKinnon, 'Creating International Law: Gender as Leading Edge' (2013) 36 *Harvard Journal of Law & Gender* 105.

17 Joy Onyesoh et al., 'Discriminatory Cultural Practices and Women's Rights among the Igbos of South-East Nigeria: A Critique' (2021) 25 *Journal of International Women's Studies* 4.

18 Simon Coldham, 'Access to Justice in Africa: Legal Aid and Traditional Justice Systems' (2021) 17 *Journal of African Law* 137. See also, Augustine Edobor Arimoro, 'Persons with Intellectual Disability and Access to Justice in Nigeria: Challenges and the Way Forward' (2019) 5 *Hassanudin Law Review* 180-198.

19 Brian Tamuka Kagoro, 'The Paradox of Alien Knowledge, Narrative and Praxis: Transitional Justice and the Politics of Agenda Setting in Africa' in Moses Chrispus Okello et al. (eds), *Where Law Meets Reality: Forging African Transitional Justice* (Pambazuka Press, 2012).

20 Olubukola Oluranti Babalola et al., 'Social Stigma and Mental Health in Sub-Saharan Africa: A Systematic Review' (2022) 12 *Frontiers in Public Health* 750778.

21 Janet Lord et al., 'Human Rights. Yes! Action and Advocacy on the Rights of Persons with Disabilities' (University of Minnesota Human Rights Center, 2009).

inequality. This may include legal and policy reforms to promote gender equality and non-discrimination, as well as community-based initiatives to challenge harmful social norms and practices. It also requires a commitment to building a more inclusive and responsive justice system that is accessible and accountable to all members of society, regardless of their identity or social status.

Corruption and Lack of Accountability in the Justice System

Corruption and a lack of accountability within the justice system itself can also pose significant challenges to accessing justice in Sub-Saharan Africa (SSA). In many countries in the region, corruption is endemic, permeating various levels of the justice system, from police and prosecutors to judges and court officials.[22]

Corruption in the justice system can take many forms, including bribery, extortion, nepotism, and political interference. It can manifest in the selective application of the law, the manipulation of evidence, and the denial of due process rights to accused persons. It can also result in the impunity of powerful individuals and entities who may use their influence to evade accountability for violations of the law.[23]

The prevalence of corruption in the justice system can have a profound impact on access to justice, particularly for marginalised and vulnerable groups who may lack the resources or influence to navigate a corrupt system. It can create a climate of impunity, where individuals may be reluctant to seek redress for violations of their rights due to a lack of confidence in the integrity and impartiality of the justice system.[24]

Corruption can also exacerbate existing inequalities and power imbalances within society, as those with resources and influence may be able to use the justice system to further their own interests, while those without may be denied access to justice altogether. This can have particularly severe consequences for individuals seeking to enforce their rights to an adequate standard of living, as they may face insurmountable obstacles in accessing legal remedies for violations of their rights to housing, health, education, and social security.[25]

The lack of accountability within the justice system itself can also serve as a barrier to accessing justice in SSA. In many countries, there are weak or

22 Chikosa Banda, 'Corruption and Its Repercussions on the Right to Development in Africa' (2021) 5 *African Human Rights Yearbook* 97.

23 Nic Cheeseman et al., 'Decentralisation in Kenya: The Governance of Governors' (2016) 54 *Journal of Modern African Studies* 1.

24 Aninka Claassens, 'Customary Law and Zones of Chiefly Sovereignty: The Impact of Government Policy on Whose Voices Prevail in the Making and Changing of Customary Law' in Aninka Claassens and Ben Cousins (eds), *Land, Power & Custom: Controversies Generated by South Africa's Communal Land Rights Act* (UCT Press, 2008).

25 Koen Vanrest, 'The Challenges of Land Governance in Africa: Lessons Learned and Current Debates' (2021) 21 *African Studies Quarterly* 97.

non-existent mechanisms for holding justice actors accountable for misconduct or corruption, such as independent oversight bodies or disciplinary procedures. This can create a culture of impunity within the justice system, where individuals may feel powerless to challenge abuses of power or seek redress for violations of their rights.[26]

Addressing corruption and promoting accountability within the justice system requires a sustained and multipronged approach. This may include legal and institutional reforms to strengthen the independence and integrity of the judiciary, as well as measures to promote transparency and oversight within the justice system, such as the establishment of independent complaint mechanisms and the publication of court decisions and other legal information.[27]

It also requires a commitment to promoting a culture of integrity and professionalism within the justice system, through the training and sensitisation of justice actors, the development of ethical codes of conduct, and the enforcement of disciplinary measures for misconduct. Ultimately, building a more accountable and transparent justice system is essential for promoting access to justice and ensuring that the rights of all individuals, including the right to an adequate standard of living, are fully respected and protected under the law.[28]

Access to Justice and the Right to an Adequate Standard of Living

Intersections between Access to Justice and Socio-Economic Rights

Access to justice and the right to an adequate standard of living are intrinsically linked, with the realisation of one often dependent on the fulfilment of the other. The right to an adequate standard of living, as enshrined in the International Covenant on Economic, Social and Cultural Rights (ICESCR), encompasses a range of socio-economic rights, including the right to adequate housing, food, water, sanitation, health, education, and social security.[29]

These socio-economic rights are essential for ensuring that individuals can live with dignity and have their basic needs met. However, the realisation of these rights is often hindered by a lack of access to justice, particularly for

26 International Commission of Jurists, 'Challenges to the Independence of the Judiciary and Accountability for Judicial Corruption in Africa' (ICJ, 2021).

27 David Pimentel, 'Reframing the Independence v. Accountability Debate: Defining Judicial Structure in Light of Judges' Courage and Integrity' (2009) 57 *Cleveland State Law Review* 1.

28 E Gyimah-Boadi, 'Dealing with Ghana's Corruption Pandemic: A Proactive Collective Responsibility' in Kwesi Aning and Kwaku Danso (eds), *Managing Election-Related Conflict and Violence for Democratic Stability in Ghana II* (Kofi Annan International Peacekeeping Training Centre, 2016).

29 International Covenant on Economic, Social and Cultural Rights (adopted 16 December 1966, entered into force 3 January 1976) 993 UNTS 3.

marginalised and vulnerable groups who may face significant barriers in asserting their rights and seeking redress for violations.[30]

Access to justice is crucial for ensuring that socio-economic rights are not merely aspirational but are enforceable and justiciable under the law. It provides individuals with the means to hold duty-bearers accountable for failures to respect, protect, and fulfil their obligations under international human rights law, as well as under national constitutions and legislation.[31]

In the context of the right to adequate housing, for example, access to justice is essential for enabling individuals to challenge forced evictions, discrimination in access to housing, and inadequate living conditions. It provides a means for individuals to assert their rights to security of tenure, affordability, habitability, and accessibility, and to seek remedies for violations of these rights.[32]

Similarly, in the context of the right to health, access to justice is crucial for ensuring that individuals can challenge denials of healthcare services, discrimination in access to care, and failures to provide essential medicines and treatments. It provides a means for individuals to assert their rights to available, accessible, acceptable, and quality healthcare services, and to seek remedies for violations of these rights.[33]

Access to justice is also critical for promoting the progressive realisation of socio-economic rights over time. By providing individuals with the means to challenge systemic failures and advocate for policy changes, access to justice can help to drive improvements in the availability, accessibility, and quality of essential services and infrastructure, such as housing, healthcare, education, and social protection.[34]

Moreover, access to justice can play a crucial role in promoting accountability and transparency in the allocation and use of public resources for the realisation of socio-economic rights. By enabling individuals to challenge corruption, mismanagement, and the misallocation of funds, access to justice can

30 Sisay Alemahu Yeshanew, 'The Justiciability of Economic, Social and Cultural Rights in the African Regional Human Rights System: Theory, Practice and Prospect' (2014) 4 *Cambridge Journal of International and Comparative Law* 297.

31 Varun Gauri and Daniel M. Brinks (eds), Courting Social Justice: Judicial Enforcement of Social and Economic Rights in the Developing World (Cambridge University Press, 2008).

32 Lilian Chenwi, 'Access to Justice and the Right to Adequate Housing: The South African Context' in Ebenezer Durojaye (ed), Strengthening the Protection of Sexual and Reproductive Health and Rights in the African Region through Human Rights (Pretoria University Law Press, 2014).

33 Obiajulu Nnamuchi, 'Bloated Remand Cells in Nigeria: An Indictment on the Criminal Justice Administration and the Right to Health' (2018) 18 African Human Rights Law Journal 485.

34 Danwood Mzikenge Chirwa, 'Privatization and the Right to Adequate Housing under International Human Rights Law in the Neoliberal Era' (2022) 70 Netherlands International Law Review 87.

help to ensure that resources are used effectively and efficiently to meet the needs of the most vulnerable and marginalised groups.[35]

Legal Empowerment of Community-Based Justice Initiatives

Legal empowerment and community-based justice initiatives are increasingly recognised as important strategies for promoting access to justice and the realisation of socio-economic rights in Sub-Saharan Africa (SSA). These approaches focus on building the capacity of individuals and communities to understand and assert their rights, and to participate actively in the processes that affect their lives.[36]

Legal empowerment refers to the process of increasing the capacity of individuals and communities to exercise their rights and participate in decision-making processes that affect them. It involves a range of strategies, including legal education and awareness-raising, community mobilisation and organising, and the provision of legal services and representation.[37]

In the context of socio-economic rights, legal empowerment can play a crucial role in enabling individuals and communities to assert their rights to adequate housing, health, education, and social security. It can help to build awareness of the legal and policy frameworks that govern these rights, as well as the mechanisms available for seeking redress for violations.[38]

Community-based justice initiatives, on the other hand, focus on promoting access to justice at the local level, through the engagement of community members and the use of traditional and informal justice systems. These initiatives often involve the training and deployment of community paralegals, who provide legal information and assistance to individuals and communities, and help to mediate disputes and facilitate access to formal justice mechanisms where necessary.[39]

Community-based justice initiatives can be particularly effective in promoting access to justice for marginalised and vulnerable groups, who may face significant barriers in accessing formal justice systems due to distance, cost, language, or cultural factors. By providing legal services and support at the local level, these initiatives can help to bridge the gap between formal and

35 Chikosa Banda (n 24).

36 Vivek Maru, 'Access to Justice and Legal Empowerment: A Review of World Bank Practice' (2010) 2 *Hague Journal on the Rule of Law* 259.

37 Lorenzo Cotula and Paul Mathieu (eds), *Legal Empowerment in Practice: Using Legal Tools to Secure Land Rights in Africa* (International Institute for Environment and Development, 2008).

38 Namati, *Pursuing Equitable Development Through Legal Empowerment: An Introduction* (Namati, 2021).

39 Aimite Jorge, 'Civic Education and Access to Justice in Namibia: The Community Paralegal Movement as an Agent of Constitutional Consciousness' (2017) 7 *Journal of Public Policy Research* 30.

informal justice systems and ensure that individuals and communities have access to the information and assistance they need to assert their rights.[40]

In SSA, legal empowerment and community-based justice initiatives have been used to promote access to justice and the realisation of socio-economic rights in a range of contexts, from land and property rights to access to health-care and education. For example, in South Africa, the Social Justice Coalition has used legal empowerment strategies to advocate for the right to sanitation in informal settlements; while in Kenya, the Kituo Cha Sheria has provided legal aid and assistance to individuals and communities facing forced evictions and land grabbing.[41]

However, while legal empowerment and community-based justice initiatives hold significant promise for promoting access to justice and the realisation of socio-economic rights in SSA, they also face a range of challenges and limitations. These include limited resources and capacity, the need for sustained funding and support, and the potential for co-optation or resistance from powerful actors who may see these initiatives as a threat to their interests.[42]

Moreover, legal empowerment and community-based justice initiatives must be carefully designed and implemented to ensure that they are responsive to the needs and priorities of the communities they serve, and that they do not inadvertently reinforce existing power imbalances or inequalities. This requires a deep understanding of local contexts and dynamics, as well as a commitment to promoting the agency and autonomy of individuals and communities in asserting their rights and seeking justice on their own terms.[43]

Case Studies and Successful Initiatives

Mobile Courts and Justice Outreach Programmes

One innovative approach to promoting access to justice in Sub-Saharan Africa (SSA) has been the use of mobile courts and justice outreach programmes. These initiatives aim to bring justice services closer to communities, particularly

40 Keita Khadija et al., 'Expanding Access to Justice for the Poor: Malawi's Search for Solutions - A Comparative Analysis with Other Select Informal Justice Systems' (2018) *65 South African Crim Quarterly* 1.

41 Jackie Dugard, 'The Right to Sanitation in South Africa: Law, Policy and Practice' (2016) 37 *South African Journal on Human Rights* 1; Rachael Njeri Mwangi, 'Forced Evictions and the Right to Adequate Housing in Kenya' (2017) 21 *East African Journal of Peace and Human Rights* 134.

42 Natalia Herbst et al., 'Legal Empowerment of the Poor: Past, Present, and Future' (2020) 19 *Annual Review of Law and Social Science* 363.

43 Sumudu Athukorala, 'The Impact of Legal Empowerment on the Rights of Women and Girls in Refugee Settings' (2022) 36 *Journal of Refugee Studies* 1.

those in remote and underserved areas, and to promote the rule of law and the realisation of human rights.[44]

Mobile courts are temporary or periodic courts that are set up in communities that are far from established courthouses or legal aid centres. They are often staffed by magistrates, prosecutors, and legal aid providers who travel to these communities on a regular basis to hear cases and provide legal services. Mobile courts can be particularly effective in addressing cases related to family law, land disputes, and minor criminal offenses which may otherwise go unresolved due to the distance and cost of accessing formal justice systems.[45]

Justice outreach programmes, on the other hand, focus on providing legal information, education, and assistance to communities through a range of strategies, such as legal clinics, community meetings, and media campaigns. These programmes often involve partnerships between government agencies, civil society organisations, and community leaders, and aim to build awareness of legal rights and processes, as well as to facilitate access to justice for marginalised and vulnerable groups.[46]

In SSA, mobile courts and justice outreach programmes have been used to promote access to justice in a range of contexts, from post-conflict settings to remote rural areas. For example, in Sierra Leone, the Mobile Courts Programme has been credited with reducing case backlogs and increasing access to justice for women and girls in rural areas, particularly in cases related to sexual and gender-based violence.[47] In Uganda, the Justice Centres programme has provided legal aid and assistance to over 400,000 individuals since its establishment in 2009, with a particular focus on land rights and family law cases.[48]

However, while mobile courts and justice outreach programmes hold significant promise for promoting access to justice in SSA, they also face a range of challenges and limitations. These include limited resources and capacity, the need for sustained funding and political support, and the potential for resistance from traditional authorities or community members who may see these initiatives as a threat to their power or interests.[49]

44 Aimite Jorge, 'Mobile Courts in Namibia: Promises and Challenges' (2018) 41 *Obiter* 217.
45 Carolyn Logan, 'Ambitious SDG Goal Confronts Challenging Realities: Access to Justice is Still Elusive for Many Africans' (Afrobarometer Policy Paper No. 39, 2017).
46 Gayathri Balagopal et al., 'Access to Justice During COVID-19: Experiences from the Justice Defenders Network' (2021) 3 *Journal of Legal Pluralism and Unofficial Law* 237.
47 Tanja Chopra, 'Expanding Access to Justice for Sexual and Gender-Based Violence in Liberia and Sierra Leone' (2019) 10 *Journal of International Peacekeeping* 70.
48 James Katorobo, 'Justice Centres Programme in Uganda (LSE International Development Working Paper No. 2020-06-01, 2020).
49 Olabisi D. Akinkugbe, 'Revisiting the Mobile Courts System in Post-Conflict Sierra Leone: Prospects and Challenges' (2017) 1 *African Journal of International and Comparative Law* 99.

Moreover, the effectiveness of mobile courts and justice outreach programmes depends on a range of factors, including the quality and accessibility of the services provided, the level of community engagement and participation, and the ability to address underlying structural and systemic barriers to justice. This requires a holistic and context-specific approach that takes into account the unique needs and priorities of each community, as well as the broader social, economic, and political factors that shape access to justice in SSA.[50]

Legal Aid and Assistance for Marginalised Groups

Another key strategy for promoting access to justice in Sub-Saharan Africa (SSA) has been the provision of legal aid and assistance to marginalised and vulnerable groups, such as women, children, persons with disabilities, and indigenous communities. These groups often face significant barriers in accessing justice due to discrimination, stigma, poverty, and other forms of marginalisation, and may require targeted interventions to ensure that their rights are protected and enforced.[51]

Legal aid and assistance can take many forms, including legal representation, advice and counselling, mediation and alternative dispute resolution, and legal education and empowerment. These services can be provided by a range of actors, including government legal aid agencies, civil society organisations, university legal clinics, and community-based paralegals.[52]

In SSA, legal aid and assistance programmes have been particularly important in promoting access to justice for women and girls, who face significant barriers in accessing justice due to gender-based discrimination and violence. For example, in Rwanda, the Haguruka Association has provided legal aid and assistance to over 50,000 women and girls since its establishment in 1991, with a particular focus on cases related to land rights, inheritance, and gender-based violence.[53] In Ghana, the Legal Aid Scheme has provided legal representation and assistance to thousands of individuals, with a particular focus on women and children in cases related to family law and domestic violence.[54]

Legal aid and assistance programmes have also been important in promoting access to justice for persons with disabilities in SSA, who face significant barriers in accessing justice due to physical, communication, and attitudinal

50 Katrina Tompsett, 'Mobile Courts and Access to Justice in Rural India' (2021) 13 *Journal of Legal Anthropology* 48.
51 Anne Daugherty-Lindsay et al. (n 16).
52 Meena Jagannath et al. (n 6).
53 Pamela Abbott et al., 'The Contribution of Rwandan Women's Organizations to Post-Genocide Reconstruction and Development' (2021) 33 *Journal of Peacebuilding & Development* 126.
54 Nana Oye Lithur, 'The Role of the Legal Aid Board in Promoting Access to Justice in Ghana' (2019) 59 *Commonwealth Law Bulletin* 117.

barriers. For example, in South Africa, the Legal Resources Centre has provided legal representation and assistance to persons with disabilities in a range of cases, including those related to access to education, healthcare, and social security.[55]

However, while legal aid and assistance programmes are crucial for promoting access to justice for marginalised and vulnerable groups in SSA, they also face significant challenges and limitations. These include limited resources and capacity, the need for sustained funding and political support, and the potential for resistance from powerful actors who may see these programmes as a threat to their interests.[56]

Moreover, the effectiveness of legal aid and assistance programmes depends on a range of factors, including the quality and accessibility of the services provided, the level of community engagement and participation, and the ability to address underlying structural and systemic barriers to justice. This requires a holistic and intersectional approach that takes into account the multiple and overlapping forms of marginalisation and discrimination that shape access to justice for different groups in SSA.[57]

Innovative Approaches to Legal Education and Empowerment

Promoting access to justice in Sub-Saharan Africa (SSA) requires not only the provision of legal services and assistance but also the empowerment of individuals and communities to understand and assert their rights. Legal education and empowerment initiatives can play a crucial role in building legal literacy and awareness, challenging harmful social norms and practices, and promoting the agency and autonomy of marginalised and vulnerable groups in seeking justice.[58]

In SSA, a range of innovative approaches to legal education and empowerment have emerged in recent years, leveraging the potential of new technologies, media platforms, and community-based strategies. For example, in Kenya, the Sheria Mtaani initiative has used street law and community theatre to educate and engage communities on legal issues related to land rights, gender-based violence, and access to justice.[59] In South Africa, the Community

55 Lisa Vetten and Tanya Charles, 'Access to Justice for Persons with Disabilities in South Africa: A Review of Legislation, Policies and Practice' (2020) 8 *African Disability Rights Yearbook* 167.

56 Dustin N. Sharp, 'Re-Thinking Access to Justice in Post-Conflict States: The Problem of Donor Assistance to Transitional Justice Processes' (2009) 32 *Liverpool Law Review* 177.

57 Rosemary Grey et al., 'Gender and Judging at the International Criminal Court: Lessons from "Feminist Judgment Projects"' (2022) 22 *International Criminal Law Review* 359.

58 David McQuoid-Mason, 'Street Law and Public Legal Education: A Viable and Effective Partnership for Increasing Access to Justice in South Africa' (2022) 35 *Speculum Juris* 103.

59 Naomi Johnstone, 'Access to Justice for Adults with Disability in Kibera, Kenya: An Application of Bourdieu's Theory of Practice' (2021) 11 *The Journal of Legal Pluralism and Unofficial Law* 285.

Advice Offices have provided legal education and assistance to over 150,000 individuals per year, with a particular focus on empowering women and youth to assert their rights and participate in local governance processes.[60]

Technology-based initiatives have also shown promise in promoting legal education and empowerment in SSA. For example, in Nigeria, the LawPadi platform has provided legal information and assistance to over 60,000 users through a mobile app and web portal, with a particular focus on issues related to housing, employment, and consumer rights.[61] In Uganda, the Barefoot Law initiative has used social media, radio, and SMS to provide legal information and assistance to over 500,000 individuals, with a particular focus on empowering women and youth to assert their rights and seek justice.[62]

However, while these innovative approaches to legal education and empowerment hold significant promise, they also face a range of challenges and limitations. These include the need for sustained funding and support, the potential for digital exclusion and inequality, and the risk of backlash or resistance from powerful actors who may see these initiatives as a threat to their interests.[63]

Moreover, the effectiveness of legal education and empowerment initiatives depends on a range of factors, including the relevance and accessibility of the information and assistance provided, the level of community engagement and participation, and the ability to address underlying structural and systemic barriers to justice. This requires a context-specific and participatory approach that centres the needs and priorities of marginalised and vulnerable groups, and that promotes their agency and autonomy in seeking justice on their own terms.[64]

Ultimately, promoting access to justice in SSA through legal education and empowerment requires a fundamental shift in power relations and a commitment to social and structural transformation. It requires challenging the deeply entrenched inequalities and exclusions that shape access to justice in the region, and building a more inclusive, equitable, and just society for all.[65]

60 Winnie Martins, 'The Role of Community-Based Paralegals in Enhancing Access to Justice in South Africa' (2022) 30 *African Journal of International and Comparative Law* 64.

61 Olanrewaju Ademola, *Access to Justice and Technology: Transformative Potential of Tech Solutions in Africa* (Africa Law Tech, 2021).

62 Douglas Glanfield, 'Access to Justice in Uganda: Examining the Impact of COVID-19 on Legal Aid Service Delivery and the Justice System' (2021) 15 *Journal of African Law* 1.

63 Annette Lansink, 'Legal Empowerment of the Poor and Its Potential for Transitional Justice: Challenges and Opportunities' (2019) 13 *International Journal of Transitional Justice* 419.

64 Yvonne Dausab, 'Access to Justice: The Use of Community-Based Paralegals to Advance the Right to Health in Namibia' (2020) 8 *ESR Review: Economic and Social Rights in South Africa* 23.

65 Sindiso Mnisi Weeks, 'Access to Justice? Dispute Management in Southern Africa's Small-Scale Fisheries' (2021) 79 *Marine Policy* 104197.

Conclusion

Access to justice is a fundamental human right and a critical enabler for the realisation of the right to an adequate standard of living in Sub-Saharan Africa (SSA). Yet, as this chapter has demonstrated, access to justice remains a significant challenge in the region, with multifaceted barriers and obstacles impeding the ability of individuals and communities to seek redress for violations of their rights and to participate fully in the justice system.

The challenges surrounding access to justice in SSA are deeply rooted in the historical, political, economic, and social contexts of the region, and are shaped by a complex interplay of factors, including the legacy of colonialism, the weakness of state institutions, the prevalence of poverty and inequality, and the persistence of discriminatory cultural practices and social norms. These factors have contributed to the creation of a justice gap, whereby a significant proportion of the population, particularly marginalised and vulnerable groups, are unable to access the legal services and remedies they need to protect and enforce their rights.

The consequences of this justice gap are far-reaching and profound, undermining the realisation of the right to an adequate standard of living and perpetuating cycles of poverty, inequality, and social exclusion. Without access to justice, individuals and communities are left without the means to challenge violations of their rights, to hold duty-bearers accountable, and to participate in the decisions that affect their lives and livelihoods.

Recognising the critical importance of access to justice for the realisation of the right to an adequate standard of living, governments, civil society organisations, and international actors have undertaken various efforts to address the challenges and barriers that impede access to justice in SSA. These efforts have ranged from legal and policy reforms to the provision of legal aid and assistance, the promotion of legal empowerment and community-based justice initiatives, and the use of innovative approaches and technologies to expand the reach and impact of justice interventions.

However, despite these efforts, significant gaps and challenges persist, underscoring the need for a more comprehensive, holistic, and transformative approach to access to justice in SSA. Such an approach must be grounded in a deep understanding of the complex and intersecting forms of marginalisation and exclusion that shape access to justice in the region, and must prioritise the needs, rights, and agency of the most vulnerable and marginalised groups.

This requires a fundamental shift in power relations and a commitment to social and structural transformation, challenging the deeply entrenched inequalities and exclusions that underpin the justice gap in SSA. It requires building more inclusive, participatory, and accountable justice systems that are responsive to the needs and priorities of marginalised and vulnerable groups, and that promote their agency and autonomy in seeking justice on their own terms.

Ultimately, realising the right to an adequate standard of living in SSA through access to justice requires a collective effort and a shared responsibility, involving governments, civil society, the private sector, and international partners. It requires sustained investment in the capacities and resources of justice actors and institutions, as well as in the legal empowerment and mobilisation of communities and individuals to claim their rights and hold duty-bearers accountable.

By embracing this vision and working towards its realisation, we can build a more just, equitable, and inclusive future for all in SSA, one in which every individual and community can enjoy the full realisation of their right to an adequate standard of living, and in which access to justice is a reality for all. While the challenges are significant and the road ahead is long, the case studies and initiatives explored in this chapter demonstrate that change is possible, and that the pursuit of justice and equality is a cause worth fighting for.

References

Abbott P et al, 'The Contribution of Rwandan Women's Organizations to Post-Genocide Reconstruction and Development' (2021) 33 *Journal of Peacebuilding & Development* 126.

Ademola O, *Access to Justice and Technology: Transformative Potential of Tech Solutions in Africa* (Africa Law Tech 2021).

Ajala T, 'Human Rights and Access to Justice in Sub-Saharan Africa' (2021) 21 *African Human Rights Law Journal* 1.

Akinkugbe OD, 'Revisiting the Mobile Courts System in Post-Conflict Sierra Leone: Prospects and Challenges' (2017) 1 *African Journal of International and Comparative Law* 99.

Akinkugbe OD, 'Towards a More Efficient Legal Aid System in Nigeria' (2022) 10 *Obiter* 25.

Arimoro AE, 'Persons with Intellectual Disability and Access to Justice in Nigeria: Challenges and the Way Forward' (2019) 5 *Hassanudin Law Review* 180–198.

Athukorala S, 'The Impact of Legal Empowerment on the Rights of Women and Girls in Refugee Settings' (2022) 36 *Journal of Refugee Studies* 1.

Babalola OO et al, 'Social Stigma and Mental Health in Sub-Saharan Africa: A Systematic Review' (2022) 12 *Frontiers in Public Health* 750778.

Balagopal G et al, 'Access to Justice During COVID-19: Experiences from the Justice Defenders Network' (2021) 3 *Journal of Legal Pluralism and Unofficial Law* 237.

Banda C, 'Corruption and Its Repercussions on the Right to Development in Africa' (2021) 5 *African Human Rights Yearbook* 97.

Cheeseman N et al, 'Decentralisation in Kenya: The Governance of Governors' (2016) 54 *Journal of Modern African Studies* 1.

Chenwi L, 'Access to Justice and the Right to Adequate Housing: The South African Context' in E Durojaye (ed), *Strengthening the Protection of Sexual and Reproductive Health and Rights in the African Region through Human Rights* (Pretoria University Law Press 2014).

Chirwa DM, 'Privatization and the Right to Adequate Housing under International Human Rights Law in the Neoliberal Era' (2022) 70 *Netherlands International Law Review* 87.

Chopra T, 'Expanding Access to Justice for Sexual and Gender-Based Violence in Liberia and Sierra Leone' (2019) 10 *Journal of International Peacekeeping* 70.

Claassens A, 'Customary Law and Zones of Chiefly Sovereignty: The Impact of Government Policy on Whose Voices Prevail in the Making and Changing of Customary Law' in A Claassens and B Cousins (eds), *Land, Power & Custom: Controversies Generated by South Africa's Communal Land Rights Act* (UCT Press 2008).

Coldham S, 'Access to Justice in Africa: Legal Aid and Traditional Justice Systems' (2021) 17 *Journal of African Law* 137.

Cotula L and Mathieu P (eds), *Legal Empowerment in Practice: Using Legal Tools to Secure Land Rights in Africa* (International Institute for Environment and Development 2008).

Daugherty-Lindsay A et al, 'Women's Access to Justice in Sub-Saharan Africa: Challenges, Opportunities and the Role of Legal Aid' (2022) 60 *Commonwealth Law Bulletin* 301.

Dausab Y, 'Access to Justice: The Use of Community-Based Paralegals to Advance the Right to Health in Namibia' (2020) 8 *ESR Review: Economic and Social Rights in South Africa* 23.

Dugard J, 'The Right to Sanitation in South Africa: Law, Policy and Practice' (2016) 37 *South African Journal on Human Rights* 1.

Gauri V and Brinks DM (eds), *Courting Social Justice: Judicial Enforcement of Social and Economic Rights in the Developing World* (Cambridge University Press 2008).

Glanfield D, 'Access to Justice in Uganda: Examining the Impact of COVID-19 on Legal Aid Service Delivery and the Justice System' (2021) 15 *Journal of African Law* 1.

Grey R et al, 'Gender and Judging at the International Criminal Court: Lessons from "Feminist Judgment Projects"' (2022) 22 *International Criminal Law Review* 359.

Gyimah-Boadi E, 'Dealing with Ghana's Corruption Pandemic: A Proactive Collective Responsibility' in K Aning and K Danso (eds), *Managing Election-Related Conflict and Violence for Democratic Stability in Ghana II* (Kofi Annan International Peacekeeping Training Centre 2016).

Harrington A, 'The Right to Health and Access to Health Care in Sub-Saharan Africa: A Perspective from the United Nations Committee on Economic, Social and Cultural Rights' (2020) 20 *African Human Rights Law Journal* 455.

Herbst N et al, 'Legal Empowerment of the Poor: Past, Present, and Future' (2020) 19 *Annual Review of Law and Social Science* 363.

HiiL, *Justice Needs and Satisfaction in Ethiopia 2020* (HiiL 2020).

International Commission of Jurists, *Challenges to the Independence of the Judiciary and Accountability for Judicial Corruption in Africa* (ICJ 2021).

International Covenant on Economic, Social and Cultural Rights (adopted 16 December 1966, entered into force 3 January 1976) 993 UNTS 3.

Jagannath M et al, 'A Rights-Based Approach to Lawyering: Legal Empowerment as an Alternative to Legal Aid in Post-Disaster Haiti' (2011) 10 *Northwestern Journal of International Human Rights* 7.

Johnstone N, 'Access to Justice for Adults with Disability in Kibera, Kenya: An Application of Bourdieu's Theory of Practice' (2021) 11 *The Journal of Legal Pluralism and Unofficial Law* 285.

Jorge A, 'Civic Education and Access to Justice in Namibia: The Community Paralegal Movement as an Agent of Constitutional Consciousness' (2017) 7 *Journal of Public Policy Research* 30.

Jorge A, 'Mobile Courts in Namibia: Promises and Challenges' (2018) 41 *Obiter* 217
Kabir M, 'Conceptualizing Access to Justice: Directions for Achieving Sustainable Development Goals in Bangladesh' (2021) 13 *Journal of Sustainable Development Law and Policy* 188.
Kagoro BT, 'The Paradox of Alien Knowledge, Narrative and Praxis: Transitional Justice and the Politics of Agenda Setting in Africa' in MC Okello et al. (eds), *Where Law Meets Reality: Forging African Transitional Justice* (Pambazuka Press 2012).
Katorobo J, 'Justice Centres Programme in Uganda' (LSE International Development Working Paper No. 2020-06-01 2020).
Kelly CL, 'Justice and Rule of Law Key to African Security' (2021) Available at https://africacenter.org/spotlight/justice-and-rule-of-law-key-to-african-security/ accessed 9 December 2024.
Khadija K et al, 'Expanding Access to Justice for the Poor: Malawi's Search for Solutions - A Comparative Analysis with Other Select Informal Justice Systems' (2018) 65 *South African Crim Quarterly* 1.
Klopp JM et al, 'Towards Development of a Global Indicator on Legal Aid to Monitor Progress on SDG Target 16.3' (2021) 6 *World Bank Policy Research Working Paper* 9598.
Lansink A, 'Legal Empowerment of the Poor and Its Potential for Transitional Justice: Challenges and Opportunities' (2019) 13 *International Journal of Transitional Justice* 419.
Lithur NO, 'The Role of the Legal Aid Board in Promoting Access to Justice in Ghana' (2019) 59 *Commonwealth Law Bulletin* 117.
Logan C, *Ambitious SDG Goal Confronts Challenging Realities: Access to Justice is Still Elusive for Many Africans* (Afrobarometer Policy Paper No. 39 2017). Available at https://www.afrobarometer.org/wp-content/uploads/migrated/files/publications/Policy%20papers/ab_r6_policypaperno39_access_to_justice_in_africa_eng.pdf accessed 9 December 2024
Lord J et al, *Human Rights. Yes! Action and Advocacy on the Rights of Persons with Disabilities* (University of Minnesota Human Rights Center 2009).
MacKinnon CA, 'Creating International Law: Gender as Leading Edge' (2013) 36 *Harvard Journal of Law & Gender* 105.
Martins W, 'The Role of Community-Based Paralegals in Enhancing Access to Justice in South Africa' (2022) 30 *African Journal of International and Comparative Law* 64.
Maru V, 'Access to Justice and Legal Empowerment: A Review of World Bank Practice' (2010) 2 *Hague Journal on the Rule of Law* 259.
McQuoid-Mason D, 'Street Law and Public Legal Education: A Viable and Effective Partnership for Increasing Access to Justice in South Africa' (2022) 35 *Speculum Juris* 103.
Mwangi RN, 'Forced Evictions and the Right to Adequate Housing in Kenya' (2017) 21 *East African Journal of Peace and Human Rights* 134.
Namati, *Pursuing Equitable Development Through Legal Empowerment: An Introduction* (Namati 2021).
Nnamuchi O, 'Bloated Remand Cells in Nigeria: An Indictment on the Criminal Justice Administration and the Right to Health' (2018) 18 *African Human Rights Law Journal* 485.

Onyesoh J et al, 'Discriminatory Cultural Practices and Women's Rights among the Igbos of South-East Nigeria: A Critique' (2021) 25 *Journal of International Women's Studies* 4.

Pimentel D, 'Reframing the Independence v. Accountability Debate: Defining Judicial Structure in Light of Judges' Courage and Integrity' (2009) 57 *Cleveland State Law Review* 1.

Sharp DN, 'Re-Thinking Access to Justice in Post-Conflict States: The Problem of Donor Assistance to Transitional Justice Processes' (2009) 32 *Liverpool Law Review* 177.

Sindiso Mnisi Weeks, 'Access to Justice? Dispute Management in Southern Africa's Small-Scale Fisheries' (2021) 79 *Marine Policy* 104197.

Thuo L et al, 'Justice for All in Sub-Saharan Africa: An Analysis of Legal Aid and Its Link to Socio-Economic Development' (2021) 2 *African Journal of International and Comparative Law* 100.

Tompsett K, 'Mobile Courts and Access to Justice in Rural India' (2021) 13 *Journal of Legal Anthropology* 48.

Ubink J et al. (eds), *Customary Justice: Perspectives on Legal Empowerment* (International Development Law Organization 2011).

UNDP, *Access to Justice and Rule of Law* (UNDP 2021).

United Nations General Assembly, 'Transforming our World: The 2030 Agenda for Sustainable Development' (2015) A/RES/70/1.

Vanrest K, 'The Challenges of Land Governance in Africa: Lessons Learned and Current Debates' (2021) 21 *African Studies Quarterly* 97.

Vetten L and Charles T, 'Access to Justice for Persons with Disabilities in South Africa: A Review of Legislation, Policies and Practice' (2020) 8 *African Disability Rights Yearbook* 167.

Yeshanew SA, 'The Justiciability of Economic, Social and Cultural Rights in the African Regional Human Rights System: Theory, Practice and Prospect' (2014) 4 *Cambridge Journal of International and Comparative Law* 297.

9 Conclusion

Introduction

The right to an adequate standard of living is a fundamental human right enshrined in various international human rights instruments, including the Universal Declaration of Human Rights (UDHR) and the International Covenant on Economic, Social and Cultural Rights (ICESCR).[1] This right encompasses a range of essential elements, such as the right to adequate food, clothing, housing, healthcare, education, and social security, which are necessary for individuals to lead a life of dignity and well-being.[2]

However, the realisation of the right to an adequate standard of living remains a significant challenge in many parts of the world, particularly in Sub-Saharan Africa (SSA). The region has long been grappling with complex and interconnected issues that hinder the full enjoyment of this right, including widespread poverty, inequality, limited access to basic services, environmental degradation, and weak governance structures.[3]

Throughout this monograph, we have explored the various dimensions of the right to an adequate standard of living in SSA, examining the challenges, opportunities, and efforts undertaken to promote its realisation. Each chapter has delved into specific aspects of this right, providing a comprehensive analysis of the current state of affairs, the progress made, and the gaps that persist.

In this concluding chapter, the aim is to synthesise the key findings and insights gained from the preceding chapters, offering a holistic perspective on the right to an adequate standard of living in SSA. The chapter begins by summarising the major challenges and complexities discussed throughout the book, highlighting the multifaceted nature of the issues at hand.

1 United Nations General Assembly, "Universal Declaration of Human Rights" (1948) Resolution 217 A (III).
2 United Nations General Assembly, "International Covenant on Economic, Social and Cultural Rights" (1966) United Nations Treaty Series, vol. 993, p. 3.
3 UNDP, The Next Frontier: Human Development and the Anthropocene – Human Development Report 2020 (UNDP, 2020).

DOI: 10.4324/9781032628974-9

Building upon this foundation, the chapter then presents a set of recommendations aimed at enhancing the realisation of the right to an adequate standard of living in SSA. These recommendations will draw upon the best practices and successful initiatives identified in the previous chapters, as well as the insights gained from the analysis of the challenges and opportunities.

Furthermore, this chapter identifies areas that require further research and investigation to deepen our understanding of the right to an adequate standard of living in SSA and to inform evidence-based policy interventions. By highlighting these research gaps, the chapter aims to provide a roadmap for future scholarly inquiry and to encourage continued efforts to advance the realisation of this fundamental right in the region.

Ultimately, this concluding chapter seeks to underscore the importance of sustained commitment, collaborative action, and evidence-based approaches in promoting the right to an adequate standard of living in SSA. It is our hope that the insights and recommendations presented here will serve as a catalyst for further dialogue, research, and action towards the full realisation of this right for all individuals in the region.

Summary of Key Findings and Challenges

The preceding chapters of this monograph have provided a comprehensive examination of the right to an adequate standard of living in Sub-Saharan Africa (SSA), shedding light on the multifaceted challenges and complexities that hinder the full realisation of this fundamental right in the region. By exploring various dimensions of the right to an adequate standard of living, including poverty and inequality, access to healthcare and education, housing and infrastructure, environmental degradation and climate change, and access to justice, the book has painted a nuanced picture of the current state of affairs in SSA.

One of the overarching themes that emerges from the analysis is the profound impact of poverty and inequality on the enjoyment of the right to an adequate standard of living in SSA. As highlighted in Chapter 4, the region continues to grapple with high levels of poverty and stark inequalities, which have far-reaching consequences for individuals' access to essential goods and services, such as food, housing, healthcare, and education.[4] The persistence of poverty and inequality in SSA is rooted in a complex interplay of historical, political, economic, and social factors, including the legacy of colonialism, weak governance structures, limited economic opportunities, and social exclusion.[5]

4 Kathleen Beegle et al., *Poverty in a Rising Africa* (World Bank, 2016).

5 Giovanni Andrea Cornia and Bruno Martorano, 'The Dynamics of Income Inequality in Sub-Saharan Africa' (2022) 133 *World Development* 106667.

Access to healthcare and education, as discussed in Chapter 5, remains a significant challenge in many parts of SSA, with limited infrastructure, inadequate resources, and socio-economic barriers hindering individuals' ability to access quality services.[6] The consequences of inadequate access to healthcare and education are far-reaching, perpetuating cycles of poverty, reducing human capital development, and undermining overall well-being.[7]

Housing and infrastructure, as explored in Chapter 6, are critical components of the right to an adequate standard of living, yet many individuals in SSA continue to face significant challenges in accessing adequate and affordable housing, as well as essential infrastructure services such as water, sanitation, and electricity.[8] The rapid urbanisation experienced in the region, coupled with inadequate urban planning and limited resources, has led to the proliferation of informal settlements and slums, where living conditions are often characterised by overcrowding, poor sanitation, and limited access to basic services.[9]

Environmental degradation and climate change, as discussed in Chapter 7, pose significant threats to the realisation of the right to an adequate standard of living in SSA. The region is particularly vulnerable to the impacts of climate change, with rising temperatures, changing rainfall patterns, and increased frequency and intensity of extreme weather events affecting agricultural productivity, food security, water availability, and human health.[10] Moreover, environmental degradation, such as deforestation, land degradation, and pollution, further exacerbates the challenges faced by communities, particularly those who rely on natural resources for their livelihoods.[11]

Access to justice, as explored in Chapter 8, is a critical enabler for the realisation of the right to an adequate standard of living, yet many individuals in SSA face significant barriers in accessing justice mechanisms and seeking redress for violations of their rights.[12] These barriers include limited legal infrastructure, inadequate legal aid services, financial constraints, cultural and social obstacles, and corruption within the justice system.[13] The lack of effective access to

6 Kathryn Strother Ratcliff, 'Health Equity and Access to Health Care in Sub-Saharan Africa' (2021) 18 *Advances in Medical Sociology* 187.

7 M Ngware et al., 'Education Challenges in Sub-Saharan Africa and SDG 4' in Brunn S and Kehrein R (eds), *Handbook of the Changing World Language Map* (Springer, 2020).

8 Sumila Gulyani and Ellen Bassett, 'Retrieving the Baby from the Bathwater: Slum Upgrading in Sub-Saharan Africa' (2007) 25 *Environment and Planning C: Government and Policy* 486.

9 Edgar Pieterse et al., 'Africa's Urban Opportunity' (University of Cape Town, 2021).

10 Doreen Stabinsky, 'Climate Change Impacts on Agriculture in Africa' (2022) 15 *Annual Review of Environment and Resources* 407.

11 James Fanzo et al., 'The Role of Ecosystem Services in the Sustainable Development Goals' in Aletta Bonn et al. (eds), *Atlas of Ecosystem Services* (Springer, 2019).

12 Ibid.

13 Chikosa Banda, "Barriers to Access to Justice in Sub-Saharan Africa" (2020) 64 *Journal of African Law* 185.

justice undermines individuals' ability to hold duty-bearers accountable and to claim their rights, perpetuating a cycle of marginalisation and exclusion.

While the challenges discussed throughout the book are significant and multifaceted, it is important to recognise that progress has been made in various areas, and there are examples of successful initiatives and best practices that offer valuable lessons for advancing the realisation of the right to an adequate standard of living in SSA. The case studies and analyses presented in the preceding chapters highlight the potential of innovative approaches, such as community-based interventions, participatory governance models, and technology-enabled solutions, in addressing some of the challenges faced by communities in the region.[14]

However, it is clear that much more needs to be done to fully realise the right to an adequate standard of living for all individuals in SSA. The challenges identified in this book underscore the need for comprehensive, holistic, and context-specific approaches that address the root causes of poverty, inequality, and marginalisation, while also promoting sustainable and inclusive development. In the following section, we will present a set of recommendations aimed at advancing the realisation of the right to an adequate standard of living in SSA, drawing upon the insights and lessons learned from the preceding chapters.

Recommendations for Enhancing the Realisation of the Right to an Adequate Standard of Living

Drawing upon the findings and insights presented throughout this monograph, we propose a set of recommendations aimed at enhancing the realisation of the right to an adequate standard of living in Sub-Saharan Africa (SSA). These recommendations are grounded in the recognition that advancing this fundamental right requires a comprehensive, multisectoral, and context-specific approach that addresses the root causes of poverty, inequality, and marginalisation, while also promoting sustainable and inclusive development.

1. Prioritise Poverty Reduction and Inequality Alleviation in National Development Agendas

Governments in SSA should place poverty reduction and inequality alleviation at the centre of their national development agendas, recognising the critical importance of these issues for the realisation of the right to an adequate standard of living. This requires the development and implementation of comprehensive poverty reduction strategies that address the multidimensional nature

14 Namati, *Pursuing Equitable Development Through Legal Empowerment: An Introduction* (Namati, 2021).

of poverty, including income poverty, human poverty, and social exclusion.[15] These strategies should be informed by a thorough analysis of the specific drivers and manifestations of poverty and inequality in each country context, and should involve the active participation of affected communities in their design and implementation.

2. Invest in Inclusive and Equitable Access to Healthcare and Education

Improving access to quality healthcare and education is essential for promoting the well-being and human capital development of individuals in SSA, and for breaking the cycle of poverty and marginalisation. Governments should prioritise investments in healthcare and education infrastructure, particularly in underserved areas, and should develop targeted policies and programmes to address the specific barriers faced by marginalised groups, such as women, children, persons with disabilities, and rural communities.[16] This may include measures such as expanding social protection systems, implementing free or subsidised healthcare and education services, and promoting community-based approaches to healthcare and education delivery.

3. Promote Sustainable and Inclusive Urbanisation

With rapid urbanisation placing increasing pressure on cities in SSA, it is crucial to promote sustainable and inclusive urban development that ensures access to adequate housing, basic services, and infrastructure for all urban residents. Governments should develop and implement comprehensive urban development policies and plans that prioritise the needs of low-income and marginalised communities, and that foster participatory governance and community engagement in urban planning and decision-making processes.[17] This may include measures such as upgrading informal settlements, investing in affordable housing solutions, and promoting integrated urban development approaches that link housing, transportation, and basic services.

4. Strengthen Climate Change Adaptation and Mitigation Efforts

Given the significant threats posed by climate change to the realisation of the right to an adequate standard of living in SSA, it is imperative to strengthen

15 Augustine Edobor Arimoro, 'Beyond Economics! The (Evolving) Role of Law in the Eradication of Extreme Poverty' (2023) 8 *Journal of Human Rights and Social Work* DOI: https://doi.org/10.1007/s41134-023-00247-2 . See also Andy Sumner and Eduardo Ortiz-Juarez, 'Multidimensional Poverty Reduction in Sub-Saharan Africa' (2022) 61 *Journal of Development Studies* 1.

16 UNESCO, 'Access to Education and Health is Key to Progress on Human Development in Sub-Saharan Africa' (UNESCO, 2022).

17 Edgar Pieterse et al. (n 9).

climate change adaptation and mitigation efforts in the region. Governments should develop and implement comprehensive climate change strategies that prioritise the needs of vulnerable communities, and that promote sustainable and resilient development pathways.[18] This may include measures such as investing in climate-resilient infrastructure, promoting sustainable land management practices, and supporting community-based adaptation initiatives. At the same time, SSA countries should actively engage in global climate change negotiations and advocacy efforts to ensure that the international community upholds its commitments to support adaptation and mitigation efforts in the region.

5. Enhance Access to Justice and Legal Empowerment

Improving access to justice and legal empowerment is critical for enabling individuals in SSA to claim their rights and hold duty-bearers accountable for the realisation of the right to an adequate standard of living. Governments should invest in strengthening the legal infrastructure and capacity of justice systems, particularly in underserved areas, and should develop targeted policies and programmes to address the specific barriers faced by marginalised groups in accessing justice.[19] This may include measures such as expanding legal aid services, promoting alternative dispute resolution mechanisms, and supporting community-based legal empowerment initiatives. At the same time, efforts should be made to address the root causes of injustice and inequality, such as discrimination, corruption, and power imbalances, through systemic reforms and social change interventions.

6. Foster Participatory and Inclusive Governance

Promoting participatory and inclusive governance is essential for ensuring that the voices and needs of marginalised and vulnerable communities are heard and addressed in the development and implementation of policies and programmes related to the right to an adequate standard of living. Governments should create and strengthen mechanisms for citizen participation and engagement in decision-making processes, such as participatory budgeting, community scorecards, and social accountability initiatives.[20] Efforts should also be made to promote the empowerment and capacity building of civil society organisations and community-based groups, particularly those representing

18 IPCC, *Climate Change 2022: Impacts, Adaptation and Vulnerability – Contribution of Working Group II to the Sixth Assessment Report of the Intergovernmental Panel on Climate Change* (Cambridge University Press, 2022).

19 Ibid.

20 Uta Gerlitz et al., Participatory Approaches to Strengthening Governance and Achieving the Sustainable Development Goals in Africa (Deutsche Gesellschaft für Internationale Zusammenarbeit (GIZ) GmbH, 2021).

marginalised and vulnerable populations, to enable them to effectively advocate for their rights and hold duty-bearers accountable.

7. Strengthen Regional and International Cooperation and Partnership

Realising the right to an adequate standard of living in SSA requires concerted efforts and partnerships at the regional and international levels. SSA countries should actively engage in regional and international forums and initiatives aimed at promoting sustainable development, poverty reduction, and human rights, such as the African Union's Agenda 2063 and the United Nations' Sustainable Development Goals (SDGs).[21] Governments should also seek to strengthen regional and international cooperation and partnerships in areas such as trade, investment, technology transfer, and capacity building, with a view to leveraging resources and expertise to support the realisation of the right to an adequate standard of living in the region.

8. Invest in Research, Data Collection, and Knowledge Sharing

To inform evidence-based policies and programmes for the realisation of the right to an adequate standard of living in SSA, it is crucial to invest in research, data collection, and knowledge sharing. Governments, research institutions, and development partners should prioritise the generation and dissemination of high-quality, disaggregated data on poverty, inequality, and access to basic services in the region, and should support research efforts aimed at identifying effective interventions and best practices for promoting the realisation of this right.[22] Efforts should also be made to promote knowledge sharing and learning across countries and regions, through platforms such as peer learning networks, communities of practice, and regional and international conferences and workshops.

While these recommendations are not exhaustive, they provide a starting point for advancing the realisation of the right to an adequate standard of living in SSA. Ultimately, the success of these efforts will depend on the sustained commitment and collaboration of all stakeholders – governments, civil society, the private sector, and development partners – working together towards a common vision of a more just, equitable, and sustainable future for all individuals in the region.

21 African Union Commission, Agenda 2063: The Africa We Want (African Union Commission, 2015).

22 Carlos Gradín, 'Poverty and Inequality in Sub-Saharan Africa: A Review of Recent Research on the Levels, Trends, Effects and Determinants' (2022) 33 *Journal of Economic Surveys* 1365.

Areas for Further Research

While this monograph has provided a comprehensive overview of the right to an adequate standard of living in Sub-Saharan Africa (SSA), it is important to acknowledge that there are still many areas that require further research and investigation to deepen our understanding of this complex issue and to inform more effective policy interventions. In this section, there is the need to highlight some of the key research gaps and areas for further inquiry that have emerged from the analysis presented in the preceding chapters.

1. Intersectionality and the Experiences of Marginalised Groups

While the book has examined the challenges faced by various marginalised groups, such as women, children, persons with disabilities, and rural communities, in accessing their right to an adequate standard of living, there is a need for more intersectional research that explores how multiple forms of discrimination and disadvantage intersect to shape the experiences of these groups.[23] Future research should seek to understand the specific barriers and challenges faced by individuals who experience multiple and overlapping forms of marginalisation, such as women with disabilities or ethnic minority children, and should identify strategies for addressing these intersectional inequalities.

2. The Role of Informal Economies in Shaping Access to Basic Services

Informal economies play a significant role in many SSA countries, particularly in urban areas, and can have a major impact on individuals' access to basic services such as housing, water, and sanitation.[24] However, the informal nature of these economies can make them difficult to study and regulate, and there is a need for more research on how informal economies shape the realisation of the right to an adequate standard of living in different contexts. Future research should seek to understand the dynamics of informal economies, the challenges and opportunities they present for access to basic services, and the potential for innovative policy interventions to support and regulate these economies in ways that promote the realisation of the right to an adequate standard of living.

3. The Impact of Technology and Innovation on Access to Basic Services

Technology and innovation have the potential to play a significant role in improving access to basic services in SSA, particularly in areas such as

23 Tina Beradze et al., 'Applying an Intersectionality Lens to Better Understand Vulnerabilities for Inequality: Experiences and Lessons from Research and Policy in Multiple Contexts' (2022) 31 *Journal of International Development* 1.

24 Caroline Skinner and Vanessa Watson, 'The Informal Economy in Cities of the Global South: Challenges to the Planning Lexicon' in Alison Brown (ed), *Rebel Streets and the Informal Economy* (Routledge, 2017).

healthcare, education, and financial services.[25] However, there is a need for more research on the specific ways in which technology and innovation are being used to promote the realisation of the right to an adequate standard of living in different contexts, and on the challenges and limitations of these approaches. Future research should seek to identify best practices and lessons learned from successful technology and innovation initiatives, and should explore the potential for scaling up and replicating these initiatives in different contexts.

4. The Role of Traditional and Customary Systems in Shaping Access to Justice

While the book has examined the challenges faced by individuals in accessing formal justice systems in SSA, there is a need for more research on the role of traditional and customary systems in shaping access to justice, particularly in rural and marginalised communities.[26] Future research should seek to understand the strengths and limitations of these systems, the ways in which they intersect with formal justice systems, and the potential for integrating them into broader access to justice strategies in ways that promote the realisation of the right to an adequate standard of living.

5. The Impact of Regional and International Frameworks on the Realisation of the Right to an Adequate Standard of Living

Regional and international frameworks, such as the African Union's Agenda 2063 and the United Nations' Sustainable Development Goals (SDGs), have the potential to play a significant role in promoting the realisation of the right to an adequate standard of living in SSA.[27] However, there is a need for more research on the specific ways in which these frameworks are being implemented and operationalised at the national and local levels, and on the challenges and opportunities they present for advancing this right. Future research should seek to understand the effectiveness of these frameworks in promoting policy and programmatic action, the extent to which they are aligned with national development priorities and plans, and the potential for strengthening accountability and monitoring mechanisms to support their implementation.

25 Banji Oyelaran-Oyeyinka and Dorothy McCormick (eds), *Industrialization and Innovation in Africa* (Springer, 2021).

26 Ibid.

27 UNECA, 2023 Africa Sustainable Development Report: Building Forward Better from COVID-19 in Africa – Fostering Inclusive and Green Economies for Accelerated Delivery of the Sustainable Development Goals and Agenda 2063 (UNECA, 2023).

6. The Long-Term Impacts of the COVID-19 Pandemic on the Right to an Adequate Standard of Living

The COVID-19 pandemic has had a significant impact on the realisation of the right to an adequate standard of living in SSA, exacerbating existing inequalities and vulnerabilities and creating new challenges and risks for marginalised and vulnerable groups.[28] While the immediate impacts of the pandemic have been widely studied, there is a need for more research on the long-term implications of the pandemic for the realisation of this right, particularly in areas such as poverty, inequality, access to basic services, and social protection. Future research should seek to understand the ways in which the pandemic has reshaped the landscape of poverty and inequality in the region, the effectiveness of policy responses and interventions in mitigating the impacts of the pandemic, and the potential for building more resilient and equitable systems in the post-pandemic recovery period.

These are just a few of the many areas that require further research and investigation to deepen our understanding of the right to an adequate standard of living in SSA. By prioritising these research gaps and investing in high-quality, context-specific research, we can generate the evidence and insights needed to inform more effective policies, programmes, and interventions to promote the realisation of this fundamental right for all individuals in the region.

Conclusion

The right to an adequate standard of living is a fundamental human right, essential for the dignity, well-being, and development of all individuals. Yet, as this monograph has demonstrated, the realisation of this right remains a significant challenge in many parts of Sub-Saharan Africa (SSA), with complex and multifaceted barriers impeding access to basic services, resources, and opportunities for large segments of the population.

Throughout this book, we have explored the various dimensions of the right to an adequate standard of living in SSA, examining the challenges, opportunities, and efforts undertaken to promote its realisation. From the pervasive impacts of poverty and inequality to the critical importance of access to healthcare, education, housing, and justice, each chapter has shed light on the complex web of factors that shape the enjoyment of this right in the region.

The analysis presented in this book underscores the urgent need for comprehensive, holistic, and context-specific approaches to advancing the right to an adequate standard of living in SSA. As highlighted in the recommendations section, this requires a multisectoral and multistakeholder effort that addresses

28 Elina Amadhila et al., 'The Impact of COVID-19 on Sustainable Development and Poverty in Sub-Saharan Africa: A Systematic Literature Review' (2022) 13 Sustainability 15515.

the root causes of poverty, inequality, and marginalisation, while also promoting sustainable and inclusive development.

At the same time, the book has identified several areas where further research and investigation are needed to deepen our understanding of the right to an adequate standard of living in SSA and to inform more effective policy interventions. From the need for more intersectional research on the experiences of marginalised groups to the potential of technology and innovation in improving access to basic services, these research gaps point to the importance of continued investment in high-quality, context-specific research to guide policy and programmatic action.

Ultimately, realising the right to an adequate standard of living for all individuals in SSA will require sustained commitment, collaboration, and innovation from all stakeholders – governments, civil society, the private sector, and development partners. It will require a fundamental shift in the way we think about and approach development, moving beyond narrow economic indicators to a more holistic and people-centred vision of progress and well-being.

The insights and recommendations presented in this book offer a starting point for this transformative agenda, providing a roadmap for action and a call to arms for all those committed to advancing the right to an adequate standard of living in SSA. By working together towards this common goal, we can build a more just, equitable, and sustainable future for all individuals in the region, one in which every person has access to the basic resources and opportunities needed to live a life of dignity and fulfilment.

As we look to the future, it is clear that much work remains to be done to fully realise the right to an adequate standard of living in SSA. The challenges are significant, and the road ahead is long and complex. Yet, as the case studies and examples presented in this book demonstrate, progress is possible, and there are reasons for hope and optimism.

By learning from these experiences, building on the successes and innovations of the past, and working together towards a shared vision of a more equitable and sustainable future, we can make meaningful strides towards the realisation of the right to an adequate standard of living for all individuals in SSA. This will require courage, commitment, and a willingness to challenge the status quo, but the stakes could not be higher – for the lives and well-being of millions of individuals in the region, and for the future of our shared planet.

In conclusion, this monograph has sought to provide a comprehensive and nuanced examination of the right to an adequate standard of living in SSA, highlighting the challenges, opportunities, and imperatives for action. It is our hope that the insights and recommendations presented here will serve as a catalyst for further research, dialogue, and action towards the full realisation of this fundamental right for all individuals in the region. By working together towards this goal, we can build a more just, equitable, and sustainable future for all.

References

African Union Commission, *Agenda 2063: The Africa We Want* (African Union Commission 2015).

Amadhila E et al, 'The Impact of COVID-19 on Sustainable Development and Poverty in Sub-Saharan Africa: A Systematic Literature Review' (2022) 13 *Sustainability* 15515.

Arimoro AE, 'Beyond Economics! The (Evolving) Role of Law in the Eradication of Extreme Poverty' (2023) 8 *Journal of Human Rights and Social Work* https://doi.org/10.1007/s41134-023-00247-2.

Banda C, 'Barriers to Access to Justice in Sub-Saharan Africa' (2020) 64 *Journal of African Law* 185.

Beegle K et al, *Poverty in a Rising Africa* (World Bank 2016).

Beradze T et al, 'Applying an Intersectionality Lens to Better Understand Vulnerabilities for Inequality: Experiences and Lessons from Research and Policy in Multiple Contexts' (2022) 31 *Journal of International Development* 1.

Cornia GA and Martorano B, 'The Dynamics of Income Inequality in Sub-Saharan Africa' (2022) 133 *World Development* 106667.

Fanzo J et al, 'The Role of Ecosystem Services in the Sustainable Development Goals' in A Bonn et al. (eds), *Atlas of Ecosystem Services* (Springer 2019).

Gerlitz U et al, *Participatory Approaches to Strengthening Governance and Achieving the Sustainable Development Goals in Africa* (Deutsche Gesellschaft für Internationale Zusammenarbeit (GIZ) GmbH 2021).

Gradín C, 'Poverty and Inequality in Sub-Saharan Africa: A Review of Recent Research on the Levels, Trends, Effects and Determinants' (2022) 33 *Journal of Economic Surveys* 1365.

Gulyani S and Bassett E, 'Retrieving the Baby from the Bathwater: Slum Upgrading in Sub-Saharan Africa' (2007) 25 *Environment and Planning C: Government and Policy* 486.

IPCC, *Climate Change 2022: Impacts, Adaptation and Vulnerability – Contribution of Working Group II to the Sixth Assessment Report of the Intergovernmental Panel on Climate Change* (Cambridge University Press 2022).

Namati, *Pursuing Equitable Development Through Legal Empowerment: An Introduction* (Namati 2021).

Ngware M et al, 'Education Challenges in Sub-Saharan Africa and SDG 4' in Stanley Brunn and Roland Kehrein (eds), *Handbook of the Changing World Language Map* (Springer 2020).

Pieterse E et al, *Africa's Urban Opportunity* (University of Cape Town 2021).

Ratcliff KS, 'Health Equity and Access to Health Care in Sub-Saharan Africa' (2021) 18 *Advances in Medical Sociology* 187.

Skinner C and Watson V, 'The Informal Economy in Cities of the Global South: Challenges to the Planning Lexicon' in Alison Brown (ed), *Rebel Streets and the Informal Economy* (Routledge 2017).

Stabinsky D, 'Climate Change Impacts on Agriculture in Africa' (2022) 15 *Annual Review of Environment and Resources* 407.

Sumner A and Ortiz-Juarez E, 'Multidimensional Poverty Reduction in Sub-Saharan Africa' (2022) 61 *Journal of Development Studies* 1.

UNDP, *The Next Frontier: Human Development and the Anthropocene – Human Development Report 2020* (UNDP 2020).

UNECA, *2023 Africa Sustainable Development Report: Building Forward Better from COVID-19 in Africa – Fostering Inclusive and Green Economies for Accelerated Delivery of the Sustainable Development Goals and Agenda 2063* (UNECA 2023).

UNESCO, *Access to Education and Health is Key to Progress on Human Development in Sub-Saharan Africa* (UNESCO 2022).

United Nations General Assembly, 'International Covenant on Economic, Social and Cultural Rights' (1966) 993 *United Nations Treaty Series* 3.

United Nations General Assembly, 'Universal Declaration of Human Rights' (1948) *Resolution* 217 A (III) available at https://www.un.org/en/about-us/universal-declaration-of-human-rights accessed 9 December 2024.

Index

Italic page references indicate figures.

Kolibri 360 GmbH
Ferdinand-Jühlke-Straße 7
99095 Erfurt, Deutschland
produktsicherheit@kolibri360.de